WISE COUNSEL
SKILLS FOR LAY COUNSELING

John W. Drakeford

Claude V. King

ISBN 0-7673-2615-6

This book is a resource in the PERSONAL LIFE category of the Christian Growth Study Plan.
Course CG-184

Dewey Decimal Classification: 361.3
Subject Heading: COUNSELING

Unless otherwise indicated, all Scripture quotations are from the
Holy Bible, New International Version,
copyright © 1973, 1978, 1984 by International Bible Society.
Used by permission.

To order additional copies of this resource:
WRITE LifeWay Church Resources Customer Service;
One LifeWay Plaza; Nashville, TN 37234-0113;
FAX order to (615) 251-5933; PHONE (800) 458-2772;
EMAIL to *customerservice@lifeway.com;* ORDER ONLINE at *www.lifeway.com;*
or VISIT the LifeWay Christian Store serving you.

Printed in the United States of America

✝

Adult Ministry Publishing
LifeWay Church Resources
One LifeWay Plaza
Nashville, TN 37234-0175

TABLE OF CONTENTS

Introduction   5

Group Covenant 11

About the Authors 12

UNIT 1: The Lay Counseling Ministry 13
> Day 1: Reasons Christians Should Provide Lay Counseling
> Day 2: Counseling as Shepherding
> Day 3: Wise Counseling
> Day 4: Introducing the Ten-Step Counseling Model
> Day 5: Asking Effective Questions

UNIT 2: Identify the Problem 28
> Day 1: Memorize Stage One
> Day 2: Time and Place; Listen
> Day 3: The Situation and Previous Counseling
> Day 4: Making Referrals for Assistance
> Day 5: Sources of Assistance

UNIT 3: Determine an Action Plan 47
> Day 1: Memorize Stage Two
> Days 2 and 3: Responsibility and Role
> Days 3 and 4: Alternatives and Outcomes
> Day 5: Information and Closure

UNIT 4: A Fundamental Skill—Listening 64
> Day 1: What Your Listening Does for People
> Day 2: Four Fallacies About Listening
> Day 3: Mental Discipline and Attention
> Day 4: Four Listening Guidelines
> Day 5: Body Listening

UNIT 5: Building Relationships 79
> Day 1: Availability for Counseling
> Day 2: Building Rapport
> Day 3: SOFTEN
> Days 4 and 5: Review

UNIT 6: Expectations and Boundaries 94
> Day 1: Expectations of the Counselee
> Day 2: The Expectation of Confidentiality
> Day 3: Establishing Boundaries
> Day 4: The Boundary of Affection
> Day 5: Practice the Ten-Step Model

UNIT 7: Counseling Sick and Grieving Persons **109**

    Day 1: The Crises of Illness
    Day 2: Resources of the Christian Counselor
    Day 3: Guidelines for Visiting the Sick
    Day 4: The Stages of a Grief Experience
    Day 5: Helping a Grieving Person

UNIT 8: Marriage and Family Counseling **127**

    Day 1: Guidelines for Marriage and Family Counseling
    Days 2 and 3: Describing the Ideal Family
    Day 4: Five Needs of a Family
    Day 5: Seven Marks of a Viable Family

UNIT 9: Providing Guidance for Behavior Change **142**

    Day 1: Behavior Change and Pinpointing
    Day 2: Praising
    Day 3: Behavior Shaping and Pairing
    Day 4: Timing
    Day 5: Time Out

UNIT 10: Counseling Youth **157**

    Day 1: Master and Mission
    Day 2: Who Will Be My Mate?
    Day 3: Coping with Sexual Desires
    Day 4: Helping Parents Communicate
    Day 5: Other Problems and Principles

UNIT 11: Counseling Singles and Senior Adults **171**

    Days 1 and 2: Counseling Singles
    Day 3: Helping Senior Adults Make Decisions
    Days 4 and 5: Life Review Techniques

UNIT 12: Resentment, Guilt, and Suicide **186**

    Day 1: The Resentment Syndrome
    Day 2: Handling Resentment
    Day 3: Handling Guilt
    Day 4: Identifying Suicidal Individuals
    Day 5: Counseling a Suicidal Individual

Unit 13: Counseling Through Group Experiences **204**

    Day 1: Spectators or Participators?
    Day 2: Counseling and Support Groups in the Church
    Day 3: Managing the Dynamics of a Group
    Day 4: Using Experiential Bible Studies in Support Groups
    Day 5: Conclusion

Notes **222**

The Christian Growth Study Plan **223**

INTRODUCTION

Probably every person who lives long enough will experience joy and grief, success and failure, hope and despair, health and sickness, life and death. Our world is filled with hurting people who need someone to help them when the going gets tough. Hurting people need someone who will listen to their woes. They need someone who can help them walk through the darkness and discover hope and light at the other side. They need someone who can help them sort through numerous options and make healthy decisions about what to do in difficult situations. They need friends who will love them unconditionally. Unless you are unusual, you have experienced needs like this at some time in your life.

Hurting people need help. You can be a helping person, a caring person, a loving person, and a friend to people in need. I want to give you training that will equip you with skills to minister to the counseling needs of persons you come in contact with from day to day. Here is our course goal:

> **Course Learning Goal:** After completing a study of *WiseCounsel: Skills for Lay Counseling,* you will understand and be able to use the Ten-Step Counseling Model and other counseling techniques to minister to the needs of persons you come in contact with from day to day.

Three words need to be defined at this point. In WiseCounsel I will use these words in the following ways.

Lay—nonprofessional, unpaid. (When referring to lay counselors, I am speaking of nonprofessional counselors. I am *not* using this word to speak of laity in the church.)

Minister—a believer who performs redemptive, loving service for people in the Spirit of Christ. (Notice that this definition does not identify a minister as the pastor. A pastor is a minister; but so is a Sunday School teacher, a New Christian Encourager, and a hospital visitor.)

Ministry—the act of performing redemptive, loving service for people in the Spirit of Christ both individually and as a church.

WiseCounsel Will Help:

- Sunday School teachers and group leaders who need to minister to members and prospects
- Deacons responsible for ministering to individuals and families
- Other church leaders who have informal counseling opportunities with their group members
- People who have family members with problems such as drug addiction, alcoholism, divorce, loneliness, depression, and suicide

- Laity who are approached by persons with broken hearts, questions, or problems
- Churches that want to provide counseling and support groups for the community
- Pastors who need trained helpers to assist with basic counseling

WiseCounsel Is Part of LIFE

WiseCounsel is a course in the LIFE learning system. LIFE stands for Lay Institute For Equipping. The Lay Institute For Equipping is an advanced approach for equipping laity for discipleship, leadership, and ministry. LIFE is an educational system that enables persons to grow at their own pace and to develop skills for ministry according to their own spiritual gifts and life goals. LIFE is designed so the local church can have its own Lay Institute For Equipping and provide a high quality of training for its laity.

All LIFE courses share some common characteristics:
- Participants interact with a self-paced workbook 30-60 minutes each day and do life related learning activities.
- They meet for a small-group session each week (often during Discipleship Training time).
- The course leader guides members to reflect on their learning and to make practical application of the study to everyday life.
- Optional videotapes provide additional content and learning experiences for a deeper study.
- An attractive diploma from the Church Study Course system is awarded for completing each LIFE course.

LIFE's Core Curriculum

MasterLife: Discipleship Training by Avery T. Willis, Jr. was the first course to be included in the Lay Institute For Equipping. In a sense, MasterLife is the core curriculum for LIFE. Though it is not a prerequisite for WiseCounsel, it provides spiritual preparation for exercising the basic disciplines and ministries of the Christian life. Thus, if you have not experienced MasterLife, you may want to consider it for your next course of study. MasterLife, or some other in-depth discipleship training, is important for the Christian who wants to mature into the image of Christ Himself. It is basic training for the Christian. That is the reason it is considered LIFE's core curriculum.

The Disciple's Cross provides a visual summary of MasterLife. Disciples of Jesus Christ must abide in Christ (John 15:5,10). To abide in Him, a disciple must exercise four basic disciplines:

- Living in the Word
- Praying in Faith
- Fellowshipping with Believers
- Witnessing to the World

As a Christian abides in Christ, he begins to bear fruit. This fruit bearing expresses itself in ministries. Five ministry areas are identified on the Disciple's Cross. They are the ministries of worship or intercession, teaching and preaching, evangelism, service, and nurture. Since WiseCounsel provides training for a practical counseling ministry to believers and unbelievers, it falls in the ministry of service category.

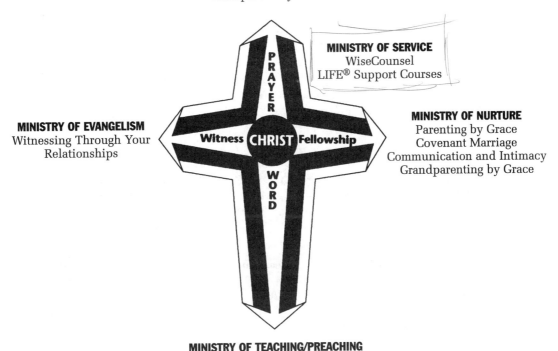

ALL MINISTRIES
Experiencing God
Life in the Spirit
MasterLife
The Mind of Christ

MINISTRY OF WORSHIP/INTERCESSION
Disciple's Prayer Life

MINISTRY OF SERVICE
WiseCounsel
LIFE® Support Courses

MINISTRY OF EVANGELISM
Witnessing Through Your
Relationships

MINISTRY OF NURTURE
Parenting by Grace
Covenant Marriage
Communication and Intimacy
Grandparenting by Grace

MINISTRY OF TEACHING/PREACHING
MasterDesign
Step by Step Through the Old Testament
Step by Step Through the New Testament

WiseCounsel Course Map

The course map on the back cover may seem complicated and even scary to you at first glance. Do not let that bother you right now. We will be working together for 13 weeks. During that time, I will use the map to show you exactly where we are and how that fits into a ministry of counseling. For instance, today I want you to get an overall view of the course.

CHRIST: SAVIOR AND LORD	CALL TO MINISTER	CHRISTIAN VALUES	SPIRITUAL GIFTS	KNOWLEDGE OF SCRIPTURE

Prerequisites. Many of the techniques and skills taught in this course could be used effectively by anyone willing to take the time to master them. This course has been written, however, to train Christians for a spiritual ministry of counseling. Consequently, I will make the assumption throughout this course that you have the prerequisites listed on the course map. I assume that you have placed your faith and trust in Jesus Christ as you *Savior* and have made Him *Lord* of your life.

Several differences exist between secular counseling and Christian counseling. One of the chief differences is that Christians who have the mind of Christ and are guided by the Holy Spirit can provide sound spiritual counsel. This spiritual ministry requires a Christian counselor through whom the love of God can be expressed in tangible ways. Biblical <u>Christian values</u> are required to adequately help a person evaluate alternatives. A <u>knowledge of</u> and ability to use <u>Scripture</u> is necessary to bring God's Word and wisdom into the decision making process. <u>Spiritual gifts</u> like helps, discernment, and wisdom are vital for a God empowered ministry. You must agree with God that you cannot meet the needs of others unless He works through you. You must make yourself available to be used by Him to meet the needs of hurting people.

According to Ephesians 4:11-12, all of God's people are called to be involved in ministry. I assume that you sense a <u>call of God</u> to be involved in ministry, perhaps a counseling ministry. As a Christian you are called and gifted for ministry in and through the body of Christ, the church.

Equipping for Ministry. A ministry of lay counseling is the ultimate goal for this course. Though Christians are called and gifted, they often need to be equipped for the ministry they have been called to. That is the task assigned to the apostles, prophets, evangelists, and pastors and teachers in Ephesians 4. WiseCounsel will help equip you for a counseling ministry.

WiseCounsel will help you gain a <u>knowledge</u> of counseling approaches and techniques. You will develop an <u>understanding</u> of these facts so that you may apply them effectively in your counseling. I also will help you develop <u>skills</u> that are necessary for effective counseling. Through group discussions, case studies, and real-life practice, you will develop <u>confidence</u> in your ability to help others.

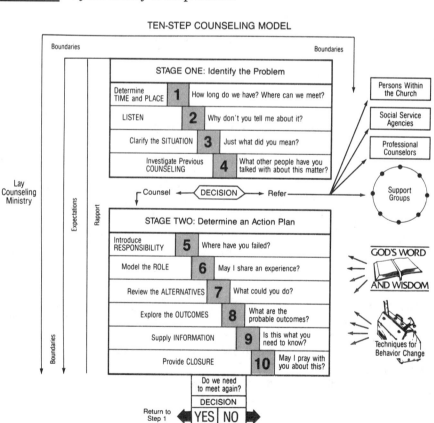

8

Counseling Ministry. Take a look at the table of contents. Notice that I will give you an overview of the counseling ministry in unit 1. I will work with the underlying assumption that

> Most of the counseling you will undertake will be brief and probably involve only one to three sessions with a counselee.

In units 2 and 3, I will introduce you to an approach to counseling called the Ten-Step Counseling Model. Many other approaches are taught in schools and books. This is a simple problem-solving model that should adequately equip you for the kind of counseling you will normally do. The Ten-Step Model is not designed for counseling children, since the problem-solving method is not appropriate for their level of reasoning abilities. I will, however, help you learn techniques for behavior change that are useful with children. In addition to the Ten-Step Model, I will help you understand the following:

- when to counsel and when to refer to a professional
- factors to be considered in the counseling process
- techniques you can use in counseling
- people that you may encounter who need counseling

From time to time, I will recommend other materials that you may use for further study on a particular topic.

A Marketplace Ministry

"Marketplace ministry" is a term that is becoming popular in Christian circles. It refers to Christian ministry that takes place anywhere in the world that a Christian finds himself. Like the counseling at the city gate that took place "amid the swirl of humanity," Christian marketplace ministry can take place at home, at church, or at work. It may take place at a party, in the supermarket (the marketplace of modern times), across the backyard fence, in a nursing home, in the hospital, at the football game—anywhere Christians encounter needy people. The counseling ministry you are preparing for is a marketplace ministry. You will find opportunities to perform this ministry for people in a wide variety of settings.

Getting the Most from the Course

WiseCounsel is an integrated course of study. For full benefit of the educational design, you must prepare your individual assignments *and* you must participate in the small-group session. Both are integral to the course.

Study Tips. Five days a week (or unit) you will be expected to study a segment of content material. You may need from thirty to sixty minutes of study time each day. If you find that you can study the material in less time, you may study more than one day's material at a time. Study at your own pace.

This book has been written as a tutorial text. Look on it as if you have the teacher sitting at your side helping you learn. When you are asked a question or given an assignment, respond immediately. Each assignment is indented and begins with a solid box at the left margin. The assignment is in **boldface type.**

SOLID →
BOX

■ **Turn to page 15 and look at the assignment in the middle of the page. Each time you see a solid box and indented boldface text you will know that you need to respond to the activity in some way. DO NOT SKIP THESE ASSIGNMENTS.**

BOLD TYPE, INDENTE AT LEFT

In most cases your "personal tutor" will give you some feedback about your response. This process is designed to help you learn the material more effectively. Do not deny yourself valuable learning by skipping the learning activities.

Set a definite time and select a quiet place where you can study with little interruption. A table or desk and good lighting will be helpful.

Make notes of problems, questions, or concerns that arise as you study. You will discuss many of these during your small-group sessions. Write them in the margins of this textbook, so you can find them easily.

Small-Group Session. Once each week you should attend a WiseCounsel small-group session. Small groups should consist of up to ten persons. This group session is designed to help you
- discuss the content you studied the previous week
- share insights you gained
- look for answers to problems you may have encountered
- develop and practice counseling skills
- consider practical application of the skills to real life situations

The small group adds a needed dimension to your learning. If you have started a study of *WiseCounsel* and you are not involved in a group study, try to enlist some friends or associates who will work through the course with you. *WiseCounsel Leader Guide* provides assistance and learning activities for these sessions. To order or inquire about this resource: WRITE LifeWay Church Resources Customer Service; One LifeWay Plaza; Nashville, TN 37234-0113; FAX order to (615) 251-5933; PHONE (800) 458-2772; EMAIL to *customerservice@lifeway.com;* ORDER ONLINE at *www.lifeway.com;* or VISIT the LifeWay Christian Store serving you. Ask for ISBN 0-7673-2676-8.

WiseCounsel
Group Covenant

Seeking to be equipped for a lay counseling ministry, I covenant with my WiseCounsel group that I will:

- *faithfully study WiseCounsel between sessions*
- *complete learning activities to the best of my ability*
- *attend weekly group sessions unless providentially hindered*
- *contribute openly during our small-group time together*
- *pray for each of the other group members on a daily basis*

- _____

- _____

- _____

- _____

Signed this _____ *day of* _____ *, 19*_____

Name: _____

Signatures of WiseCounsel Group Members:

_____   _____

_____   _____

_____   _____

"Study to shew thyself approved unto God, a workman that needeth not to be ashamed, rightly dividing the word of truth" (2 Tim. 2:15, KJV).

MEET THE AUTHORS

JOHN DRAKEFORD

CLAUDE KING

John W. Drakeford, a native of Sydney, Australia, is Distinguished Professor of Psychology and Counseling, Emeritus and Writer in Residence at Southwestern Baptist Theological Seminary, Fort Worth, Texas. John holds graduate degrees from The University of Sydney, New South Wales Baptist Theological Seminary, Texas Christian University, and Brite Divinity School. He earned the Doctor of Religious Education and the Doctor of Education Degrees at Southwestern Seminary. He served as a pastor, chaplain, and youth director before coming to the faculty of Southwestern. He is the author of more than thirty books including: *The Awesome Power of the Listening Ear, Integrity Therapy, People to People Therapy, Wisdom for Today's Family,* and *A Christian View of Homosexuality*. He writes a weekly column titled "Dear John" in *The Baptist Standard*. He and his wife, Robina, spend most weekends conducting Family Enrichment Conferences. They have presented over 1,000 such conferences across the United States and around the world.

Claude V. King is a former Design Editor in the Leadership Development Section of the Discipleship Training Department, Baptist Sunday School Board. Claude also serves as Church Planter, Tentmaker (volunteer) for the Concord Baptist Association. A native of Tennessee, he received the Bachelor of Science degree from Belmont College and Master of Divinity and Master of Religious Education Degrees from New Orleans Baptist Theological Seminary. He lives in Murfreesboro, Tennessee, with his wife Reta and daughters Julie and Jenny.

UNIT 1

The Lay Counseling Ministry

This Week's Learning Goal

After studying this unit, you will understand the value of a lay counseling ministry and one approach to use in helping people with their problems.

Why You Will Find This Study Useful

You will recognize the important ministry you can perform as a lay counselor, and you will examine a structure for that ministry. The questions you learn to ask will become vital tools in your ministry of helping people.

Day 1: Reasons Christians Should Provide Lay Counseling

> **Today's Objective:** You will be able to write three reasons Christians should provide lay counseling.

In the year 1793 the city of Philadelphia went through a four-month period of agony. A yellow fever plague killed ten percent of the population. Dr. Benjamin Rush, probably the single most important professionals of that day, threw himself into the task of helping his unfortunate fellow citizens.

Periodically Dr. Rush met with the College of Physicians. They speculated and argued about the cause and cure of the disease. They never came close to either. For controlling the dread disease, many other speculators suggested such things as lighting fires on the street corners, spreading soil on the floor of the victims' houses, and washing the whole house with vinegar.

Amidst all this confusion a letter appeared in *Dunlap's American Daily Advertiser,* signed by a citizen who designated himself A. B. He suggested that the problem was with rain barrels outside the houses. They provided a breeding place for mosquitoes. These mosquitoes were poisonous and distressing. To cope with this problem, he proposed that each citizen pour a glass of oil on the water of each rain barrel. This would cover it with a film of oil and prevent mosquitoes from breeding.

The historian of the plague commented about A. B.'s suggestion, He "spelled out the source of the trouble (and the remedy) with pinpoint accuracy."[1] If his suggestion had been followed, the cities of Baltimore, Mobile, and New Orleans could have been saved from the agony of yellow fever. A hundred years later Walter Reed demonstrated the validity of A. B.'s ideas. If his suggestion had been followed the course of history might have been changed. Why didn't they listen to A. B.? He was not a professional. He was a layman.

Many people believe that only well-trained professional counselors can help needy people. As you can see in the above example, sometimes lay people can do what professionals cannot do. Christians can and should serve as lay counselors. Today, we will look at three reasons.

> **Reasons Christians Should Provide Lay Counseling**
>
> 1. Laypersons can counsel effectively.
> 2. Professional counselors cannot meet all the needs.
> 3. Christians have a responsibility to minister to others.

Reason 1: Laypersons Can Counsel Effectively

■ **As you read the following section, underline at least three statements that indicate laypersons can counsel effectively. Remember to write in the margins any problems, questions, or concerns that arise.**

The modern equivalent of A. B. is the nonprofessional or layperson who, unaware of the scientific investigations and detailed descriptions of the social scientists, has proceeded with his work. He has become part of a powerful lay movement that has produced remarkable results. A monument to the workers on the Alaska pipe line identifies one reason for the success of laypersons: "They didn't know it couldn't be done." The yellow-fever tragedy in Philadelphia happened because professionals did not listen to a layman. Today, in the area of counseling, professionals are recognizing the value of the layperson.

"Evidence is mounting to show that the social and clinical services that are available have not been very effective. (And) many of the traditional credentials and authorities are coming under question, and a sense is developing that common people may have more abilities than they have been credited with."[2]

Hundreds and thousands of lay counselors effectively help their fellowmen and women. Dr. Walt Menninger has written about laypersons who work in the mental health field. He says, "A key to the self help [groups] is nonprofessional leadership." For instance, while mental health professionals are welcome to attend meetings of Recovery (a self-help organization) and participate as members, "they are specifically denied leadership roles." The non-professionals often get good results.[3]

■ **Summarize the three statements you underlined that indicate laypersons can counsel effectively.**

    1. _____

    2. _____

    3. _____

This was your first learning activity in WiseCounsel. Have you completed it? If not, please keep in mind that these activities are here to help you learn. By responding to the activity, you will process the content in such a way that you will learn more effectively. Complete each activity as you come to it. Then I will give you some feedback on your response. Here is the feedback:

You may have selected other statements to summarize. That is okay. I selected these three: (1) "They didn't know it couldn't be done." (2) "Common people may have more abilities than they have been credited with." (3) "Nonprofessionals often get good results." In summary, laypersons can provide effective counseling because they:
• approach opportunities with optimism
• possess ability to meet the needs of others and
• get the job done.

■ **Write in the first reason Christians should provide lay counseling.**

    1. _____

    2. **Professional counselors cannot meet all the needs.**

    3. **Christians have a responsibility to minister to others.**

Reason 2: Professional Counselors Cannot Meet All the Needs

Many problems that society finds so troublesome, such as alcoholism, drug addiction, obesity, compulsive gambling, phobic reactions, and antisocial behavior have been stubbornly resistant to the best efforts of professional counselors. Yet these are the very areas in which laypersons and self-help groups have been most successful.

This is fortunate. If we had to wait for mental health professionals to do the job, many people would never get the help they need. There are simply not enough professionals to do the job. The training of a professional is a lengthy process. As one authority said: "As the population has grown, health and welfare service has failed to keep pace; consequently there are not enough professionals to meet the demands for help."

■ **Which of the following best illustrates this point? Circle your choice.**

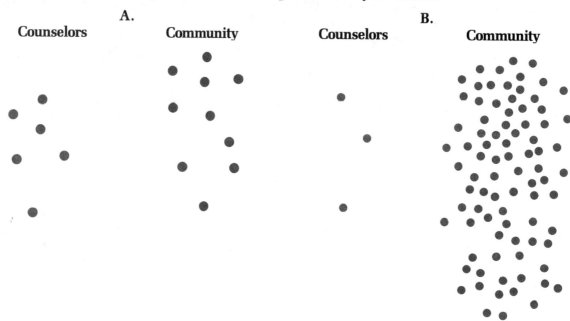

A.
Counselors   Community

B.
Counselors   Community

In most communities more needy people exist than professional counselors to help them. More than likely your community is no different. You should have circled B. Notice the Proverb we included on the front cover of WiseCounsel: "Where no counsel is, the people fall: but in the multitude of counsellors there is safety" (Prov. 11:14).

■ **Write in two reasons Christians should provide lay counseling.**

1. _____

2. _____

3. **Christians have a responsibility to minister to others.**

Reason 3: Christians Have a Responsibility to Minister to Others

The idea of using laypersons as counselors ties in with our concept of Christian ministry. One important doctrine of our faith is called, "The priesthood of all believers." Every believer is a priest. Each Christian has a place to fill in the ministry of the church. Each is to be concerned about others. We must be willing to help meet the needs of others.

■ **You evidently have a concern to help others, or you would not be studying WiseCounsel. Why did you decide to take this course? Write your answer here:**

_____

_____

_____

_____

_____

_____

_____

_____

In the introduction, one prerequisite I mentioned was a sense of calling to ministry. You may or may not feel that kind of calling to a counseling ministry right now. By your participation in WiseCounsel, however, you will be equipped for a lay counseling ministry. Begin praying that God will clearly reveal to you ways you can and should use this training in ministry to others.

■ **Pause to pray right now.**

Pastors and church leaders urge laypersons to share the gospel and lead others to faith in Christ. We trust laypersons with this all-important task. We also must be willing to let a layperson assist this same person in emotional and relational problems.

The layperson does, however, face certain limitations. I will seek to make you aware of some of these limitations during the course. I will provide you with training and experiences that will help you become an effective counselor. I will also help you know when and how to refer persons to others when you cannot or should not try to help.

■ **Write the three reasons Christians should provide lay counseling.**

1. _____

2. _____

3. _____

Day 2: Counseling as Shepherding

> **Today's Objective:** You will be able to describe in your own words five demands of counseling.

The image of the work of the shepherd is heavily impressed on the Christian faith. In the Old Testament God's care for His children is described as a Shepherd's care for His sheep. "He tends his flock like a shepherd: He gathers the lambs in his arms and carries them close to his heart; he gently leads those that have young" (Isa. 40:11). Christian leaders are exhorted to "Be shepherds of God's flock" and to be "examples to the flock." For doing so, they will be rewarded by the Chief Shepherd (1 Pet. 5:2-4).

The Shepherd and His Sheep

Methods of modern-day shepherding contrast vividly with the eastern shepherd of biblical times. A major difference is the relationship of the shepherd and his sheep.

■ **In the following paragraph look for two ways Jesus describes this relationship between the shepherd and his sheep.**

Jesus said, "I am the good shepherd; I know my sheep and my sheep know me" (John 10:14). He further reminded His followers of the special relationship of the shepherd, "When he has brought out all his own, he goes on ahead of them, and his sheep follow him because they know his voice. But they will never follow a stranger; in fact, they will run away from him because they do not recognize a stranger's voice" (John 10:4-5).

■ **What are two ways Jesus describes the relationship between a good shepherd and his sheep?**

    1. _____

    2. _____

A shepherd and his sheep spend so much time together they *know* each other intimately. They *care* about each other. Consequently, the sheep trust in and follow the leadership of the shepherd. The shepherd leads his sheep to green pastures and still waters. He leads them away from dangerous places. In similar ways, you will build relationships with those you counsel.

I made my commitment to Christ as I lay in a hospital bed. Mrs. Bull came to visit me. She challenged me and led me to make this all-important decision. Later, I accepted a call to a church related vocation. On the night of my ordination this good lady came by to congratulate me. She handed me a present. She had painted a copy of the Good Shepherd on the mountainside reaching out to rescue a lamb that had been captured in the thicket. Her admonition still rings in my ears, "This is your task, John."

The Demands of Counseling

David, the shepherd boy, became the great king of Israel. His shepherding experiences helped prepare him for much of the work God called him to. Many parallels can be drawn between the work of the counselor and the work of the shepherd.

■ **Read these five demands of counseling and circle a key word or phrase in each one that describes the demand.**

1. Counseling is difficult work. David attested to the difficulty of shepherding when he spoke of fighting the lion and the bear. In a counseling ministry you will confront many difficult situations. Counseling is not the work of the fainthearted. If you are not willing to face difficult and challenging situations do not try to counsel.

2. Counseling demands time. The shepherd spent long hours with his flock. Counseling is similarly demanding of our time. Like the sheep, very frequently the individuals we work with have not made intelligent choices. The movement of people from some of their self-defeating behavior is often a slow and tedious process that demands patience and time.

3. Counseling requires a special concern for families. "He tends his flock like a shepherd: He gathers the lambs in his arms and carries them close to his heart; he gently leads those that have young" (Isa. 40:11). This reminds us that in our work the family will always be a major consideration. Some of these families are seriously mixed up and call for careful handling. Children of future generations may be blessed because we took time to help.

4. Counseling requires tolerance. David's sheep sometimes wandered into trouble. They were not necessarily defiant, just wanderers. We will find that our counselees are frequently foolish but not deliberately wicked. We must be just as tolerant with them as the shepherd was with his flock.

5. Counselees demand attention. The shepherd stayed and watched over his flock no matter what. He could never leave them alone for fear that a lion or bear might attack the flock. This required a responsible person. Most people need some attention at one time or another. As a counselor, you too must be observant and try to help protect your counselees from unforeseen dangers. The counselor must maintain a watchful eye over those he is helping.

■ **On the lines below list the words or phrases you circled. Then briefly describe the demand in your own words.**

1. _____

   _____

2. _____

   _____

3. _____

   _____

4. _____

   _____

5. _____

   _____

Close your book. Try to remember the key idea in each of the five demands. Check yourself with the list in the book. Now on seperate paper write the five demands of counseling in your own words without looking at your book.

> "Be shepherds of God's flock."—This is our calling.

Day 3: Wise Counseling

> **Today's Objective:** You will be able to list sources of wisdom for the process and the content of counseling.

People turn to a variety of sources for "counseling." Some are sources for wise counseling. Others may be sources for foolish counseling. Still others may even be sources for evil counseling.

■ **Make a list of some of the sources people turn to for counseling help.**

Yes, the list could be quite lengthy. You may have included such sources as pastors, doctors, teachers, psychologists, psychiatrists, and mental health clinics. You also may have included books, magazines, newspapers, television, horoscopes, palm readers, bartenders, gurus, friends, salespersons, "Dear Abby," or others. Some of these would be fairly reliable sources for wise counsel and others would not be reliable at all. In fact, some of the least reliable often times may be the most popular. Wise counseling with Christian values is much needed in our world.

The Wise

In the Old Testament days people known as "the wise" began to appear in countries around the Mediterranean shoreline. For years respect had been growing for people who were able to help others with their problems. They primarily achieved their reputations as being wise because their counsel proved helpful to others. As the value of these wise people became recognized, they were added as important members to the king's court.

Wise people were included in the court of King David. One roll call of the significant people in the kingdom included, "Jonathan, David's uncle, was a counselor, a man of insight and a scribe. . . . Ahithophel was the king's counselor. Hushai the Arkite was the king's friend" (1 Chron. 27:32-33). Although women did not enjoy a very high status in the society of that day, some were recognized as possessing these helping skills also. As David went through a struggle in his relationships with his son Absolom, his friend Joab perceived that he needed some help. Joab called in a "wise woman" from Tekoa to help the troubled king (2 Sam. 14:2).

Helps for Wise Counseling

Process. As you can readily see from the title of this course, our goal is to equip you to provide *wise counseling* to needy persons you come in contact with from day to day. WiseCounsel will help you in the *process* of counseling. For example, you will find answers to such questions as:
- How do I identify the real problem?
- Which people should I refer to professional counselors?
- What boundaries should I set up for a counseling session or relationship?
- What steps can I take to help a person make wise decisions?
- What are the dynamics of a counseling relationship that I should recognize?
- How can I help people change patterns of behavior?
- How long should a counseling relationship last?

Content. You do need wisdom in the process of counseling. But you also need godly wisdom in the *content* of your counseling. God's Word and the leadership of the Holy Spirit will be your primary sources for this wisdom. Wisdom should guide the "content" of your counseling in ways like the following:
- What is this person's responsibility for this particular problem?
- What biblically based alternatives do we need to examine?
- What biblical principles should be used in evaluating the probable outcomes of various alternatives?
- Can teachings from Scripture provide practical information in this situation?

WiseCounsel will help you know how to counsel people. It will also provide you with Scriptures related to issues you may face. WiseCounsel is not, however, intended to provide you with all the principles and values a Christian should know and live by. God's Word and the Holy Spirit will help you know what you should say and do in many of the situations that arise in your counseling. For God's help, however, you must walk in the Spirit and abide in Christ. Study God's Word regularly and pray for His wisdom to fill your mind.

■ **Circle the letter of the correct answer in the following questions.**

1. WiseCounsel is primarily intended to provide you with wisdom in what area(s)?
   a. the process of counseling
   b. the content of counseling
   c. both the process and the content of counseling

2. What are your primary sources for wisdom in the *content* of counseling?
   a. WiseCounsel
   b. the Bible
   c. leadership of the Holy Spirit
   d. all of the above
   e. both b and c

As stated in the introduction, I am assuming that you already have a biblically based Christian value system. A working knowledge of God's Word is also invaluable as you seek to help persons make wise decisions. This course is not intended to provide you with all the biblical principles involved in the problems you will encounter as a counselor, though we will try to help. We are focusing primarily on helping you learn the process of counseling. Answers: 1-a; 2-e. Even though the name of this course is WiseCounsel, I will focus primarily on the process of counseling. I am depending on you to seek godly wisdom from God's Word and the Holy Spirit.

Whole books are devoted to the Christian's view of subjects like divorce, aging, ethics in the workplace, marriage and family life, life as a single, retirement living, coping with grief, and so forth. You may want to study some of these in subject areas you confront regularly. I encourage you to study the Bible and other sources to discover what the Bible has to say about the subjects you will encounter most often.

At the very least, I do want to stimulate your thinking about these subject areas and some of the biblical teachings involved. I will challenge you from time to time to examine Scriptures to discover biblical principles. You will have opportunity in your small-group sessions to discuss the biblical teachings you have studied. If you find disagreement in certain areas, you may want to do more detailed study to develop a better understanding of the issues and the biblical principles involved. This series of assignments will be titled "God's Word and Wisdom." Here is the first of these assignments.

■ **Write a brief summary of what the following Scriptures have to say about sources of wisdom.**

Psalms 111:10 _____

_____

_____

GOD'S W

Proverbs 2:6 _____

_____

AND WIS

_____

2 Timothy 3:14-17 _____

_____

_____

James 1:5 _____

_____

_____

List some sources you intend to use that will provide you with wisdom for the

process of counseling: _____

_____

the content of counseling: _____

_____

Day 4: Introducing the Ten-Step Counseling Model

> **Today's Objective:** You will be able to identify the basic structure of the Ten-Step Counseling Model and describe the importance of using questions.

TEN-STEP COUNSELING MODEL

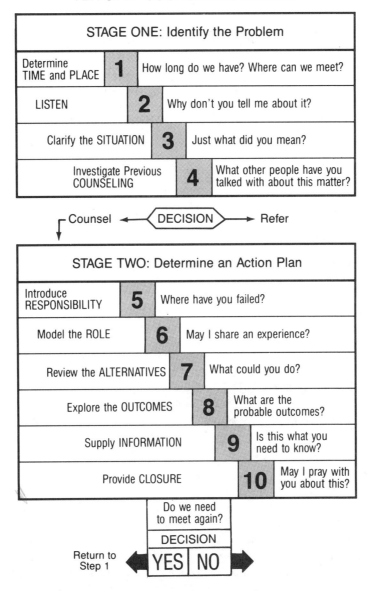

As you look at the course map on the back cover, you can see that the Ten-Step Counseling Model is the heart of the counseling process. These ten steps are vital to your counseling with confidence. I will help you memorize each of the ten steps and the questions that guide you from step to step. Once memorized, you will be able to use this process anytime you have an opportunity to help a person solve a problem or make a decision.

Stages. Notice that the model is divided into two stages. The first four steps help you begin a counseling relationship and *identify the problem.* At that point you make a decision about whether you should counsel the person or refer him to others for help. We will focus on identifying the problem in unit 2.

When you decide to continue counseling the individual, you enter stage two. You will use steps five through ten to *determine an action plan.* In unit 3 you will learn to help a counselee determine an action plan. You will use these ten steps again and again to counsel the individuals you work with.

Questions. One or more questions is used at each step to guide your formal or informal counseling. Part of the secret of the plan lies in its use of questions. By using the questions, your counseling will flow very naturally from one step to the next.

■ 1. Take a few minutes to study the course map. You will be studying each part in detail later. For now, see if you can begin to grasp the relationship between parts.

2. Use the information above and the course map to answer the following questions.

    A. What are the two stages of the Ten-Step Counseling Model?

        Stage One: _____

        Stage Two: _____

    B. Which steps of the Ten-Step Model are used at each stage?

        Stage One: Steps 1—_____   Stage Two: Steps 5—_____

    C. What key decision do you make at the end of stage one?

        _____

    D. What decision do you make at the end of stage two?

        _____

I have asked you these questions to help you identify the structure of the Ten-Step Counseling Model. Stage one is "Identify the Problem" and stage two is "Determine an Action Plan." Use steps one through four for stage one and five through ten for stage two. At the end of stage one, you decide whether to counsel or refer the person. At the end of stage two, you decide whether you need to meet for another counseling session or not.

The Importance of the Question

Question-and-answer is one of the oldest teaching techniques known to educators. Questions challenge people to think. Well-worded questions direct attention to the key ideas under discussion. Jesus, the greatest of all teachers, frequently had a question on His lips. If you watch an effective teacher at work, you will be impressed by his or her skillful use of the question. Questions are valuable tools for education. The question also serves as a powerful tool for the counselor who is skillful in its use.

In the course of a presentation, the outstanding Methodist pastor Dr. Charles Allen told an audience of seminary students that he had developed a marvelous new counseling technique. Allen, already known for some of his books such as *God's Psychiatry* and *Twelve Ways to Solve Your Problems,* caused the students to listen even more intently.

Allen presented his counseling method in his own matchless way. When someone came to him for counseling he said he would ask, "What seems to be your situation?" His counselee would then proceed to recount all the difficulties he was facing, sometimes taking a considerable amount of time.

Next, the pastor would ask a second question, "What do you think you should do?" His counselee then advanced his ideas about the course of action he should take. By the time this plan of action had been presented, the time had come to conclude the counseling session. As Allen saw it most people's problems could be handled by using the two-question method.

Dr. Allen's "new counseling technique" was a practical way to help persons identify their problems and look at alternative solutions. It points out the value of the question in counseling. As a counselor, you must keep in mind, however, that not all people have Christian values and a spiritual background that will lead them to solve their problems with God's wisdom. This fact reinforces the need for you to be spiritually attuned to God's will and ways. In the Ten-Step Model, you will use additional questions to guide your counseling and provide opportunity for you to help the counselee examine God's will and ways.

■ **Write a summary of the importance of using questions.**

_____

_____

_____

What relationship do you see between Dr. Allen's two-question method and the Ten-Step Model?

_____

_____

_____

Your summary should have included some of the following ideas. Questions are important teaching tools. They cause people to think. They focus attention on the key ideas or concepts. They are helpful in guiding a conversation or counseling session. Dr. Allen's two-question method is seen in the two stages of the Ten-Step Model. His first question about the counselee's situation is stage one—Identify the Problem. His second question about what the counselee plans to do is stage two—Determine an Action Plan.

Day 5: Asking Effective Questions

> **Today's Objective:** You will be able to apply the guidelines for effective questioning to identify effective questions.

One simple rule of thumb for opening conversation with a question is:

> Never ask a question that can be answered by "yes" or "no"
> unless you have a follow-up question ready.

■ **See if you can restate this rule in a positive way.**

_____

_____

You will discuss this rule in your group session this week.

Open Questions

The best conversation openers do not just seek simple one-word answers. Neither do they ask just about facts. They focus on a person's feelings, attempting to help him or her verbalize emotional reactions, opinions, ideas, and so forth. For example: Assume that you are talking with Joe Jones, who seems to be greatly troubled by a family problem. One way of approaching his problem would be to ask him, "Do you like living with your brother?" The obvious answers are either yes or no. After one or the other is given, looking at each other is about all you have left to do.

■ **Try rephrasing this question to receive a more involved response.**

_____

A better question would be something like, "How do you feel about living with your brother?" or "What are the joys and problems you encounter living with your brother?" These questions may evoke his feelings and ideas thereby stimulating further discussion. Open questions seek the help of the six words about which Rudyard Kipling wrote:

> I keep six honest serving-men,
> (They taught me all I knew)
> Their names are What and Why and When
> And How and Where and Who.[4]

These "honest serving-men" invite the counselee to express his or her ideas on a variety of subjects. Here are some guidelines for developing your skills at questioning:

> ### Guidelines for Effective Questioning
>
> - Take every possible chance to ask a searching question. Then keep quiet and listen for the response.
> - Questions that come close to the other person's true interest get the best answers—providing you are interested too.
> - Be prepared to wait. Sometimes a long silence can be more rewarding than another question.
> - In every case the quality of an answer depends on the quality of the attention given by the questioner.
> - Questions that deal with a person's feelings are more provocative than those that deal with facts.

■ **Try out your ability to identify effective questions. The following list contains some good questions and some poor ones. On the lines at the left, write G in front of the good questions and P in front of the poor ones.**

_____ 1. Did you have a good day today?
_____ 2. How do you feel about this?
_____ 3. Do you like your work?
_____ 4. What is your reaction?
_____ 5. What ideas do you have on the subject?
_____ 6. Would you explain this to me?
_____ 7. Will you accept this new offer?
_____ 8. Oh, really?
_____ 9. Why do you think she responds to you that way?
____ 10. When did you begin to feel this way?

Questions that can be answered with a noncommittal yes or no are poor questions for use in counseling. Thus, you should have placed a P beside 1, 3, 7, and 8. You should have placed a G beside 2, 4, 5, 6, 9, and 10, because they stimulate further conversation. Here are a few more examples of good open questions:

- How do you think your husband should go about handling this problem?
- What have you done about getting this matter under control?
- Why is this relationship so important to you?
- How do your daughter's attitudes look to you?

A famous preacher was asked the secret of posing a good question. His reply was, "I suppose the secret, if there is one, is to realize that questioning and listening are inseparable. The asking of good questions represents listening on its highest plane, and that of course can never be faked or turned on—it must come from within. I believe it is the quality of attention that makes all the difference."

Congratulations! You have just completed your first unit of WiseCounsel.

UNIT 2

Identify the Problem

This Week's Learning Goal

After studying this unit, you will understand the steps to take in identifying a counselee's problem. You will understand when to make a referral to others for help.

Why You Will Find This Study Useful

I want to help you develop the skill of identifying a counselee's problem. In this unit you will memorize four steps to take in identifying a problem. Then, I will help you determine whether you should counsel the person or refer him to a professional counselor or agency for help.

Day 1: Memorize Stage One

> **Today's Objective:** You will be able to write the steps and
> questions used in stage one of the Ten-Step Counseling Model.

Why Should I Memorize the Ten Steps?

Good question. You probably are not fond of memorizing. Usually, we only memorize
what is of practical value. I would guess that you have memorized your address, your
phone number, your Social Security number, and other such practical things. Sometimes
we memorize items in a certain sequence. See if the following sequence sounds familiar.

1. open door
2. get into car
3. close door
4. put on seat belt
5. place key in ignition
6. press gas pedal
7. turn key
8. release key
9. move gear shift to "R"

10. look in rearview mirror
11. press gas pedal slowly
12. turn wheel at appropriate times
13. step on brake
14. look forward
15. move gear shift to "D"
16. press gas pedal slowly
17. drive away

"That's simple," you might say. "I don't ever have to stop and think about those steps.
They just come naturally."

Exactly! You do not have to think about each step now. You have memorized what to do
and when to do it. Suppose you were to try and teach this process to an adult from a
primitive country who had never driven a car. What would happen if he did step 9 before
steps 7 and 8? The car would not start. What if he left out step 12 altogether? Crash!
Sometimes we memorize steps in a sequence for a reason. We can perform a complicated
task without having to stop and think through each step first. We save time and can
perform the task in a natural way.

This is why I want you to memorize the Ten-Step Counseling Model. Memorizing the
model will help you:
- perform a complicated task without having to stop and think through each step
- save time for more intense listening
- accomplish tasks in the best order (Imagine trying to review the alternatives before you
  have identified the real problem.)
- counsel in a natural way
- have confidence in the direction you are going
- get back on track if your counselee decides to "chase a rabbit"

You will be memorizing the model in two stages. Let's begin work on the four steps of
stage one. Your goal in stage one is to identify the counselee's problem. Then you will
decide whether you will counsel this person yourself or refer him to others for help.

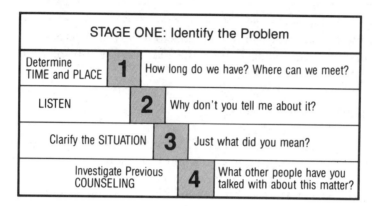

1. Read through the four steps and the questions that go with them.

2. Circle the following words in the diagram above: *time and place, listen, situation,* and *counseling*.

3. Try to capture a mental picture that will help you remember each word. You may want to include the step number in your picture. Crazy or humorous pictures may be the most memorable. (For example: for *time* you could visualize a huge wrist watch set at 1 o'clock. For *situation* you could visualize a person on top of a stool with three mice on the floor.) Write a brief description of your mental images on these lines:

   Time and Place: _____

   Listen: _____

   Situation: _____

   Counseling: _____

4. Write the key word(s) for each step.

   Step 1: Determine _____

   Step 2: _____

   Step 3: Clarify the _____

   Step 4: Investigate Previous _____

5. Draw a line from each question on the left to the step where it is used.

   Just what did you mean?   **Step 1: Time and Place**

   Where can we meet?

   What other people have you   **Step 2: Listen**
   talked with about this matter?

                                                          Step 3: Situation
   How long do we have?

   Why don't you tell me about it?   **Step 4: Counseling**

6. Now read *aloud* the four steps and the questions for each. Reread the steps two more times.

7. See if you can write the four steps (without the questions) from memory.

   Step 1: _____

   Step 2: _____

   Step 3: _____

   Step 4: _____

8. Now see if you can write the questions for each step. They do not have to be exact at this time as long as you get the essence of the question.

   Step 1: Time and Place _____

   Step 2: Listen _____

   Step 3: Situation _____

   Step 4: Counseling _____

Using the course map, check your work for these assignments.

Write the steps and questions on an index card. Carry it with you through the day for review. Keep reviewing the steps and the questions whenever you have an opportunity. We will work on understanding each step in the days to come.

Day 2: Time and Place; Listen

> **Today's Objective:** You will be able to (a) explain a way to determine a time, (b) describe the ideal counseling setting, and (c) explain one value of listening.

Determine TIME and PLACE	**1**	How long do we have? Where can we meet?
LISTEN	**2**	Why don't you tell me about it?

Step 1: Determine Time and Place

Time. Time is an important ingredient in counseling. When someone initiates a contact with you, he will frequently say, "This will only take a minute," or "Can you spare a moment?" In actual practice, however, few counseling experiences reach a successful conclusion in a moment or a few minutes.

You cannot carry on a good counseling relationship if either party is worried about passing time. You may catch yourself glancing at your watch, hoping that your counselee will pause for a moment so you can bring the conversation to an end. On the other hand, the counselee may suddenly realize she has to get to the bank or pick up her child.

Get off to a good start by asking the question, "How much time do we have?" The discussion may be saved from aimless wandering if you have limited the amount of time available. Time will be wisely used. You also will be able to conclude the session more effectively. Some people are afflicted with the inability to say good-bye. A good counselor who has set time limits at the beginning finds it relatively easy to say, "Thank you so much for sharing this with me, but you will remember that we had thirty minutes and it seems as if our time has gone."

■ 1. **Write two reasons for setting a general time limit on a counseling session.**

   _____

   _____

2. **What question will you generally use to determine the time available?**

   _____

3. **Suppose you have decided to visit a senior adult in a nursing home. He did not ask you to come, but you are aware of his need for your counseling ministry. How could you go about setting a time limit in this situation?**

   _____

   _____

   _____

   _____

   _____

Setting a general time limit helps you use time wisely. It also helps you conclude a session more effectively. Generally you will use the question, "How much time do we have?" When you have initiated a counseling session (as in the nursing home), you could say something like, "I heard about your son's illness. I had an extra thirty minutes and just stopped by to see you." Thus, you have indicated about how much time you plan to stay.

Not all ministry encounters lend themselves to hard and fast time arrangements. Time limits can be changed if necessary. When you are going to need more time, you can say, "If it is all right with you, we can take a few extra minutes." On the other hand, you may find yourself caught in a difficult situation where you need an escape hatch. In those situations you can remind your counselee of the time arrangement decided on at the beginning.

Place. The place arrangements will depend on many factors. Brief counseling, like you will be involved in, may take place in a variety of settings. Semiprivate settings are probably best. Brief counseling can be carried on with other people around. People accidently thrown together often establish easy and helpful relationships under less than ideal circumstances. Yet, these relationships provide opportunities for God to use trained laity to minister to the needy.

I once spoke at a ladies luncheon. As I went through a serving line, I encountered a lady who said, "I understand you are a psychologist, and I have a major problem I must talk to you about." We found two convenient chairs and the lady began to pour out her tearful story. Although the room was comfortably filled with women, they acted as if nothing unusual was happening. Eventually, I was able to break loose from the conversation and arrange to continue later. In that later discussion, she said the experience had been very helpful.

A crowded room is not an ideal setting for counseling; but counseling can take place there, if necessary. If you need to meet again, seek a less public setting. When you have opportunity to adjust or plan for the place of your counseling, the question to use is "Where can we meet?" or "Where can we talk?"

The ideal counseling setting will be a private situation in a semipublic place. This could be one of the Sunday School class rooms or a meeting place near the church. The most important feature is to provide at least some privacy. A certain psychological value lies in the feeling that everything else is temporarily excluded. Do not sit behind a desk or other barrier. Sitting in a chair by the counselee's side, you convey the impression of functioning as a helper.

■ 1. **When you have an opportunity to plan or adjust the place for your counseling, what question will you use?**

_____

2. **Describe the ideal counseling setting.**

_____

_____

_____

3. **Suppose you are planning to counsel a person of the opposite sex. You ask the question, "Where can we meet?" He or she responds, "How about my apartment?" How would you respond and why?**

_____

_____

_____

_____

_____

4. **In a case like #3, would you choose a different approach to determining a place? If so, describe that approach.**

_____

_____

_____

_____

_____

_____

5. **Examine this counseling setting. If you were the counselor, what would you do differently?**

_____

_____

_____

_____

_____

_____

_____

_____

_____

_____

6. **What are the two questions you will use as guides for step 1?**

_____

_____

(1) The question you use is: "Where can we meet?" (2) You would seek a private situation in a semipublic place. "Private" means a place where you can talk with few interruptions or distractions. "Semipublic" means a place where you are not totally alone. You do not need people close enough to overhear the conversation, but someone in the near vicinity would help. This builds boundaries that will help avoid problems that could arise when you happen to be counseling a person of the opposite sex. We will talk more about boundaries in unit 6. (3) Normally you would not go to a person's apartment—that is too private for counseling a person of the opposite sex. You need to "abstain from all appearance of evil" (1 Thess. 5:22). Suppose, however, that this is a marriage counseling situation, and you are going to the apartment to meet with the spouse. This is a more acceptable situation. Be wise; use discretion in selecting a place. (4) If a person of the opposite sex seeks you out as a counselor, you can recommend an appropriate place rather than asking the person for a suggestion. (5) In this counseling setting, you would do well to turn the stereo off so you can hear clearly. You also will improve rapport and communication by sitting beside the counselee rather than behind the desk. (6) Check your course map for these two questions.

Step 2: Listen

If you are going to be a counselor, you must be a listener. Help your counselee start talking with the question, "Why don't you tell me about it?" Then listen. A good listener gives the impression that he really wants to understand all about the other person. He puts aside every other thought, so he can try to understand just what his subject is grappling with. Listening is a fundamental skill for counseling. I have devoted all of unit 4 to helping you develop or improve that skill. For now keep this rule in mind:

> **A Listening Rule:** Spend two thirds of the available counseling time listening.

■ **Write from memory the first two steps and the questions you will use to guide each step.**

Step 1: _____

    Questions: _____

                             _____

Step 2: _____

    Question: _____

Use the course map to check your work.

Day 3: The Situation and Previous Counseling

> **Today's Objective:** You will be able to describe ways to clarify the situation and investigate previous counseling.

Clarify the SITUATION	**3**	Just what did you mean?
Investigate Previous COUNSELING	**4**	What other people have you talked with about this matter?

Step 3: Clarify the Situation

■ **As you read the following section, look for answers to these questions:**
  • *What* do I need to clarify?
  • *Why* do they need to be clarified?
  • *How* can I ask for clarification?

Clarify Words and Phrases. The person who seeks counseling from you may be under stress. Stressed people often experience great difficulty in expressing themselves. Your subject may stumble around trying to think of a way to tell you the difficulty she is struggling with. The story may not be at all logical. It may come tumbling out in a confused stream of language.

Some people use confusing language. Words and phrases like, "and stuff, and everything" are space filler expressions. The subject can't think what to say next and throws in a few space fillers that confuse the listener. To clarify words and phrases use the question, "Just what did you mean?"

Clarify the Order of Events. Walter Mathau once said, "I like a story which has a beginning, a middle, and a conclusion, preferably in that order." A counselor generally feels the same way. Frequently you will find that the counselee is not concerned about chronology. He or she may give a confused recital of events.

Clarify the Real Problem. Sometimes the person who comes for counseling will say, "I know I need help but I don't know what to say." My answer in this situation is to say, "Just talk about whatever seems to be worrying you most at this time."

As the counselee begins to talk you will begin a process of evaluating the need of this individual. As a beginning counselor you may sometimes be surprised to discover the problem first presented is not the real problem. The problem first presented is the "presenting problem." The real problem may be in some other area of life.

You must learn not to jump to a conclusion. In these situations, accept the problem presented, but do not become too immersed in it. Suspend judgment until you feel reasonably certain that you have discovered the real problem. Keep an open mind in the early stages of the counseling relationship and remain alert for any turn the presentation may take.

One pastor told of a man who said he would become a Christian if the preacher could show him where Cain got his wife. The pastor tried to explain. It turned out, however, that it was not Cain's wife who was worrying him. The man was worried about his relationship to somebody else's wife.

If the statements of the counselee are really confused, the situation may call for specific questioning. The counselor must gently but firmly ask, "Will you please explain just what you mean when you say you want to get out of it," or "Will you please explain what this relationship has to do with your brother's sister-in-law?"

■ **Fill in this chart with your findings.**

CLARIFY THE SITUATION		
What do you clarify?	**Why do you clarify them?**	**How do you ask for clarification?**
WORDS AND PHRASES		
ORDER OF EVENTS		
REAL PROBLEMS		

Step 4: Investigate Previous Counseling

Part of identifying the problem involves this step. Efforts of a counselee to consult with other people may indicate something about the seriousness of the situation. The question you will use is: "What other persons have you talked with about this matter?"

Suppose the subject responds, "Well, there was a time when I went to see a social worker, later I had some sessions with my pastor, and for a period of time I was in therapy with a psychologist. Last year, after one interview with a psychiatrist, I was admitted to the psychiatric ward of All Saints Hospital." In this situation you will realize you have a "therapy gypsy" on your hands. This type of person is emotionally disturbed. He may be doing more to seek attention than a solution to his problems. As a counselor, you will probably be able to do very little to help.

Suppose this person says, "I can't remember ever talking to anyone other than a few close friends." A person with this response will be more likely to benefit from the counsel you have to offer.

■ **Why do you need to investigate previous counseling? Check the best answer.**
   □ a. **Because I'm curious.**
   □ b. **Because I may want to talk with some of these other people to find out what they think about this problem.**
   □ c. **Because the number of people this counselee has talked with may tell me something about the seriousness of the problem.**
   □ d. **Because I do not want to waste my time on someone that no one else can help.**

   Describe how you will investigate previous counseling.

   _____

   _____

   _____

Discovering the seriousness of the problem is your real reason for asking the question, "What other persons have you talked with about this matter?" If the counselee has talked with many different people, he or she may be emotionally disturbed and in need of professional help. You should have checked item "c." Curiosity is no reason to probe into a person's privacy. Lay counselors are not likely to benefit from talking with others about the person's problem. If the problem is so serious that you need to consult other counselors, you probably should refer the counselee to begin with.

Counseling with someone should not be considered a waste of time, even if others have failed to help. For instance, you may sense that the person has a spiritual problem, but he has only talked with secular counselors. In such a case, your spiritual counsel may be the help he is searching for.

Be careful, however. Christians correctly believe that all things are possible with God. However, this belief could encourage you to counsel a person that has serious emotional problems you are not trained to handle. You could do more harm than good. In such cases, you should consider referral.

■ **Write from memory steps three and four and the question you will use to guide each step.**

Step 3: _____

      Question: _____

Step 4: _____

      Question: _____

Identifying the problem is very important, but it is just a beginning. Tomorrow we will consider one outcome of this assessment as we look into the process of making a referral.

Day 4: Making Referrals for Assistance

> **Today's Objective:** You will be able to (a) define what a referral is, (b) identify emotional difficulties that call for referral, (c) identify the correct way to make a referral in given cases.

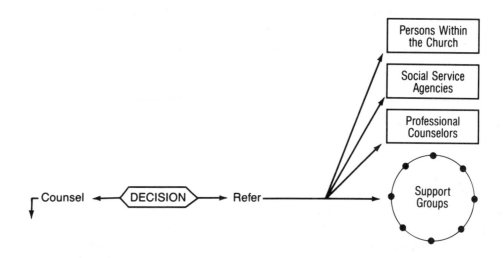

As a counselor, you do not have the training, ability, resources, or experience to help every counselee who comes to talk with you. Some needs can best be met by a person or agency that is especially prepared to provide specific types of assistance. Some psychological problems should be referred to a professionally trained counselor. You would be wise not to venture into areas like severe emotional disorders or physical disorders. You have not been trained to handle these situations. Certain professionals are highly trained and capable of providing this help. Getting counselees in touch with the appropriate assistance is called referral.

■ 1. **Write a definition for:**

    referral—_____

_____

2. **True or False? This is an example of referral. Mark each example as T (True—this is a referral) or F (False—this is not a referral).**

_____ A A homeless person comes by the church Wednesday night looking for shelter from the bitter cold. You drive him to the local rescue mission for help.

_____ B A homeless person comes by the church Sunday morning looking for food. You drive her to the Pancake Shop and pay for her breakfast.

_____ C A class member's father died suddenly. You let her talk, but you have difficulty relating to her feelings. You loan her a copy of a book about the grief process.

_____ D Jeff has had some real emotional problems at home. They seem to be causing severe headaches. You suggest that he first visit his family doctor for a physical check-up.

_____ E Bill and Sonja are separated and seeking a divorce. They are unwilling to accept your conclusions about the teaching of Scripture concerning God's plan for marriage. You ask them to agree to talk with your pastor. Then you call him to set up the meeting.

A referral is an instance where you send a person to someone else for assistance. This may be a professional counselor, an agency, other helping person, or organization. In the True/False quiz A, D, and E are True. Notice that in each case the person or persons is directed to someone else for help—the rescue mission, the family doctor, your pastor. B and C are False. You met the need in B; that is obviously not a referral. You may have missed C; it was a bit tricky. By allowing the grieving person to talk and by providing information (a book) you have provided the counseling. In one sense you *are* referring her to an expert on the grieving process, but you are still the counselor. We will not consider this action as a referral. You should follow-up with another visit to discuss what she discovered while reading the book. We will discuss the idea of bibliotherapy (providing helpful literature as a counseling technique) in a future unit.

The process of referral begins when, after due consideration of all the aspects of the counselee's problem, you realize the problem is beyond your ability to help. You should then tell the counselee of your inadequacy in this area and suggest someone else who can be of greater help to him or her. Let's examine types of emotional difficulties that you should refer and those you may be able to help yourself.

Emotional Difficulties

Many strange motivations are at work in emotional illness. These sometimes cause the sufferer to turn to the fellowship of the church for help. Some turn to religion as a "last straw" in an effort to cope with apparently unmanageable emotional problems. While you can help with many of these problems, some are so serious that you cannot handle them. Individuals with serious problems need professional help. As you assess an individual's emotional problems try to answer this question: How disturbed is this person? Emotional difficulties can be classified in the following four categories:

Neurotic Reactions. Neurotic reactions are the milder types of emotional maladjustment than the psychotic conditions described below. Individuals with neurotic reactions are uncomfortable and perhaps even distressed. They may experience mild physical ailments, anxieties, or fears. But, they are still capable of functioning at a fairly effective level. They need help and you can offer them opportunities, through counseling, to move toward achieving their potential.

Psychotic Conditions. Psychotic conditions are out of the sphere of the lay counselor. You need to become aware of some warning signals. While observing the prospective counselee, note if he shows signs of severe emotional difficulty. Some of these are that the person:

1. Shows big changes in behavior.
2. Has strange periods of confusion or loss of memory.
3. Thinks people are plotting against him, watching him, or talking about him.
4. Has grandiose ideas about himself saying he is George Washington, Superman, or Jesus Christ.
5. Talks to himself and hears voices.
6. Sees visions, smells strange odors, or has peculiar tastes.
7. Complains of bodily changes that are not possible.
8. Is plagued by scary thoughts.
9. Suffers from the need to perform repetitive acts many times over.
10. Shows markedly depressed behavior.
11. Behaves in a way that is dangerous to himself or others.

These criteria need to be used cautiously. In their milder forms, these experiences come to all normal people. However, when they are gross or exaggerated, they are serious. Another consideration is that just one of them may not be enough. When there is a cluster of several of these symptoms, they have to be seriously considered. In such cases you should seek a good referral person.

Physiologically Based Conditions. Physiologically based conditions have their origin in the functions of the body. They may be due to toxins in the body, chemical imbalances, or a host of other physical causes. Some of the psychotic conditions may be the result of a physiologically based condition, but you probably would not be able to tell. Refer the psychotic conditions to a reputable Christian psychiatrist or psychologist. Physiologically based conditions like headaches, dizziness, fainting spells, loss of appetite, sudden weight changes, and so forth are outside the scope of the lay counselor. They need to be referred to a capable physician.

Character Disorders. Character disorders have to do with the value system or conscience. An individual with a character disorder is apparently devoid of socially acceptable values. He can commit a crime or immoral act with no sense of guilt that he has done wrong. He is often referred to as a sociopathic personality. He needs special attention. He can be helped, but it must be done carefully and preferably in specialized group therapy.

■ This may seem pretty complicated to you. Do not worry. That is why professionals require years of education and experience. This may be an area in which you will want to do further study as time goes by. For now, see if you can match the problem on the left with the category on the right. Draw a line from the problem to the category.

Problem	Category
1. Joe complains of fainting spells, memory losses, and headaches.	a. Neurotic Reaction
2. Vick's parents have asked you to talk with him. He is 13. He is constantly vandalizing property. He has been arrested twice for shoplifting. He does not see anything wrong with his behavior.	b. Psychotic Condition
3. Maria claims to be Mother Teresa. She says she can perform miracles. As you talk, she rocks back and forth. She occasionally turns her head and responds to inaudible "voices."	c. Physiologically Based Condition
4. Brenda says she has good days and bad days. She gets so depressed that she eats to pamper her emotions. She has mood swings that take her from joy to depression. This has really been a problem since her mother's death last year.	d. Character Disorder

Brenda appears to be suffering from a grief reaction over her mother's death. This is probably just a normal neurotic reaction. You should be able to help. Maria exhibits several of the warning signals I gave you. This sounds like a psychotic condition that requires professional help. Vick seems to lack any sense of moral values. His anti-social behavior seems to indicate a character disorder. He needs special help that you are not trained to provide. Joe has some indication of physical problems. His best course of action would include a physical checkup looking for a physiologically based condition. Answers are 1-c; 2-d; 3-b; 4-a.

Two Possible Problems in Making Referrals

The skill of referral is not easily learned. Some professionals say that a large proportion of referrals are unsuccessful. However, if you observe some of the precautions suggested here, you will improve the effectiveness of your counseling ministry. Referral will call for tact, skill, and patience; but it is a necessary skill for any counselor to develop.

Two possible problems can arise when you try to make a referral. The counselee may feel rejected and never follow through with the person or agency you recommend. The second possible problem can arise because you are anxious to avoid giving the impression of rejection. You may oversell the person to whom the referral is being made. This can create expectations about the outcome of the contact that are too high to be met. Then the counselee may feel that you misled him. To avoid these two pitfalls:
• Give assurance of your continued interest and
• Realistically present the possibilities of assistance.

■ Which of the following counselors did the best job in trying to avoid the pitfalls of rejection and unrealistic expectations? Circle your choice.

A Sue realized that Sara had some very serious emotional problems. She related her inadequacy to help in this area, but she affirmed her concern. She agreed to take her to a Christian psychologist in a nearby city. Sue said she would continue to be available to Sara anytime she just needed someone to talk to. Sue explained that this psychologist was well trained and could help her solve her problems more quickly.

B As Jimmy listened to Phil's problems, he began to think some chemical imbalance or other physical ailment was the root of the problem. He explained his inadequacy to help in this situation. Jimmy told Phil that a medical doctor should be consulted. He said, "Until you get a doctor's help, I can't be of any help to you. Give me a call after you have seen your doctor."

C Lela felt helpless. She knew that Maggie's emotional problems were too complex for her limited training. Lela explained her inadequacy. She suggested, "Maggie, I want you to talk with my pastor. He used to be a chaplain in a hospital. I think he may be able to help you sort through some of your problems better than I can." She helped make an appointment. She also scheduled a time to get together with Maggie for a friendly lunch the following week.

Write two ways to avoid rejection and unrealistic expectations.

_____

_____

_____

All three of these counselors have done some commendable things. Each one was aware of his or her limitations. Each explained his or her inadequacy. Each knew of a good resource person to refer the counselee to. However, Lela probably treaded between the pitfalls most successfully. Notice that she did not oversell her pastor. She explained his qualifications (a former chaplain) and expressed hope within limits. She limited the expectations by using such words and phrases as "I think," "may be able," and "some." She avoided giving the impression of rejection by setting up a time to meet with Maggie again.

Sue did a great job avoiding rejection. She stayed involved. She remained available. She set Sara up, however, by claiming that this counselor could "solve her problems" and "quickly." Some problems may not have a good or easy solution. They may never be "solved." Deep emotional problems do not develop quickly; and they are seldom, if ever, overcome quickly. Keep these two DON'Ts in mind:

> DON'T promise that a person's problems will be solved.
> DON'T give a definite time frame in which improvement can be expected.

Jimmy may have been correct that a medical doctor was the person to consult. He certainly did not oversell the doctor's skills. However, Jimmy was rather blunt about making the referral. He offered no support while Phil went through the medical tests. In a sense, Jimmy refused to help anymore until Phil followed through with the doctor. Phil may feel rejected after this encounter.

Do not worry if you did not see all these details. I am going to help you learn to improve your ability to make good referrals. I do not want to oversell you, though. Referrals are not always successful—even when a professional does the referring. When assistance is needed for an individual or family you have several sources to turn to for assistance. Let's examine two sources.

Day 5: Sources of Assistance

> **Today's Objective:** You will be able to list three sources of assistance and match qualifications and training with the appropriate titles of professional counselors.

Assistance Source 1: Persons Within the Church

Church staff members may have fine counseling backgrounds. If they do, they can be excellent sources for referral. The lay counselor should be careful to keep in touch with these leaders. Without burdening the pastor or staff with little problems, you should notify them of circumstances where they need to be involved. The busy minister is sometimes unaware of what is going on in the grass roots of church life. By keeping him informed, you perform an important service. Make sure that people who really need to talk with the pastor are put in touch with him.

Within the membership of churches in your community are school teachers, physicians, psychologists, social workers, school counselors, and other professionals. Many of these have experience that could be invaluable in helping some of their fellow church members with their problems. A wise counselor can help make arrangements for a consultation with one of these individuals.

■ **On a separate sheet of paper, list people you readily think of who could provide assistance when a referral is needed. Bring this list with you to your group session.**

Assistance Source 2: Social Service Agencies

A large percentage of people turn to their church in time of trouble. However, the church is not prepared to help in every situation. Social service agencies have the expertise and resources to provide much of the assistance that churches may not be prepared to provide. These agencies are supported by the community. Members of your church may play a large part in supplying the finances to keep some of these agencies going. You should use these resources when they can provide for needs you cannot meet.

You should familiarize yourself with the social service resources within your community. Most cities have some type of directory of social service agencies. If there is no directory in your town you can make a card file on which you can place information about each of the agencies.

To develop a knowledge of community resources, Dr. Charles Kemp has suggested that the counselor find answers to the following questions:

> - Where do you go if a man wants a job?
> - Where do you go if a transient wants a meal and a room for the night?
> - Where do you go for help for an alcoholic?
> - Where do you go when parents wonder if their child is retarded?
> - Where do you go if a husband and wife are having difficulty and it seems to be a deeper problem than you can handle?
> - Where do you go if a family does not have sufficient clothing to send a child to school?
> - Where do you go if there is an older person who needs nursing home care but does not have the funds to provide it?
> - Where do you go if a boy wants to study for the ministry but isn't sure whether he has the intellectual capacity to finish college?
> - Where do you go to find a foster home for a neglected child?
> - Where do you go to find help for a family that needs legal assistance but cannot afford to hire an attorney?
> - How do you find out if a person or family has been consulting other agencies?[1]

Making contact with the agency will probably be the responsibility of the counselor. A telephone call may be sufficient. Your counselee may, however, need help filling out a form or with another initial procedure. You could be of great help by accompanying him to the agency. Social service agencies, when properly used, are a valuable resource for the counselor.

■ **Look at the questions above. For the questions you can answer, write the agency or person's name in the margin beside the question. You will begin to identify other helping persons and agencies during your group session this week. Bring a yellow pages telephone directory to your group session this week.**

What are two sources you can look to for assistance?

_____

_____

You will want to look for persons inside the church who could help. You will also need to identify community social service agencies who provide assistance.

Assistance Source 3: Professional Counselors

Psychiatrist—A person with medical training for his M.D. degree who has had an internship and special training in psychiatry.

Psychoanalyst—This person has similar training to a psychiatrist with the addition of training in Freudian theory and practice. Generally, psychoanalysts are not sympathetic to Christian beliefs.

Psychologist—This person is licensed by the state and holds a doctor's degree in psychology with a clinical major.

Marriage and Family Therapist—This person may be licensed in some states. Generally, this term is applied to someone who has a graduate degree in marriage and family counseling with supervised counseling experience. Preferably, this person should be a member of the American Association of Marriage and Family Therapists.

Social Worker—This person has earned a Master of Social Work degree.

Pastoral Counselor—This person has a graduate degree and work in clinical pastoral education. He is a member of the American Association of Pastoral Counselors. This term, however, may be loosely used to describe a pastor or church staff person who does counseling.

Licensed Professional Counselor—In some states this person is licensed if he has an appropriate graduate degree and supervised counseling experience.

■ **Match the following definitions with the correct professional. Write the correct letter of the definition beside each professional title.**

A. **Has earned a Master of Social Work degree.**
B. **Has a state counseling license with an appropriate graduate degree and supervised counseling experience.**
C. **Has a graduate degree in marriage and family counseling with supervised counseling experience.**
D. **Has similar training to a psychiatrist with training in Freudian theory and practice. Is generally not sympathetic to Christian beliefs.**
E. **Has a graduate degree and work in clinical pastoral education. May be a pastor or church staff person who does counseling.**
F. **Has M.D. degree with an internship and special training in psychiatry.**
G. **Holds a doctor's degree in psychology with a clinical major.**

Professional Titles:

____1. **Psychiatrist**   ____5. **Social Worker**

____2. **Psychoanalyst**   ____6. **Pastoral Counselor**

____3. **Psychologist**   ____7. **Licensed Professional Counselor**

____4. **Marriage and Family Therapist**

Answers to the matching are 1-F; 2-D; 3-G; 4-C; 5-A; 6-E; 7-B.

Selecting a Trustworthy Counselor

Many people set themselves up as counselors. Some are very competent and successful. Others may do more harm than good for your counselee. You must make a decision as to whom you recommend. Here are some criteria you can use to select a counselor to recommend.

Criteria for Counselor Selection

★ Is the counselor a Christian? Does he counsel from a Christian perspective?

★ Who sponsors this counselor? If the counselor is sponsored by a church or some reputable agency, you will have more confidence in sending your counselee.

★ Has this counselor been in the community for very long? The longer the person has been in the community, the more reason to feel he has stood the test of time. If he is a new arrival, he may need to prove himself first.

★ Has the counselor had reasonable success in dealing with other people's problems? The pragmatic test can always be applied to a counselor's work. He should have had a certain amount of success in helping other people. You or your counselee may want to talk with an individual who has been involved in counseling with the counselor.

★ Does this person promise much and do little? Beware of people who are constantly boasting about what they have accomplished. A reputable counselor does not brag and is willing to acknowledge that he is not always successful. Constant boasting may be a cover-up for inadequacy.

★ Has this counselor been adequately trained for his task? By looking back at the list of professional counselors, you will notice the distinctive preparation required for the status of helping people with deep emotional problems.

■ **What are three sources you can look to for assistance?**

_____

_____

_____

Remember to bring a yellow pages telephone directory with you to your group session this week.

UNIT 3
Determine an Action Plan

This Week's Learning Goal

After studying this unit, you will know the steps to take in helping a counselee determine an action plan.

Why You Will Find This Study Useful

After you have identified a counselee's problem, you next help him determine an action plan to begin resolving the problem. In this unit, I will help you learn six steps of the Ten-Step Model that will guide you in this process.

Day 1: Memorize Stage Two

Today's Objective: You will be able to write the steps and questions used in stage two of the Ten-Step Counseling Model.

■ **By way of review, fill in the chart below with the four steps in stage one.**

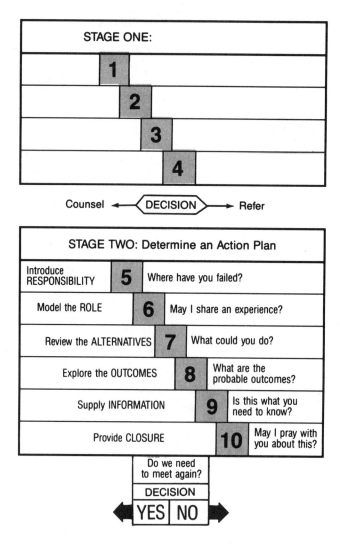

1. **Read through steps 5-10 and the related questions.**

2. **Circle the following words in the diagram:** *responsibility, role, alternatives, outcomes, information,* **and** *closure.*

3. Try to capture a mental picture that will help you remember each word. You may want to include the step number in your picture. (For example: for *responsibility* you could visualize your dog and the neighbor he just bit. Your neighbor is holding up five fingers to indicate the number of teeth marks on his leg.) Write a brief description of your mental images on these lines:

   Responsibility: _____

   Role: _____

   Alternatives: _____

   Outcomes: _____

   Information: _____

   Closure: _____

4. Write the key word(s) in the appropriate spaces:

   Step   5: Introduce _____

   Step   6: Model the _____

   Step   7: Review the _____

   Step   8: Explore the _____

   Step   9: Supply _____

   Step 10: Provide _____

5. Draw a line from each question to the step where it is used.

What are the probable outcomes?	**Step 5: Responsibility**
May I share an experience?	**Step 6: Role**
Do we need to meet again?	**Step 7: Alternatives**
Where have you failed?	**Step 8: Outcomes**
What could you do?	
May I pray with you about this?	**Step 9: Information**
Is this what you need to know?	**Step 10: Closure**

6. Now read aloud the six steps and the related questions in stage two. Read through the list two more times.

7. See if you can write the six steps (without the questions) from memory.

   Step   5: _____

   Step   6: _____

Step 7: _____

Step 8: _____

Step 9: _____

Step 10: _____

8. **Now see if you can write the questions for each step. They do not have to be exact at this time as long as you get the essence of the question.**

Step 5: Responsibility _____

Step 6: Role _____

Step 7: Alternatives _____

Step 8: Outcomes _____

Step 9: Information _____

Step 10: Closure _____

_____

Using the course map, check your work for these assignments. Write these six steps on the index card you prepared last week. Keep reviewing the steps and the questions whenever you have an opportunity. We will work on understanding these steps in the days to come.

■ 1. **Below is a mixed up list of all the steps in the Ten-Step Model. Write them in the correct order.**

Model the Role	**Step 1:** _____
Investigate Previous Counseling	**Step 2:** _____
Supply Information	**Step 3:** _____
Provide Closure	**Step 4:** _____
Determine Time and Place	**Step 5:** _____
Explore the Outcomes	**Step 6:** _____
Listen	**Step 7:** _____
Clarify the Situation	**Step 8:** _____
Introduce Responsibility	**Step 9:** _____
Review the Alternatives	**Step 10:** _____

2. **Close your eyes and see if you can state each step in order and the question or questions you will use with each step.**

The next two lessons deal with four steps. Both lessons are longer than normal. You will have three days to study them. Notice that the first lesson is for days 2 and 3 while the second includes days 3 and 4. Feel free to adjust the daily schedule to meet your needs.

Days 2 and 3: Responsibility and Role

> **Today's Objective:** You will be able to write from memory steps 5 and 6 and the related questions. You will be able to describe the technique of modeling the role.

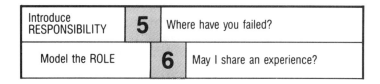

Introduce RESPONSIBILITY	**5**	Where have you failed?
Model the ROLE	**6**	May I share an experience?

Step 5: Introduce Responsibility

Lack of Responsibility. Rudolph Guiliani, a 1986 US Attorney, said that in the 50's and 60's "We socialized the responsibility for crime." In the process we broke down the line between explanations and excuses. The result? *Explanations* of the why and how of behavior have become socially acceptable *excuses* for bad behavior. He said, "It is all too easy to say in effect, 'Oh well you're not responsible for what you did. Your parents are responsible for it, your neighborhood is responsible for it, or your society is responsible for it.'" According to Guiliani, the individual not the group must be held responsible. He claimed:

> **"We elevate human beings by holding them responsible."**

'S WORD

WISDOM

■ **Examine the following Scriptures. Each states a biblical principle related to "Responsibility." Summarize each principle. Prepare to discuss these in your group session this week.**

Ezekiel 18:20—_____

_____

_____

Matthew 12:36—_____

_____

_____

Romans 14:12—_____

_____

_____

Accepting Responsibility. Our society has taught people that blaming someone else for their behavior is acceptable. As you have discovered, the Bible clearly states that each person is responsible for his or her own behavior. Before a counselee can determine an action plan, he or she must assume responsibility for his or her own life and behavior. The question you can use is: "Where have you failed?"

Counselees cannot just wait on others to change. The desired change may never happen. Then the counselee feels helpless and victimized. Instead, he needs to work on changing his own behaviors and his own responses to others.

Here is an example from the Daytop Lodge, a center for rehabilitating drug addicts. The court gave the addict an opportunity to commit himself to program. Upon arrival he was interviewed.

Interviewer: Why do you shoot dope?
    Addict: I grew up on the wrong side of the tracks.
Interviewer: Not good enough, go on.
    Addict: My father left home when I was young and I did not have a role model in life.
Interviewer: Not good enough, go on.
    Addict: I am really the victim of racial prejudice.
Interviewer: Not good enough.
    Addict: What do I have to say?
Interviewer: There is only one reason for shooting dope, stupidity.
    Addict: I'm stupid.
Interviewer: Welcome stupid, we're glad to have you.

■ **What did this interviewer do to help the addict accept responsibility for his own behavior? Circle all that apply.**
    a. He talked about the addict's poor lot in life.
    b. He focused on the addict's past to find reasons for his behavior.
    c. He refused to let the addict blame someone else for his behavior.
    d. He rewarded the addict with acceptance when he finally accepted responsibility for his own behavior.

Some approaches to counseling focus almost exclusively on understanding the past. They assume that once a person understands what makes him act and feel the way he does he will be able to work through past problems and achieve a healthy life. One criticism they receive is that this takes a long time and is frequently unsuccessful. The Ten-Step Model focuses on the importance of now. It focuses on what the individual can do now to change his circumstances. It requires a person to accept personal responsibility for his behavior and feelings. The interviewer of the drug addict did not do a or b. He did do c and d.

If people are to realize their potential, they must learn to accept personal responsibility and quit blaming others. No doubt life is tough for many people. We accomplish nothing when we encourage people to blame others and wallow in their misery. We must insist that they take charge of their own lives. The emphasis on responsibility saves people from the hopeless bogged down feeling that characterizes so many of our counselees.

The situation is frequently seen in marital difficulties which are often reported in terms of a spouse's failure, "It's my wife. She always . . ." or "I can't stand it when my husband . . ."

An effective way to handle this is for the counselor to say, "Suppose your husband is 90% wrong, would you be 10%?" Most people are willing to accept a meager 10% and the counselor says, "Let's talk about your 10%. We don't have your spouse here. The most effective work we can do is to help you do what you can and should."

■ **Write step 5 and the related question you will use.**

Step 5: _____

Question: _____

Step 6: Model the Role

Counseling often can be a slow and tedious process, particularly in the early stages of the relationship. Often the person being counseled is "testing the waters." Inwardly, he or she is trying to decide whether it is safe to really share a problem. One of the best ways to build confidence is to use a technique generally referred to as "modeling the role." To understand this technique let's look at an example. As you read about Bob and Suzan, look especially at what Bob models for Suzan.

Bob is a retired auto salesman. At the conclusion of the Senior Citizen's Club meeting, he meets Suzan and notes she is not her usual cheery self. Bob greets Suzan with a friendly, "Hi, how are things?"

Suzan, a widow, responds with a long recital of what is happening between her and Agnes Simpson with whom she shares a house. They argue over the trivial matter of sweeping the front porch. Suzan had reminded Agnes that she had not done this chore in days. She delivered her judgment that their home looked like a haunted house. In reaction to this statement Agnes turned on Suzan. She said she resented being spoken to like a child. A pall of silence had fallen over the house.

Suzan owns and drives the only car they possess. She came to the meeting today without even asking Agnes if she wanted to come. Now she is feeling guilty about the situation.

Bob listens quietly and encourages Suzan to talk. When at last she has finished her story, he says, "May I share an experience with you?" Suzan nods yes. "Well, I remember a time when I was supervisor of a group of salesmen. We had a very good salesman named Frank who was careless with his paperwork. One day I discovered he had not filled in a report I needed. I called him into the office and bawled him out.

"Frank, who was our top producer, turned around and walked off. I kept telling myself that he was careless and deserved to be rebuked. I wasn't going to make the first move toward him. Our strained relations went on for several weeks. Then I heard a rumor that he had been approached by another dealership. I suddenly realized I could not afford to lose Frank. I went to his office and apologized for jumping all over him.

"To my amazement, he quickly replied, 'No, Bob, that's not necessary, I had been careless, and I should not have reacted the way I did.' We warmly shook hands. I decided I was going to be more careful how I spoke to my co-workers."

Bob looked Suzan in the eye and asked, "Does my experience in anyway relate to yours?"

■ **What role did Bob model for Suzan? Check all the correct answers.**
   ☐ a. The role of a person who never holds a grudge.
   ☐ b. The role of being an open person.
   ☐ c. The role of being a person who also has failed.
   ☐ d. The role of a person who has overcome the same problem.

Bob helped Suzan take a fresh look at her behavior by using the technique of modeling the role. Bob modeled openness, his own failure, and probably even a person who has overcome the same problem or a similar problem.

Some Guidelines in Modeling the Role. First, in the counseling experience you do not want to emphasize your victorious, problem-free living. If you imply that you have never had a problem, most counselees will feel that you cannot understand them or help them. Place the emphasis in your modeling on admitting to personal irresponsibility and the difficulties that it brought in your experience. We are saying model the role, not, be a role model. Your goal is for the counselee to feel you can understand and that he can openly share his own problems with you.

Second, some people feel that if they are going to model, they must tell about some experience similar to that which is troubling their counselee. Bob was able to do this with Suzan. However, some of the people you counsel may have lived a rough life. They may have been involved in situations that you have never encountered. You *do not* have to be able to say, "I'm a prostitute, too." Or, "I was unfaithful to my wife once." Or "I can understand; I was a shoplifter when I was a teenager." Let us see how Lester Johnson handled this kind of situation.

Herman: "Lester, I don't think you can really help me very much. You see I got caught up in this gambling racket and I want to quit. I suppose I really need to talk with someone who has been a gambler."

Lester: "Well I've never had any trouble with gambling, because I never got started on it. But I don't mind telling you that I have a terrible temper. I've had to learn to keep it under control. It hasn't been easy, but I've gradually learned some lessons along the way."

Lester has not tried to make out that he has had exactly the same experiences as Herman. He is, however, letting him know he has been irresponsible, even though it was in a different area. This modeling technique has three advantages:

Advantages of Modeling

1. Modeling builds confidence. It helps the counselee feel he can trust the person to whom he is talking.

2. Modeling saves time. It helps you get to the problem more quickly. This is a particularly important factor in the short-term method you will most frequently use.

---

3. Modeling teaches openness. The word *teach* means "to show." Modeling the role is sometimes referred to as "observational learning" or "imitative learning." This means that the counselor teaches his counselee to become open by demonstrating openness.

■ 1. **In your own words, describe the technique of modeling the role.**

_____

_____

_____

2. **Write step 6 and the question you will use to guide you into the process.**

    Step 6: _____

        Question: _____

In your description of modeling the role, you should have included some of the following ideas:
• demonstrate openness to talk about weaknesses or problems
• demonstrate acceptance of personal responsibility for my actions
• indicate something of the problems created by my irresponsibility
Check the course map for correct wording of step 6 and the question.

Days 3 and 4: Alternatives and Outcomes

Today's Objective: You will be able to write steps 7 and 8 and the related questions.

Review the ALTERNATIVES	**7**	What could you do?
Explore the OUTCOMES	**8**	What are the probable outcomes?

Step 7: Review the Alternatives

When people are under stress, facing a crisis, depressed, or anxious, they may become confused and overwhelmed. They may find it difficult to see the variety of options they may face. They may have tunnel vision and only see one possible line of action. Later they will confess, "At the time I felt hedged in with only one way to go." Your task as counselor will be to help the counselee brainstorm the various options that are available.

As you identify options, keep in mind that you will explore the outcomes in step 8. Do not hinder the brainstorming by evaluating or automatically eliminating possibilities. You will sometimes identify an option that you know is impossible. However, by making a complete list you will come closer to finding a viable alternative.

Consider writing the alternatives or options on a note pad or a tear sheet if you are in a place where this is possible. This will help you both remember all the options as you begin to explore the outcomes in step 8. It will also allow you to see possible relationships between options. Sometimes two improbable or seemingly impossible alternatives can be combined to provide the very best alternative. A visible, written list will be helpful.

Sheila, a twenty-year-old college student, explained to her deacon **Harry** Bladman that she is in love with Graham Harris, a divorced man with the custody of his two teenage children. Her parents are opposed to the idea of her marrying Graham. She confides that Graham and she are contemplating marrying without her parent's approval. Having heard her out, Harry asked a number of questions to clarify the situation. In answer to one she said she thought that due to her homely appearance this might be the only marriage opportunity she'd ever have. Harry then said, "Why don't we think about some of the possible actions you can take."

■ **Before we look at Harry's and Sheila's list, try to write down in rapid fire order all the options you can think of for Sheila. What could Sheila do?**

_____

_____

_____

_____

_____

_____

_____

_____

_____

_____

_____

_____

Here are the options Sheila and Harry identified:
1. She could go ahead and get married without her parent's permission.
2. She could be patient and continue cultivating a relationship between Graham and her parents trying to win their consent.
3. She could break up with Graham and try to make a fresh start of her life in new relationships.
4. She could take two weeks off, leave town, and try to evaluate her real feelings toward Graham and this marriage.
5. She and Graham could go through some premarital counseling with a professional counselor and reevaluate their marriage plans with his help.
6. She could get a third party to counsel her and her parents to identify the problems and seek a solution.
7. She could go out of town to college and finish her degree before making any lasting commitments.

While she sees no easy solution to her problem, Sheila realizes that she has more than two alternatives to choose from.

■ **Try one more situation. Suppose you are counseling Gary, a forty-year-old man who is going through a mid-life crisis. He is tired of his job and wants a new challenge. His problem is that he does not have the professional skills to get any good-paying job he knows of. Together you brainstorm answers to the question: "What could you do?" Gary could:**

_____

_____

_____

_____

_____

_____

_____

_____

_____

Bring this list with you to your group session. You will join your group in working on this case study together.

Step 8: Explore the Outcomes

In *Fiddler on the Roof,* Tevye, a Jew, is faced with his daughter Chava's desire to marry a Gentile. He begins a soliloquy with a statement of shock. He continues to think aloud in a reasoning process punctuated, from time to time, with the expression, "on the other hand." At last he reaches a conclusion, "there is no other hand," and makes his terribly difficult decision. Tevye had to go through the processes of stating a situation then moving on to the opposing point of view "on the other hand" to get to his conclusion.

Sometimes the counselor has to take the opposing point of view in which he says, "Let me suggest another possibility." Using this technique the counselor is able to help his counselee face up to possible outcomes of plans of action.

In an earlier case study, we saw Harry helping Sheila evaluate her plans to marry Graham against her parent's wishes. Harry and Sheila reviewed the alternatives. Then they began to explore the outcomes. Here are some of Harry's comments:

1. You may be marrying for the wrong reason. Opportunity is not the best reason to take on a ready made family that may give you some awkward moments.
2. You can decide to delay marriage at this time realizing that if it is true love it will not be hurt by waiting another year.
3. You can take up your college studies realizing that whatever happens you need to establish yourself with an education and establish a professional identity. If you do marry Graham, statistics indicate you will probably outlive him by several years.

4. You may want to study the Scriptures that relate to divorce and remarriage to examine the biblical principles that are involved in this relationship. I'm sure our pastor would be happy to discuss these principles with you. Or, if you prefer, I could recommend a book from our church media library that deals with the subject.

■ **Read again the list of alternatives Harry and Sheila brainstormed. What other outcomes would you want to explore with Sheila?**

_____

_____

_____

_____

_____

_____

_____

Harry could raise the issue of her marrying a man with two children not so many years younger than she is herself. They are entering on their teen years and may be particularly difficult to manage. Harry could discuss with Sheila her own difficulties with her parents and point out that she would now be the authority figure. The children might see her as the "bad guy."

Come to your group session this week prepared to further explore the outcomes of Sheila's alternatives.

Another Example of Exploring Outcomes. In the case of Sheila and Harry, Sheila has not made a definite decision about what to do. She and Harry are working through their list of alternatives. They will eventually explore outcomes for all the alternatives that seem practical. Notice in the following example that the counselee has already made up her mind about what she plans to do. Watch how Sunday School teacher/counselor helps her explore the outcomes of her action plan.

Mrs. Bratton is mad at her husband. Without consulting her, he invested all their savings in a grandiose scheme to make a lot of money. Now their life savings are gone. Humiliated that he did this behind her back, thoughts of revenge soon took over.

She announces that she intends to divorce her husband. She looks defiantly at her counselor. "There's really no sense talking about it. I've had enough. I don't care how much he protests that he still loves me and wants to reconcile our differences. I want a divorce."

Her counselor responds, "I can understand your distress. I wonder, however, if you have considered what you will do when you get your divorce. Here are some of the things we should consider:
1. How will you live after you have divorced? You have not worked outside the home for many years. Do you have a marketable skill?
2. Where will you live? From what you have told me, I gather the payments on your present home are pretty steep and these losses may have intensified the situation.
3. What will happen with your three children? Apparently your husband has been a good father. Will this breakup effect them adversely?

4. How will this fit in with your Christian convictions? Will you feel guilty for getting a divorce that lacks a scriptural basis?"

■ 1. **What did this counselor do when the counselee stated that her decision had been made?**

_____

2. **Suppose that Mrs. Bratton realizes that divorce is not in her best interest. What should the counselor do next?**

_____

The counselor helped her counselee explore the outcomes of her plan of action. If Mrs. Bratton realizes that divorce is not in her best interest, the counselor should move back to step 7 and review alternatives with her. In this way Mrs. Bratton can begin to determine a new action plan.

Ease of divorce has created a situation wherein an offended spouse can all too easily threaten divorce as a reflex attitude and later live to regret having adopted the attitude. As a counselor, particularly one committed to Christian values, you should do everything you can to help people like Mrs. Bratton avoid actions they may regret.

In each of these cases the counselees may proceed with their plan of action. They are responsible for their own decisions. At least the counselor has caused them to stop and think about the implications of their actions. Hopefully, they will make good and sensible decisions.

Wait a Minute! In Mrs. Bratton's case, the counselor seems to have jumped right from step 3 (Clarify the Situation) to step 8 (Explore the Outcomes). Now is a good time for us to talk a little more about the Ten-Step Model. In this case the counselor was wise in moving directly to explore the outcomes. Mrs. Bratton had already made up her mind about what to do. This points out that you must be flexible and sensitive as a counselor. The Ten-Step Model is your guide. You should not follow it so closely, however, that you fail to meet your counselee's needs. What Mrs. Bratton needed next was to explore the outcomes of her action plan. That is exactly what her counselor did. Good job, Sunday School Teacher/Counselor!

■ **Write steps 7 and 8 and the question you will use at each step.**

Step 7: _____

Question: _____

Step 8: _____

Question: _____

Check your responses with the course map.

Day 5: Information and Closure

> **Today's Objective:** You will be able to write steps 9 and 10 and the related questions.

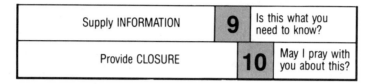

Supply INFORMATION	**9**	Is this what you need to know?
Provide CLOSURE	**10**	May I pray with you about this?

Sometimes additional information is needed to make a wise decision. Biblical principles may speak to the issue. Helpful information may be available in pamphlets, books, articles, videotapes, or other resources. To be able to supply information, you will have to take time to become familiar with the matter under consideration. You should be able to supply resources or put the counselee in touch with someone who can help by supplying the needed information. At times you may need to say, "I don't know about that. Why don't you give me a couple of days to find out what you need to know. Then we can meet again, say on Friday, to talk about this further."

Step 9: Supply Information

A person may seek a counselor because she wants information. If this is the case, the obvious thing to do is to give her the information she needs.

Suppose I am sitting in my office and a student comes by and and asks me, "I am considering what psychology course I will take next semester. I am considering signing up for PSY-433. Could you tell me something about it?" It would be ridiculous for me to say in my best Rogerian manner, "You want to know what PSY-433 is about? Why don't you tell me more?"

What I must obviously do is say, "This is a course on the psychology of religion and personality. In it we consider aspects of psychology, religion, and personality theory and the way they relate to each other. This semester we will be focusing on a study of David." If she asks for information you cannot provide, help the person think of sources of information that may be of help.

Provide Some Literature. Books often provide excellent resources. One counseling technique is known as bibliotherapy. Using this technique the counselor guides the troubled person to read applicable books.

One doctoral student carried out a research project in which he had three groups of people. One group was involved in a group therapy experience. The second was in group therapy and read certain suggested books. The third group was given the same books to study without any form of therapy. All three groups were given psychological tests before and after the experience. The results showed that the group who concentrated on reading did just as well as any of the others.

The important aspect of this research was that the reading was directed. This would indicate that you, as the counselor, must search out the best appropriate books and make them available. Here are some considerations in making your choice of books:

Guidelines for Selecting Books as Counseling Resources

1. Watch for reviews in reputable publications.
2. Consult your local or church librarian.
3. Beware of cure-all literature. Some writers over simplify the issues.
4. Look for books that will lead you to other sources for help.
5. Recommend books that have an optimistic, encouraging note.
6. Is the book published by a reputable publisher?
7. Make sure the book is written for the layperson rather than a professional.
8. Read the book carefully to be sure that it will not contain anything that is objectionable. You may be judged by its contents.

Keep in mind that people under emotional pressure may make a commitment to return a book, then later forget. If you get in the practice of loaning out books, buy the cheapest editions available.

Depending on the situation, the question you will normally use at this step is: "Is this what you need to know?"

■ 1. **Write step 9 and the related question.**

    Step 9: _____

        Question: _____

  2. **What is bibliotherapy?**
     It is a counseling technique in which _____

_____

Step 10: Provide Closure

This final step is not to be taken lightly. Two traps should be avoided. The first is that of prematurely dismissing the counselee so that he feels rejected or as though he has unfinished business to address. The second trap is to invite the counselee to become dependent on you and seek your help in every situation that arises. The sweetest word to a counselor's ears should be, "Thank you so much for your help. I feel as if I can handle this matter now."

■ **Why do you want to avoid the trap of the counselee's feeling:**

Rejection? _____

_____

_____

_____

Dependence? _____

_____

_____

_____

If the counselee feels that you and he have more business to attend to, premature closure could add to his frustrations. His feeling of rejection may keep him from coming back to you for help at a later time. Allowing a counselee to develop feelings of dependence is bad for you and him. He needs to face the reality that he has to make his own decisions. Feelings of dependence can actually lower his self-esteem. More than likely, you do not have time to help a counselee make every decision that he or she faces. The potential you have of falling into these two traps is the reason step 10 is important.

Prayer. Now has come the opportunity for the Christian counselor to invoke the blessing of the Wonderful Counselor. After asking the question, "May I pray with you about this?" bring the experience to a conclusion with a brief word of prayer.

> Our heavenly Father, we commend our discussion into Your hands. I pray that You will guide our sister by Your Holy Spirit into making a wise decision. Give her strength to take the actions that will bring glory to Your name and blessing into her life. Through Jesus Christ our Lord we pray. Amen.

Unfinished Business? We are focusing your training on brief counseling. In this process some unfinished business may become evident. The counselee may need more help. You may want to have a check-up period in which you evaluate the results of the counselee's action plan. Some of the other methods advocated in the following chapters may be needed. Consequently, you should leave the door open so that the counselee will not feel cut off and abandoned. The final question will reflect this attitude: "Do we need to meet again?"

Notice on the course map that another decision is made at this point. If the counselee says yes, return to step 1 and Determine Time and Place. If the counselee says no, then you have completed this particular ministry opportunity. Sometimes you may reach the end of the counseling session and realize that a referral would be appropriate. If this is the case, you will proceed to make the referral to the appropriate helping agency or professional counselor. Another referral possibility we will explore in unit 13 is to a support group.

As mentioned in the introduction, WiseCounsel focuses on brief rather than long-term counseling. The underlying assumption is that most of the counseling you will undertake will probably involve no more than one to three meetings with the person. In some cases you may counsel a person on several occasions as they work through a problem step by step. You probably should not plan to go beyond five or six meetings without additional training or making a referral to a professional.

■ **Write steps 9 and 10 and the questions related to them.**

    Step 9: _____

            Question: _____

    Step 10: _____

            Question: _____

Check your responses with the course map. Continue reviewing the Ten-Step Model until you can state the ten steps and all of the questions in order (without peeking).

UNIT 4
A Fundamental Skill—Listening

This Week's Learning Goal

After studying this unit, you will understand ways to improve your active listening skills.

Why You Will Find This Study Useful

The fundamental skill for the counselor is listening. Listening is more than just hearing. It is an active process that requires discipline and practice. In this unit, I will help you understand some of the dynamics of listening. You will learn ways to improve your listening skills. Listening is a skill that is valuable not only in counseling but also in all your human relationships.

Day 1: What Your Listening Does for People

> **Today's Objective:** You will be able to match the way listening helps people with a given case that illustrates it.

Probably the most important skill for you to develop as a counselor is the skill of listening. You already have learned that step 2 calls for you to listen. Step 2 helps your counselee begin to talk about his or her problem. Certainly you want to listen at that time in order to begin identifying the problem. Listening, however, is a fundamental skill that is also used throughout the counseling session. Because listening is such an important skill, we will focus on that subject for this entire week. Your listening does at least four things for people. Let's examine each one of these separately.

1. Listening Helps People Break Out of Isolation

There is a peculiar sense in which every individual is born in isolation. As he grows, he breaks out of his isolation by beginning a process of establishing work linkages with the world around him. As family members and friends listen to the new arrival, they enable him to enter into the community of experience.

Born a normal child, stricken nineteen months later by a mysterious illness, Helen Keller lingered at death's door. Then suddenly and unaccountably she recovered. She was left deaf and blind and, because of her deafness, mute.

Helen became, in her own words, "a Phantom living in a world that was no-world." She described herself as, "wild and unruly, giggling and chuckling to express pleasure; kicking, scratching, uttering the choked screams of the deaf-mute to indicate the opposite." She was condemned to stay in this isolation for five years.

Then the dedicated teacher, Annie Sullivan, began to work with Helen. At first there was little response. After a frustrating month, a moment of breakthrough finally came. Down at the well, Annie placed one of the little blind girl's hands under the flowing stream of cold water. In Helen's other hand she spelled out the word water again and again. Suddenly, "the mystery of language was revealed to me!" Helen recalled. "I knew then that 'w-a-t-e-r,' meant the wonderful cool something that was flowing over my hand . . . . That living word awakened my soul, gave it light, hope, joy, set it free."

Words now had a significance. Previously Helen had struggled to learn a meaningless series of letters. Now they combined into words representing something. She learned many words that day, just how many she could never recollect. However, "I do know that mother, father, sister, teacher, were among them—words that made the world blossom for me 'like Aarons's rod with flowers.'"[1] When Helen Keller finally was able to communicate with others, she escaped from the "no world" that had entrapped her.

Listening helps people like Helen break out of isolation. Many Helen Kellers are around us today. They need the all-important listening ear to help them develop their tremendous potentialities and possibilities.

■ **Write the first way listening helps people. Listening helps people:**

_____

2. Listening Helps People Evaluate Their Thoughts

When a person has a chance to verbalize his thoughts, to bring them out in the open, to hear them, and then see how another responds to them, he often sees some of the irrationalities of his thought processes.

When people verbalize their thoughts, they are better able to evaluate them. One man expressed it beautifully, "How can I know what I think until I hear myself say it?" Listening to a troubled person encourages him to verbalize and evaluate his thoughts.

■ **Write the second way listening helps people. Listening helps people:**

_____

3. Listening Helps People Say Something to Themselves

Most of us need to say something to ourselves. The best way to do this is not to sit and think furiously. The best way is to tell someone else and in the process say it to ourselves. "Every speaker has two audiences—the people before him and himself." As you listen, mirroring back the emotion, you facilitate the process of the counselee saying something to himself.

■ **Write the third way listening helps people. Listening helps people:**

_____

4. Listening Helps People Express Their Emotions

The frustrations of life cause emotional intensities to build up rapidly, creating a condition of uneasiness. Some form of emotional release is highly desirable. Like a blocked hose these emotional pressures may cause the individual to erupt in vulnerable areas. Speech has been described as man's most readily available safety valve. Counselors often find that when people are allowed to talk about the things that are worrying them the emotinal intensity frequently subsides. During emotional outbursts, a listening counselor can provide a channel for draining the emotions. This kind of listening requires you to be mature, objective, and permissive enough not to become emotionally involved or defensive when the outburst comes.

The listener has a tremendous potential for helping others. As he listens people frequently mobilize their own internal resources and discover new and meaningful ways of living—all because someone listened.

■ 1. Write the fourth way listening helps people. Listening helps people:

_____

2. Match the way listening helps people with the case that illustrates it. On the line beside each case write the number of the way listening helps.

> **Ways Listening Helps People**
>
> 1. **Break Out of Isolation**
> 2. **Evaluate Their Thoughts**
> 3. **Say Something to Themselves**
> 4. **Express Their Emotions**

_____ A. Tom is listening to Robert discuss the financial problems that seem to overwhelm him. Tom asks Robert to try and identify the sources of his problems. Robert mentions two or three. Then he reflects, "You know, if I would just quit buying unnecessary things with my credit cards, I think I could eventually dig my way out of these problems."

_____ B. Janet went by the funeral home to see her friend Carol. Carol was seated near the casket of her mother. They talked for a while. Then Janet said, "Carol, I know you and your mom had some really good times together. What is your favorite memory of her?" Carol began to weep as she related some of her fond childhood memories of her mom.

_____ C. Mozelle has a ministry with senior adults in her church. Someone recommended that she go by and see Mrs. Snell. Mrs. Snell lives alone and seldom leaves her home. Mozelle asked a couple of questions to get acquainted. Mrs. Snell began to talk about her preretirement days. An hour later Mozelle graciously says good bye. Mrs. Snell thanks her for the visit and begs her to come back soon.

_____ D. Danny has had some serious problems at work. He has just about decided to resign his job to get away from the problems. He is confident that he can find another job fairly quickly. As he tried to explain his plan to Gene, he began to ask questions of himself: "What will my family do financially while I look for a new job? Will a new employer consider me if I'm unemployed? Have I tried everything I can at work to resolve my problems?" Without any counsel from Gene, Danny decided he had better not rush into a resignation.

Nearly every counseling session could demonstrate more than one of the ways listening helps people. In the above cases Robert had an opportunity to say something to himself about his use of credit cards. Carol had an opportunity to express some pent-up emotions. Mrs. Snell was able to break out of her isolation. Danny was able to evaluate his thoughts about his plan to resign. Answers are A-3; B-4; C-1; and D-2.

Day 2: Four Fallacies About Listening

> **Today's Objective:** Given a list of statements about listening, you will be able to identify the correct and incorrect statements in the list.

When we examine the subject more closely, we discover problems as to what listening really is. You need to understand the nature of listening and the way the skill is developed and used. Let's examine several fallacies or myths concerning listening.

Fallacy 1: Intelligent People Are Good Listeners.

Many people believe that people with a high intelligence level will automatically be able to listen and comprehend well. No evidence shows this to be true. Because intelligent people have a pretty good self-image, they often feel no need to be concerned about such a skill. In fact, pride may hinder them from acknowlcging the need to study or develop listening skills.

Intelligence may actually hinder listening. The very intelligent person often becomes impatient with the slower-speaking individual. Because he cannot be bothered waiting around to hear the complete message, he tunes the speaker out. Listening skills must be learned, practiced, and developed regardless of intelligence level.

■ 1. **Which of the following are reasons an intelligent person may not be the best listener. Check all correct answers.**
   - ☐ a. **Impatient with slower-speaking individual**
   - ☐ b. **Not concerned about developing the skill**
   - ☐ c. **Pride**
   - ☐ d. **May see no need for the skill**

2. **Mark the following statements as either T (True) or F (False).**

   _____ a. **Listening is a gift that is especially prominent in people with high intelligence.**

   _____ b. **Listening is a skill that must be developed and practiced.**

You probably checked all four of the answers in #1 above. All of these are reasons an intelligent person may be a poor listener. Keep in mind, however, that an intelligent person who is willing to work at the skill of listening can indeed be a good listener. Listening is a skill to be developed and practiced. In #2, a is false and b is true.

Fallacy 2: Everyday Listening Builds Listening Skills.

Some people believe that constant listening experiences improve listening skills. However, practice does not always make perfect. We too easily practice our mistakes. To improve listening skills you must practice good listening habits.

Fallacy 3: Reading Develops Listening Ability.

Because we acquire much of our knowledge through reading, some may assume that reading makes us better listeners. Considerable differences exist between reading and listening. At its best, reading is a solitary experience, requiring isolation in order to concentrate. It may even foster the development of a withdrawn or antisocial individual. In contrast, listening is a social experience always involving as least two people.

Moreover, the reader chooses his own pace; but the listener must follow the speaker's pace. If the listener does not seize the speech and take possession of it in the moment of its birth, it dies and is lost to him. Considerable evidence indicates that listening skills may increase reading ability, but good reading skills do not necessarily increase listening ability.

■ **Mark the following statements as True (T) or False (F).**

_____ a. **The listener chooses his own pace.**

_____ b. **Reading skills improve listening skills.**

_____ c. **Everyday listening provides good practice for listening skills.**

_____ d. **Good listening requires practice of good listening habits.**

A hearing problem could be the cause of poor listening, but it certainly is not the only reason. Poor listening is more likely to be due to bad habits. Depending on reading skills or everyday listening to improve listening will probably not help. Good listening *does* require practicing good listening habits. Answers to the above exercise are: True—d; False—a, b, c.

Fallacy 4: The Words *Hearing* and *Listening* Are Synonyms.

To many the words hearing and listening are synonyms. In actual fact they are quite different. *Hearing* describes the process whereby a sound wave travels through the air, hits the ear, is translated into neural current, and proceeds to the brain. *Listening* describes the sorting out process by which we choose and decide which stimuli will have our attention.

Since listening is often confused with hearing it is assumed hearing problems are the reason some people do not listen. Investigation shows, however, that many with perfectly good hearing are poor listeners. What we do with our listening equipment is the all-important consideration. We may use excellent equipment for the wrong purpose and be poor listeners.

The whole operation of a sound wave's transmission to the brain takes place with lightning speed. The brain itself is programmed by years of experience and conditioning to handle the auditory impressions it is fed. Like a busy executive's efficient secretary who sorts out the correspondence, keeping only the most important for his personal attention, some sounds are similarly rejected, while others have total attention focused on them. This selective process in listening is the main distinction between hearing and listening.

■ 1. Here are definitions of *hearing* and *listening*. Identify the correct definition for each, and write the word beside its definition.

   a. _____ is a process by which we choose which stimuli will have our attention.

   b. _____ is a process by which a sound wave is translated to neural current and sent to the brain.

2. What is the major difference between hearing and listening?

   _____

   _____

   _____

   _____

   _____

The process of choosing which stimuli (sights, sounds, and so forth) receive our attention is listening. This is the main difference between listening and hearing. You may hear many things. You selectively choose which of those things you will listen to. In #1, a is listening and b is hearing.

■ In each pair of statements below, select the correct statement about listening. Place an X in the box beside the correct statement.

   ☐ a. Intelligent people have a special gift for good listening.
   ☐ b. Listening is a skill that must be developed and practiced.

   ☐ c. Good listening requires practice of good listening skills.
   ☐ d. Everyday listening will give a person plenty of practice for good listening.

   ☐ e. Reading will help a person develop listening skills.
   ☐ f. The listener must follow the speaker's pace.

   ☐ g. Hearing and listening describe the same process.
   ☐ h. Listening is selective and, thus, different from hearing.

If you marked b, c, f, and h, you have done a good job with today's study. If you marked a, d, e, or g, go back and review the related fallacy.

In the days that follow you will continue your study about listening. I will try to help you understand the process and the way you can use it in the important work of counseling.

Day 3: Mental Discipline and Attention

> **Today's Objective:** You will be able to write specific suggestions that will help improve your listening.

Most of us are so anxious to express ourselves that we do not bother to listen to others. A bore has been described as, "someone who keeps on talking after you have thought of something clever to say." Listening is an art. Like any other art form, listening requires effort. Listening requires discipline, concentration, and comprehension.

■ **As you read the sections about discipline, concentration, and comprehension, underline specific suggestions that can help you improve your listening. I have underlined one suggestion in the first section to give you an example.**

Listening Requires Discipline

Mastering this skill is complicated for many people. Many have mastered the skill of talking, but not of listening. Discipline requires self-control and practice. You must constantly <u>reprimand yourself when you catch yourself drifting.</u> When you should be listening, you must curb your impulses to express yourself. You must learn to be receptive and responsive. This may be an about-face from any formal training you may have had. This will call for much self-discipline.

Listening Requires Concentration

A partially deaf man went on a trip with a group of friends. He wore a hearing aid and was able to enter freely into conversation with the group. Whenever he became weary or bored his simple technique was to switch off the hearing aid. Although most of us do not have a mechanical aid, we all have the capacity to mentally turn people off. Our listening is selective. As a counselor you must be intellectually active and concentrate on all that your counselee has to say. You must beware of the dazed look in the eye, the furtive glance at the watch, or rearranging the desktop. You must give the speaker your undivided attention.

Listening Requires Comprehension

Some people can speak at the rate of 125 words per minute. The person on the receiving end can think as much as four times quicker than that. This means that when you are listening to someone speak you have leftover time on your hands. The temptation is to go off on a side excursion in this period of surplus time. This is fatal to comprehension. A good listener forgets his own difficulties and spends all his energies comprehending his subject's situation. An effective listener will sometimes indicate his desire to comprehend the speaker by asking a short question.

■ **What specific suggestions did you underline? Write them below and on the following page. Add any other suggestions you can think of that will help you listen with discipline, concentration, and comprehension.**

REPRIMAND MYSELF WHEN DRIFTING

_____

_____

_____

_____

_____

_____

_____

_____

Other suggestions you may have underlined include: "curb your impulses to express yourself," "learn to be receptive and responsive," "be intellectually active," "concentrate on all that your counselee has to say," "bends all his energies to comprehend his subject's situation," and "indicate his desire to comprehend the speaker by asking a short question." You may have suggested other specifics like: If the person is a slow-talker, I will use the extra time I have to think by evaluating what the speaker has to say. Or: I will fold my hands to keep from fiddling with other objects.

Day 4: Four Listening Guidelines

> **Today's Objective:** You will be able to recognize the correct application and the violation of listening guidelines in given case studies.

1. Do Not Display Feelings of Disapproval.

As people talk with you, they will sometimes exibit a wrong attitude. A person may be belligerent, rude, or offensive. Your natural reaction to such an attitude may be to condemn the behavior or show resentment. This may either stop or infuriate the counselee. If you want to help this person and keep him talking, you should not show signs of disapproval. Let him continue to talk. In a counseling situation when a person gets an opportunity to express his hostility and negative feelings, he will often follow such outbursts with more positive expressions and maybe even an apology.

This is often described as "accepting" people. This trait is seen in the ministry of Jesus when He did not condemn the woman taken in adultery but accepted her as a person. Accept people for what they are and listen to them. You will help them grow to what they can be by first allowing them to express their feelings.

■ **Explain guideline 1 in your own words.**

_____

_____

_____

_____

_____

2. Develop Helpful Responses.

Helpful responses can be verbal or physical. Some authorities think there are only four good listening responses. These are "Mmmm", "Uh-huh", "Oh", and "I see." The best responses in listening are short and contain an invitation to continue to talk.

I remember sitting with a skillful counselor as a woman poured out a sordid story. At the conclusion of her statement, she fixed her eyes on the counselor. Through her tears, she said, "What do you think of that?" The counselor responded with a kindly expression on his face, wrinkling his nose. That wrinkled nose said more than any words. A response can take the form of a nod of the head, an understanding smile, or a gesture of the hand. These physical responses are indicators of a good listening technique.

■ **Explain guideline 2 in your own words.**

_____

_____

_____

_____

3. Listen for the Sound of Silence.

One of the most difficult things for a counselor to do is to say nothing. Silence can be the most creative time in a counseling session. Like any other creative activity, silence calls for self-control and diligent practice. For most of us ten seconds of silence can seem like ten hours. Life is sometimes a carnival of noise when we need a chapel of silence. Rushing in to cover over periods of silence may hold up the redemptive process of a troubled individual. He may be building up his courage to make a clean breast of it all. Or he may be trying to put things together in a way they can be expressed. He needs some quiet time to do his thinking.

A troubled man with a list of anxieties and fears went to visit his doctor. The wise physician told his patient to take a day off work and visit the beach. At the end of the consultation, the doctor placed an envelope in his hand with instructions to open it when he reached his destination.

The man found a quiet spot at the beach and opened the envelope. On a small piece of paper he read the words, "Listen carefully." Later he told of the rewards that came to him as, for the first time in years, he heard the lapping of the waves, the songs of the birds, and the sighing of the wind.

Sometimes a silence does grow too long and must be broken. A good way to do this is to ask the person to elaborate on a point about which he has been talking. A woman was working with young marrieds and was somewhat discouraged. After pouring out her problems she lapsed into a painfully long silence. The counselor softly said, "Would you care to tell me about some of the techniques you have tried with those young marrieds?"

■ 1. **Explain guideline 3 in your own words.**

_____

_____

_____

_____

2. **What is one way to break a silence that has grown too long?**

_____

4. Make Reflective Statements.

One important function of the counselor is to reflect the emotional content of what the counselee expresses. A good listener is like a mirror or a sounding board. Through the technique of reflection, the counselee comes to know himself better. An example of this type of response is in this conversation between a pastor and a deacon.

Mr. Daniel: I told you that the doctor advised me to give up my church work. He didn't really say that, it just seemed at the time that this would be the easy way out.
Pastor: What you are saying sounds as if you feel pretty guilty about this.

The pastor did not get himself into a complicated discussion about what the doctor said or did not say. Instead, he responded to the emotional overtones of the statement of his deacon. He reflected a sense of guilt in the deacon's voice. Another good reflective technique is seen in this conversation between the pastor and a disgruntled church member.

Mrs. Carol: I don't know what is wrong with this church. It used to be different.
Pastor: It used to be different?

The essence of this technique is to pick up on the last remark of the counselee and reflect it back. In reflective counseling you are saying in effect that you are aware of the feelings of the counselee. You invite him to continue. You encourage the subject to keep on talking by saying in effect, "The ball is in your court, please tell me more."

■ **Explain guideline 4 in your own words.**

_____

_____

_____

_____

Guidelines for Listening

1. Do Not Display Feelings of Disapproval.
2. Develop Helpful Responses.
3. Listen for the Sound of Silence.
4. Make Reflective Statements.

■ In each case below, one guideline is followed and one is violated. Write the numbers of the guidelines in the appropriate blanks.

A. **Counselor:** Bill, I can tell from what you just said that you are pretty sensitive about this relationship to your sister. Do you want to talk about it?

   Bill: No, I do not! That's none of your business. I would appreciate your not trying to pry into my private life.

   Counselor: Well, if that's the way you are going to treat me, I don't know why I'm wasting my time trying to help you.

   Guideline Followed: #_____   Guideline Violated: #_____

B. **Tonya:** When I told Leon to go to his room until he could behave, he held up his fist and said, "Make me!"

   Counselor: Mmmm.

   Tonya: I just don't know what I'm going to do with him.

   Counselor: Why don't we work together on this. What could you do?

   Tonya: Well, uh . . .

   Counselor: We need to think of some possible actions you could take. Can you name some?

   Tonya: I've never had this problem before. I guess I . . . uh . . .

   Counselor: Maybe we should talk some more about things you have already tried.

   Guideline Followed: #_____   Guideline Violated: #_____

The counselor in A did a good job of making a reflective statement (#4). He lost his cool, though, and clearly indicated his feelings of disapproval (#1). The counselor in B gave a helpful response (#2) with his "Mmmm." Tonya responded to it. She seemed to need some time to think. The counselor kept pumping her, however, to keep the discussion moving. He did not allow silence to enter the conversation (#3).

■ 1. **How could the counselor have responded to Bill's outburst in a way that would not violate guideline 1?**

   _____

   _____

   _____

   _____

2. **When and what should the counselor have done with Tonya to follow guideline 3?**

   _____

   _____

   _____

   _____

You will discuss these points in your group session this week.

Day 5: Body Listening

> **Today's Objective:** You will be able to describe ways to "listen" with your total body.

Many people believe that listening is something we only do with our ears. A closer examination, however, shows it is also done with eyes, head, hand, skin, and other parts of the body. Listening is a very complex multisensory experience. Many sensory impressions are given and received in a variety of ways. In today's study, we are going to consider some of these different levels of listening.

Eye Listening or Looking

In many ways, listening begins not with the ears but with the eyes. Although we can listen to someone talking over the phone, this is never as satisfactory as when we can look that person in the eye. Counselees need listening eyes (your eyes) focussed on them.

> "The eyes of men converse as much as their tongues, with the advantage that the ocular dialect needs no dictionary, but is understood the world over."—Emerson

■ **What is one good way to "listen" with your eyes?**

_____

Feedback on today's questions will come later in the lesson.

Ear Listening or Focused Hearing

This would seem to be the most obvious aspect of listening. Some counselors may have physiological problems that hinder their hearing. Noise, the relative position of the speaker, or the way the counselee enunciates may also interfere with communication. You must learn to cope with or compensate for these hindrances to listening.

Head Listening or Positioning

A man belonged to a rural church pastored by a poor preacher. This sensible man said, "I've discovered a way to help my preacher. As he preaches I begin to nod my head. You should see him respond! My head is like the handle on a pump; the more I nod the more he spouts." The preacher was responding to a listening head. Counselees will often respond in a similar way.

■ 1. **What must be done to "listen" with your ears when noise and a soft-spoken counselee hinder your hearing?**

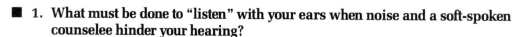

2. **What is one good way to "listen" with your head?**

_____

Hand Listening or Gesturing

I once watched an actor recite the Gospel of Mark. In the congregation sat a little girl. The actor recited the words of Jesus, "Suffer the little children to come unto me." He paused and made a gesture of invitation. The little girl rose from her seat and walked down the aisle to the platform. The gesture was a compelling summons the little girl could not resist. A counselor uses gestures that convey important nonverbal messages to a troubled counselee.

Tactile Listening or Touching

The skin is the largest organ of the body containing something like five million sensory cells. Many people stand in need of some sort of touching experience. A dying man had requested that his wife remain by his bedside. An observer noted that she gently stroked his hand. This wife was listening with her hands.

A word of caution. This is a nondemanding, nonsexual touch that conveys messages that cannot be expressed in words. The unlovely and the elderly particularly need our touch. Remember the leper; "Jesus reached out his hand and touched the man" (Matt. 8:3).

■ 1. **What is one good way to "listen" with your hand?**

_____

2. **What is one good way to "listen" with your touch?**

_____

Third-Ear Listening or Intuition

A counselor must listen for the unspoken message contained in the emotional overtones of the speakers's voice. This ability to listen to the "words in between the lines" is often referred to as third-ear listening. A good counselor will learn to perceive emotions and reflect them back to the counselee.

One counselor reported a case of a woman who said, "I hate my husband." The counselor commented, "The very intensity with which she made the statement indicated that she loved him very much." Taking the woman's statement literally could have had some important effects on the outcome.

■ **What are you listening for when you listen with your "third ear"?**

_____

Feedback

Looking your counselee directly in the eyes helps listening. In fact his eyes may tell you something as you listen with the third ear. You listen with your "third ear" for emotional content that is not being expressed verbally. When noise or a soft-spoken counselee hinder your hearing, you must make adjustments like getting closer, closing the window, moving to a quieter place, and so forth. Nodding your head in agreement or disagreement or tilting your head to indicate confusion are two ways to listen with your head.

Gestures of the hands can say "Wait just a minute," "I don't know," "I'm thinking about it," "I've got an idea," and many other things. The hand is often used in tactile listening as well. Your hand touching the counselees hand can say, "I understand." An arm around the shoulder can communicate that you really care.

Total Listening

Total listening may be described as the activity in which the listener uses every part of his body to listen to another person.

■ **This equation says that total listening involves many parts of the body. Describe at least six ways that you can listen with your body.**

1. _____

2. _____

3. _____

4. _____

5. _____

6. _____

> **For Further Study**
> ☐ *The Awesome Power of the Listening Ear* by John Drakeford. Waco: Word Books, 1967.

UNIT 5

Building Relationships

This Week's Learning Goal

After studying this unit, you will understand ways to begin and develop open relationships with others.

Why You Will Find This Study Useful

Opportunities to counsel will come only if people know you can help them. I will help you identify some ways you can make your availability known. You also will learn to develop open relationships with your counselee through rapport building. You will spend two days reviewing key ideas you have already studied. In this way, you will "nail down" the basics before going further.

Day 1: Availability for Counseling

> **Today's Objective:** You will be able to list ways you can make your availability to counsel known to others.

 Availability to Counsel

By now you are probably convinced that you would like to be a counselor. You have spent time learning the process, but you may not have had any counseling opportunities. Many people are desperately in need of the help of a counselor. The problem is to discover a way the willing counselor and the needy counselee can get together.

Practical Availability

On the staff of a modern hospital, many professionals are trained in specialized techniques for helping needy people. These professionals include such people as the doctor, the psychiatrist, the social worker, and the chaplain. Despite the presence of these helpers, some investigators claim that the nurse is the person to whom most patients open their hearts and pour out their fears and apprehensions. This is because she is readily available to the patient as many as eight hours a day. Sometimes the chaplain feels bad because the patient has told his spiritual problem to the nurse instead of sending for him. The situation arises because the chaplain is officially available, but the nurse is practically available.

Similarly, availability is a factor the lay counselor has going for him. The Sunday School teacher, the Church Training leader, the deacon, or leader in youth work will be faced with many opportunities to help. You must constantly watch for opportunities. The variety in your life brings you into close contact with people. You may call on people in their homes or meet them at various church gatherings such as socials, picnics, and church meetings. In many ways lay leaders are much closer to needy people than the staff members of the church. Consequently, lay leaders will often be presented with unusual opportunities to counsel.

This informal type of ministry was dramatized in the life and work of our Jesus. He looked into a tree, saw Zachaeus, and called him down to talk. He met a woman and talked to her beside the well. He met and talked with two who trudged along the road to Emmaus. He listened as they recounted their story of disappointment. In like manner, you will have many contacts with people that will provide you with opportunities for ministry.

A man who is now an outstanding counselor tells of an experience at a church social. He began a conversation with a young woman. Though they attended the same church, he had never talked with her before. He happened to mention that he had an interest in counseling people. The young lady said she had a problem and would like for him to counsel with her. Chance contacts can open doors for meaningful opportunities to help others.

■ **The places where you are practically available will provide opportunities for counseling. Write down the names of places where you come in contact with people during a normal week. Think back over the past few weeks. List as many places as possible. Be specific (for example: instead of church you might list Sunday School class, WMU study group, worship services, and so forth).**

_____

_____

_____

_____

_____

_____

_____

_____

_____

_____

_____

Now look back over your list. Think about your lay counseling ministry. Where are you most likely to have practical opportunity to counsel persons who have needs? Circle those places.

You should have many different places listed. If you had trouble thinking of places, try again and mentally walk through several normal days. You would include places like home, work (work station, cafeteria, or break room), church, school, grocery store, gas station, and so forth. These are places for your "marketplace" counseling ministry. Begin to watch for counseling opportunities in these places. You already have learned enough of the basic counseling process to provide some help to needy people.

Your Availability Through Church Organizations

A modern church is highly organized, but it is still mainly staffed with laypersons. The closeness of the leader to those within his organization gives him counseling opportunities. A good Sunday School teacher knows the members of his class and often can see the symptoms of problems in the lives of individual members. A class member whose attendance is sporadic, shows signs of stress in the class session, or in discussion reveals an attitude of resentment or disillusionment, may be seen as one who is in need of help. Even the prayer time may alert the teacher to problems in the lives of members.

The leader of a youth group sees who dates whom, how free they are with members of the opposite sex, attitudes towards parents, and feelings about school and authority. Degrees of involvement that a parent may never see may be discerned by the watchful youth leader.

Children in Sunday School often talk freely and tell that Daddy stayed away all week, grandmother is staying with them and she and mother are having quarrels, and so on. Sometimes excessively bad behavior of a child may be an acting out of the frustrations or stress of home life. The astute and perceptive leader is again in the position to see the distress signals and move into action.

Teaching activities can provide openings for counseling experiences. Within a small group, the teacher seeks to apply the lesson to the experiences of the class members. The teacher may speak in the first person, stating what she said to her children, how her husband pleased or annoyed her, or how she felt about the relatives who dropped in unexpectedly. A woman who sits in the class comes to feel that the teacher understands something of her own frustrating experiences. Consequently, she will be more willing to talk with her teacher than she would be to other people.

Committee work can offer unusual opportunities for group interaction. If the committee becomes an intimate group, members will often let down their defenses and express themselves more freely. From being an experience to be dreaded, the committee meeting can become a therapeutic experience and also lead to a counseling relationship.

■ **In the previous section, several practical suggestions are given that will communicate your availability. Other practical suggestions may be implied. Check the activities below that should increase the probability that people will come to you for counseling or that will help you identify problem situations where you may need to offer your help.**
  - ☐ 1. **Watch for changes in mood or behavior to identify symptoms of a problem.**
  - ☐ 2. **Get to know members so I will notice when something seems to be wrong.**
  - ☐ 3. **Watch for abnormal child behavior.**
  - ☐ 4. **Listen to prayer requests and prayers for possible problem situations.**
  - ☐ 5. **Impress people with how busy I am.**
  - ☐ 6. **Watch for over involvement of youth with members of the opposite sex.**
  - ☐ 7. **Listen to what a child says about problems at home.**
  - ☐ 8. **Listen for attitudes of class members toward family members.**
  - ☐ 9. **Give others the impression that I always have the right answer to any problem situation that arises.**
  - ☐ 10. **Listen to the discussion for clues that a problem exists.**
  - ☐ 11. **Give others the impression that I never have a problem.**
  - ☐ 12. **Model my openness to discuss my own struggles with others.**
  - ☐ 13. **Watch for attitudes of guilt, resentment, discouragement, or depression.**
  - ☐ 14. **Watch for opportunities in group sessions to teach or counsel.**

Most of the above suggestions will improve the chances that you will be approached by others for counseling. Many will help you identify problem areas where you may want to offer help. Certainly you will want to proceed with caution when you plan to intervene in a problem situation.

I hope you did not check 5, 9, or 11. These three suggestions will help you stand on the sidelines of a counseling ministry. If you appear to be overwhelmed with work, people will think you are too busy. They will not want to impose on your time. They will not ask you to take time to help them. If you always seem to have the right answer to every problem, most people will not see you as a real person. They do not like a smart aleck. They also do not believe that all of life's problems have easy answers. If they sense that you never have problems, they will not believe you can understand their problem. When a counselor reveals his own weaknesses, his vulnerability becomes a strength. It increases his ability to relate to the problems of others.

Other Ways to Make Your Availability Known

★ Show an attitude of concern.
★ Listen when people need someone to talk to.
★ When giving a devotional mention that you are interested in counseling.
★ Mention that you are taking a course in counseling.

Churches are usually successful to the extent to which they have involved the laity in ministry. You have an opportunity to make a great contribution to the work of the kingdom of God. Much of this will depend on the way you succeed in making your availability known.

■ **What ways do you believe you can best make your availability known? Use the suggestions given in today's lesson, and list on the lines below the suggestions you think will work best for you.**

_____

_____

_____

_____

_____

_____

Day 2: Building Rapport

> **Today's Objective:** You will be able to explain three ways to build rapport with other people.

While still working as a shepherd of his father's flocks, David was invited to the royal court by Saul; "Send me your son David, who is with the sheep" (1 Sam. 16:19). After watching him in action Saul was greatly impressed with the boy and wrote again to Jesse, "Allow David to remain in my service, for I am pleased with him" (1 Sam. 16:22).

David came to occupy a unique position in the court of King Saul. Not only did he serve in the king's bodyguard, but he also developed an interest in the monarch's emotional well-being. When Saul struggled with severe emotional disturbances, David was at hand to help the distressed ruler. Caring came naturally to a shepherd boy. He was accustomed to long periods of time on the lonely hillside concentrating on the well-being of his flock. In modern counseling language, we would say that David developed rapport with King Saul.

> **Rapport:** "A comfortable and unconstrained relationship of mutual confidence that comes to exist between two people."[1]

■ **Take a minute to study this definition of *rapport*. Then write a definition of *rapport* in your own words.**

_____

_____

_____

_____

Rapport is marked by harmony, conformity, accord, or affinity. David had developed his ability to build rapport to a high degree. He used this ability many times in the years ahead. I want you to develop a similar ability to develop rapport with others, especially those with whom you counsel. Today we are going to look at three factors that build rapport. Tomorrow we will study six more things you can do to build warm, comfortable relationships with your counselees.

Listening Builds Rapport

David the shepherd boy had learned to listen on the hillside. He had quiet days to attune his ear to sounds many people never hear. Listening became second nature to him. He took this skill with him when he went to the palace to minister to King Saul.

Free, unguided talk is always important in building a relationship with another person. As a person tells his story, he soon has the feeling that the listener is no longer just another individual. He is an insider with whom the speaker can share his inner thoughts. We really feel good toward people who take time to listen to us. In his book *How To Win Friends and Influence People,* Dale Carnegie suggests: "Be a good listener. Encourage others to talk about themselves."[2] When you listen to another person, you build rapport.

■ **List and explain specific things you can do to build rapport through listening.**

_____

_____

_____

_____

_____

I will give you feedback at the end of today's lesson.

Assurance of Confidentiality Builds Rapport

Assurance of confidentiality is the second factor in building rapport. You must be able to give your counselee the assurance that everything said will be kept confidential. I want to make sure you understand what I mean by "confidential."

■ 1. **Check the words or phrases below that describe "confidential." Mark through those words or phrases that do not describe "confidential."**

☐ disclose   ☐ private
☐ top secret   ☐ blab
☐ intimate   ☐ gossip
☐ keep to yourself   ☐ secret
☐ don't tell anybody   ☐ tattle
☐ make others promise not to tell

2. **In your own words, define "confidential."**

   Confidential means: _____

   _____

Some counselors make the mistake of thinking that confidential means "It's okay to tell someone as long as he/she promises not to tell." If you practice this approach to confidentiality, in a matter of time your reputation as a counselor will be tarnished. Sooner or later a counselee will discover that you shared a confidence with another person. Things discussed in confidence should normally be private, secret, intimate, and kept to yourself. You should not tattle, gossip, blab, or disclose that information unless there is compelling reason to do so.

In some cases you may be compelled by law or for the protection of the individual or community to reveal information gained in a counseling session. I will go into much more detail about guidelines for confidentiality next week. For now, I will give you this suggestion: Give your assurance of confidentiality. But, if asked the question: "Will all I say be held in complete confidence?"—Answer: "I will keep it all in confidence unless there is some compelling reason to tell."

■ **Explain the way you would assure your counselee that his statements will be kept confidential.**

   _____
   _____
   _____
   _____
   _____
   _____

Interest and Concern Build Rapport

A third factor in building rapport is the ability to make our interest and concern clearly understood.

Bill Sands was his name. The son of a California judge, Bill was serving a life sentence in San Quentin Penitentiary. While there, he became embroiled in a senseless prison riot and was placed in solitary confinement. As he lay on his prison cot, he heard the click of a lock as the door was opened and someone entered his cell.

A voice said, "Bill Sands."

The convict didn't even look up, "Go away nobody's interested in me."

The voice responded, "Bill I care."

Bill looked up and saw Clinton Duffey, the warden of the penitentiary. When an interviewer asked Sands how he felt in that moment, he replied, "With three words: 'Bill I care' Clinton Duffey gave me back my life."

> We are in the business of giving people back their lives; and, in a large measure, we do this when we master the skill of showing people that we care for them.

■ **Explain some ways you think you can demonstrate your interest and concern for your counselee.**

_____

_____

_____

_____

_____

You will have an opportunity in your group session to compare responses to today's activities. However, you probably listed some of the following ways to build rapport: encourage free, unguided talk; take time to listen; encourage the counselee to tell his story; listen intently; encourage others to talk about themselves; assure the counselee of confidentiality. Many of these things show your interest and concern. Spending time to help shows concern. Trying to understand, to comfort, or to encourage will also indicate your concern.

Day 3: SOFTEN

> **Today's Objective:** You will be able to list six more ways to build rapport in a counseling relationship.

When the counselor and the counselee meet for the first time, a process of evaluation begins. The prospective counselee is seeking to discover whether or not he can trust this counselor. He wants to determine how much he should tell. He may have been worried for quite a long time, trying hard to build up enough courage to come and talk. Once counseling begins, he is filled with misgivings and wondering whether he should have come.

Faced with this difficult situation, the counselor realizes that if he is going to achieve anything with this person, he must build rapport. The building of rapport is facilitated by a number of factors. Some of these can be gathered around an acrostic on the word *SOFTEN:*

Smile
Open gesture
Forward lean
Touch
Eye contact
Nod

Smile

A male flight attendant was fired from his trial position, because he did not smile. He took a legal action against the airline claiming a case of sexual discrimination. A federal judge ruled that a smile was part of the job and upheld the dismissal.

A smile is an absolute necessity for a counselor. Your face must carry a message of welcome and friendliness. You can learn to do this. Think smile! Practice smiling!

Open Gesture

You must be particularly careful about the nonverbal messages that you pass on to your counselee. If you sit with your arms crossed, you may send a message of defense, defiance, or withdrawal. If you sit with legs crossed and a foot moving in a kicking movement, you nonverbally say that you are bored. You should sit relaxed and attentive in a manner that conveys that you are open-minded and receptive to anything your counselee might say.

■ **Fill in the first two factors that can help you build rapport.**

S_____

O_____

Forward lean
Touch
Eye contact
Nod

Forward Lean

The nonverbal message of a counselor leaning back in his chair with both hands clasped behind his head is that he is smug, superior, and considers himself to be an authority. This will give your counselee the wrong message. Avoid this by leaning slightly forward in a friendly posture.

Touch

I once worked in a drug addiction facility. While conducting our group therapy sessions, I was aware that I did not have a rapport with these men. Then came a memorable day when we had a real breakthrough. I felt for the first time we had achieved an experience as a cohesive group. The chaplain arrived just as we were concluding. He remarked that we had obviously had a good experience. Then he explained, "I couldn't help but notice the way they each came and touched you. That is an indication that they accept you."

Touch conveys a message that may be difficult to verbalize. In the ministry of Jesus He reached out and touched the leper. Many people in our society today feel just as much like outcasts as the leper must have felt. When we touch them, we bring them back into contact with another individual. The touch we are discussing is the nondemanding touch. People who most need touching are the elderly and the unattractive. We will look more closely at the boundaries related to touching next week.

■ **Fill in the first four factors that can help you build rapport.**

S_____

O_____

F_____

T_____

Eye contact

Nod

Eye Contact

In setting up the budget in a large organization, the comptroller was a key figure. One department head sent a lady on his staff to make a plea for a special allocation of funds. When she returned, she told of one of the reasons she had been unsuccessful, "He looked out the window most of the time, never once did he look me in the eye."

Communication between two individuals is hampered without eye contact. Attention is the greatest reward one individual can give to another. Attention begins with looking. The good counselor fixes his eye on his counselee, not in a staring match, but in an interested coaxing way that assists the person to respond.

Nod

The slight movement of the head that we call a "nod" has awesome possibilities. The humorist Woodehouse told about a group of "yes men" who surrounded the movie director. Whenever he made a pronouncement, they all hastened to say yes. The process was never considered to be concluded until another man moved his head. He was the nodder, the one who gave the final affirmation of the group.

A counselor who sits like a "bump on a log" will not accomplish very much. There must be some movement. A nodding head is a valuable asset for building a relationship with another person. Do all this in a restrained manner, however. If you become too enthusiastic, the counselee may call up his latent resistance to "salesmen."

■ **Fill in the six factors that can help you build rapport.**

S_____

O_____

F_____

T_____

E_____

N_____

Next time you join in conversation with another person, check yourself on these six factors. Refer back to these questions to evaluate your rapport-building practices.

- Do you smile?
- Do your gestures indicate openness?
- Do you indicate your interest by a forward lean?
- Do you use nondemanding nonsexual touch appropriately?
- Do you maintain eye contact?
- Do you nod your head occasionally to indicate your attention?

Days 4 and 5: Review

> **Objective:** You will be able to successfully respond to activities reviewing some of the key points studied in units 1-5.

Believe it or not, we are approaching the mid-point of the course. I want us to take two days for review of some of the key points covered thus far. Work through the following activities. If you have trouble with one of them, refresh your memory by referring to the course map or to the material on the pages I have referenced for the activity.

Since I am allowing two days for these activities, take your time. Read again any material that is not quite clear. Thoroughly study any subjects that you have trouble with. Pace yourself and take a break between days whenever you choose.

Effective Questions

■ 1. **Turn to pages 26-27. Review the rule of thumb for questions and the guidelines for effective questioning.**

2. **Write an example of a poor question:**

_____

3. Write an example of a good question:

    _____

4. In your own words, state a principle for asking effective questions.

    _____

    _____

Two Stages

■ 1. What are the two stages of the Ten-Step Counseling Model?

   Stage One: _____

   Stage Two: _____

2. Which steps of the Ten-Step Model are used at each stage?

   Stage One: Steps 1—_____   Stage Two: Steps 5—_____

3. What key decision do you make at the end of stage one?

   _____

4. What decision do you make at the end of stage two?

   _____

Ten Steps

■ Write each of the ten steps in the counseling model.

   Step 1: _____

   Step 2: _____

   Step 3: _____

   Step 4: _____

   Step 5: _____

   Step 6: _____

   Step 7: _____

   Step 8: _____

   Step 9: _____

   Step 10: _____

The Questions

■ **Write the questions that are used in the Ten-Step Counseling Model.**

Step 1: _____

_____

Step 2: _____

Step 3: _____

Step 4: _____

Step 5: _____

Step 6: _____

Step 7: _____

Step 8: _____

Step 9: _____

Step 10: _____

_____

Use the course map to check your work on the questions and steps. By now, you need to have memorized the Ten-Step Counseling Model. If you have not done so, spend some extra time today reviewing units 2 and 3.

This may be a good place to stop for today. Start reviewing referrals tomorrow. If you want to continue, go ahead.

****

Referrals

■ 1. **Turn to page 41 and review "Two Possible Problems." Write and explain the two problems here:**

_____

_____

_____

_____

_____

_____

_____

_____

_____

2. Read through the list of questions on page 44. Place a check mark beside those questions you have already found answers to. On a separate sheet of paper, make a list of the questions you have yet to answer. See if you can find answers to those questions in the next few days.

3. Review the descriptions of the four emotional difficulties beginning on page 40. Which of these are you probably trained to help? Which should be referred?

I can help: _____

I should refer: _____

Listening

■ Mark the following statements as T (True) or F (False).

_____ a. Listening is a skill that must be developed and practiced.

_____ b. Reading will help a person develop listening skills.

_____ c. Listening helps people evaluate their thoughts.

_____ d. Intelligent people have a special gift for good listening.

_____ e. Hearing and listening describe the same process.

_____ f. Listening helps people express their emotions.

_____ g. Good hearing is the same as good listening.

_____ h. Good listening requires practice of good listening skills.

_____ i. Listening helps people break out of isolation.

_____ j. Everyday listening will give a person plenty of practice for good listening.

_____ k. A person can have good hearing and be a poor listener.

_____ l. The listener must follow the speaker's pace.

_____ m. Listening helps people say something to themselves.

_____ n. Listening is selective and, thus, different from hearing.

Four of the above statements describe the ways listening helps people (pp. 65-66). These are true. The other ten statements relate to the fallacies about listening (pp. 68-69). Five of the statements are true and five are false. You should have marked T (True) for a, c, f, h, i, k, l, m, and n. The false statements are b, d, e, g, j.

■ Assume that a friend has come to you for help to become a better listener. Place an X beside each of the listening guidelines below that you think you could explain to him. Place an O beside those you could not explain.

_____ Do not display feelings of disapproval.

_____ Develop helpful responses.

_____ Listen for the sound of silence.

_____ Make reflective statements.

Review pages 72-74 for those you do not understand well enough to explain.

■ **Describe at least five ways you can "listen" with your body.**

_____

_____

_____

_____

_____

_____

_____

_____

_____

_____

Review day 5 on pages 76-78 to check your work.

Building Rapport

■ **Using the word *SOFTEN* as an acrostic, list six factors that help build rapport.**

S_____

O_____

F_____

T_____

E_____

N_____

Check your work on page 87.

UNIT 6
Expectations and Boundaries

This Week's Learning Goal

After studying this unit, you will understand the dynamics of expectations and boundaries in counseling relationships.

Why You Will Find This Study Useful

Counseling relationships are very delicate. I will help you identify and understand expectations the counselee has of the relationship. You do not want to lose your opportunity to help by failing to recognize these expectations.

Boundaries for responsibility, time, and affection need to be set in a counseling relationship. Appropriate boundaries protect you and help the counselee derive the greatest benefit from the session. I will show you how to set and use these boundaries effectively.

Day 1: Expectations of the Counselee

> **Today's Objective:** You will be able to identify four counselee expectations in real life counseling situations.

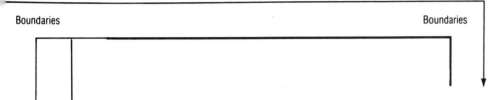

Boundaries   Boundaries

Expectations

Rapport

Boundaries

As you become involved in counseling persons, you need an understanding of some of the dynamics of a counseling relationship. As the counselee comes for counseling, he has certain expectations. These are different from those of a normal social relationship. Let's examine some of these expectations.

Counselee's Remorse

Many people experience what salespeople call "buyer's remorse." When an individual wonders if he is an idiot for making a purchase, he is experiencing buyer's remorse. A similar feeling of remorse, sorrow, or regret may characterize the counselee. As the counselee comes for counseling, her major reaction may be one of apprehension. She may have been concerned about the session for some time. She may expect the counseling to be a terrible experience. At last she has found courage and made arrangements to talk with you. Now that she is approaching the meeting place, she is growing more uncertain. What is going to happen? Was she foolish to come at all? When the counselee arrives, she may be in the grip of "counselee's remorse."

Your first task will be to relieve these fears. Either verbalize your awareness of this anxiety or chitchat on nonthreatening subjects until the counselee feels more comfortable.

■ **In your own words, define "counselee's remorse."**

_____

_____

The Expectation of Dependency

When a person comes to a counselor for help, he admits that he cannot manage life and needs the help of someone else. This contrasts vividly with our normal cultural expectation that a person should be self-sufficient. Society seems to expect everyone to be capable of handling any situation that may come along. Now he is admitting that he is not self-sufficient. He realizes his need to depend on someone else for help.

This expectation of dependency may be a strong motivating force toward seeking counseling. You will be tempted to enjoy the dependence of your counselee. You must deny yourself that satisfaction. Your ultimate objective as counselor is for your counselee to be independent. Keep your counselee moving toward the goal of an independent existence.

The goal of independent living does not mean independence from God. We are all dependent on Him for our very lives. Independence does mean, however, that the counselee can handle feelings, emotions, and decisions without having to depend on another human to guide him each step of the way. Dependence is okay in certain circumstances, but constant dependence is not healthy.

■ **In your own words, define the expectation of dependency.**

_____

_____

The Expectation of Self-Orientation

In a normal social setting, people are not expected to spend their time talking about themselves. If an individual persists in this type of talk, he is considered an ill-mannered bore. When an individual comes to a counselor, however, he has every reason to believe that the total focus of the conversation will be on him, his life, his family, his relations, his problems, and his difficulties. This focus on the counselee is characteristic of a counseling relationship and is quite appropriate.

■ **In your own words, define the expectation of self-orientation.**

_____

_____

The Expectation of Nonretaliation

In a good counseling relationship, the counselee should feel that you will not strike back at her. The counselee should be able to speak without fear of ridicule or criticism from the counselor. Moreover, she should feel that she can speak of subjects not generally discussed in polite company. The counselor says in effect, "You can talk about anything you want to no matter how bad it seems."

■ **1. In your own words, define the expectation of nonretaliation.**

_____

_____

   2. Review your four definitions. Identify the expectation involved in each of the following situations. On the line below each situation, circle the expectation you think is involved.

A. Janet's husband died last week. She has never held a job outside the home. Her husband kept the checking account balanced and paid all the bills. She is devastated. She does not know how to start putting her life back together. Janet has asked you to tell her what to do. What is Janet's expectation?

   Remorse   Dependence   Self-Orientation   Nonretaliation

B. Leon lives in a very deprived environment. He feels like the whole world is against him. When you try to tell him you understand how he feels, he lets his pent up anger loose on you. After a five minute verbal beating, you come right back with some choice words of your own. Leon decides that you are probably not the person who can help him. He apologizes and then leaves. What was Leon's expectation?

   Remorse   Dependence   Self-Orientation   Nonretaliation

C. Mary Beth has just moved to your town. She is in your Sunday School class. After your monthly class meeting, she discovers your interest in counseling. She asks for your help. She begins to explain the problem she is having adjusting to the changes. You remember experiencing similar problems the last time you moved, so you spend twenty minutes telling her all you went through. She leaves feeling that you have done little to help. What expectation did Mary Beth have?

   Remorse   Dependence   Self-Orientation   Nonretaliation

D. George frequently travels out of town for his business. He had been sexually involved in an affair. He finally realized his sin and broke off the relationship. No one else knows about the relationship, but he is experiencing a heavy load of guilt. He feels that you are a person who can help him. He also believes you will keep the matter confidential. When he finally sits down to talk with you, he gets "cold feet" and never mentions the real problem he is having. What is George's expectation?

   Remorse   Dependence   Self-Orientation   Nonretaliation

George is a good example of one who presents a different problem, not his real problem, to the counselor. He expects this session to be a disaster. He is experiencing counselee's remorse. Mary Beth needed to talk about her problems. She did not come to you for counsel in order to hear about your problems. She expected self-orientation. You shocked Leon when you struck back at him. Angry people sometimes just need someone to vent their anger on. Leon expected nonretaliation. When that expectation was shattered, he decided to find another counselor. Janet is immobilized in the grief process. That is a very normal experience. In such cases the grieving person needs someone she can depend on for help. She may have been overly dependent on her husband. She is expecting a dependent relationship with you. You have a big but potentially rewarding challenge as you help move Janet toward independence.

NOTE: On day 5 you will need at least five sheets of paper for your assignment. Plan on spending up to one hour for that assignment.

Day 2: The Expectation of Confidentiality

> **Today's Objective:** You will be able to distinguish between situations that demand strict confidence and those that will compel you to tell someone.

One of the reasons most people go to see a counselor, rather than a close friend or relative, is because they believe the counselor will keep this information in the strictest confidence.

■ **Before studying further, go back to page 85 and review "Assurance of Confidentiality Builds Rapport." Rewrite your definition of *confidential* here:**

_____

_____

You must be very careful to maintain a reputation as one who will keep a confidence. Make sure no one would ever have any question about your ability to keep a confidence. You may be asked to make talks, and you will be tempted to refer to a counseling experience in which you have been involved. One way to avoid this is to spend more time preparing your talk. In that way you will not be reaching around in your mind for extra material.

The Problems of Confidentiality

Another aspect of confidentiality is the commonly held belief that the counselor cannot be required to reveal anything told to him in a counseling session. Some exceptions to this may present a problem to the counselor.

In 1984 a man was accused of sexually molesting a six-year-old girl. He went to his pastor to surrender himself and ask that the minister accompany him to the police. At the trial the prosecutor subpoenaed the pastor and asked him to reveal what the accused had told him. The preacher refused to answer on the grounds that he had the right to confidentiality about conversations with a person with whom he was counseling. He was sentenced to sixty days for contempt of court!

This situation has arisen from the rightful alarm over child abuse. Numerous state laws now require anyone who knows about such a crime to inform authorities. In at least twenty states, toughened child abuse laws have led to the elimination of the long established legal and social recognition of the clergy-penitent privilege.[1]

Another rare situation reminds us that we must be careful in assuming the privilege of confidentiality as counselors. After an attempted assassination of President Reagan, reports came out that the FBI had interviewed the attempted assassin's psychiatrist. He was asked if the privilege of the psychiatrist had been compromised. The answerer referred to the guidelines of the American Psychiatric Association's Principles of Medical Ethics which say,

"A physician may not reveal confidences entrusted to him in the course of medical attendance . . . unless required to do so by law or it becomes necessary to do so to protect the welfare of the individual or the community."[2]

Because the law requires that any threat on the president's life be reported, confidence was not breached in this incident. However, the troublesome aspect of this guideline is the clause about protecting the welfare of the individual or the community.

■ **Mark the following statements as True or False.**

_____ 1. **The privacy of a counselor-counselee relationship is protected by law.**

_____ 2. **Some state laws require a counselor to report certain crimes he/she learns about in counseling sessions.**

_____ 3. **Sometimes the circumstances shared in a counseling session will compel you to tell.**

_____ 4. **Sharing confidential information with your spouse is not a breach of confidentiality as long as he or she promises not to tell.**

_____ 5. **You will sometimes need to share a confidence for the protection of the individual or society.**

Maintaining confidentiality cannot always be based on a clear-cut decision. Confidential matters learned in counseling are not always protected by law. Laws may require you to report a confidential matter. You will sometimes need to report a confidential matter for the protection of the individual. In dealing with a suicidal person for instance, you may need to involve family and close friends in the helping process. Though your spouse may be completely trustworthy, sharing a confidence is a breach of confidentiality. Answers to the true-false questions are: True—2, 3, and 5; False—1 and 4.

No Guarantees

I once counseled with a man who insisted that I assure him that everything he told me would be kept in confidence. After I had given him this assurance, he said, "I have committed a murder." I was on the horns of a dilemma. You do want your counselee to feel assured of confidentiality. At the same time, you cannot promise complete confidentiality for all circumstances. You should be careful in the way you assure your counselee about confidentiality.

A counselee may ask, "Will all I say be held in complete confidence?" As I suggested earlier, you should answer, "I will keep it all in confidence unless there is some compelling reason not to do so."

Guidelines for Deciding on Issues of Confidentiality

1. Operate on the basis that you are not going to divulge anything that is told to you by a counselee.
2. In some specialized instances, you should not guarantee confidentiality.
3. In telling a counselee about everything being kept confidential, you should add the phrase, "unless there is a compelling reason to do so."
4. If process notes are kept about the session for later reference, they should be done in such a way as to guard the counselee's identity.
5. Become aware of the laws of your state regarding the concept of counselor's privilege.
6. Make an agreement with your spouse that you will not discuss the contents of counseling sessions.
7. If, for some reason, you believe your pastor should be informed about a particular situation, ask for the counselee's permission to share the information with the pastor.

■ 1. **Suppose you are asked the question: "Will you promise not to tell anything to anyone about what I am about to say?" How would you respond?**

   _____

   _____

   _____

   _____

   _____

2. **Decide whether you will keep the following matters confidential or not. Circle Yes (I will keep this confidential) or No (I will not keep this confidential). Briefly explain why in each case.**

   YES or NO   A **Melinda (age 15) has been involved sexually with a boy her age. She came to talk to you out of a deep sense of guilt.**

   Why? _____

   YES or NO   B **Bill has asked you to help him learn to control his temper. He was an abused child. He finds himself beating his own son when he gets mad. Thus far, the son has not been seriously injured physically. Bill thinks you can help him stop. Your state law requires persons who are aware of child abuse to report it.**

   Why? _____

   YES or NO   C **You visit Benton in a nursing home. From several things he says, you believe he might attempt suicide if given the opportunity and means.**

   Why? _____

   YES or NO   D **A next door neighbor talks to you about a marriage problem. Your spouse quizzes you about the subject of your talk. You did not actually promise to keep the matter confidential.**

   Why? _____

YES or NO   E   Barry and Jill are in your youth department at church. They have been dating seriously for a year. Jill confides in you that she is pregnant. She is considering an abortion and does not want her parents to know about her condition.

Why? _____

YES or NO   F   A church member you do not know learns that you are a trustworthy counselor. He seeks your help with a grudge he is carrying toward another church member. He was mistreated quite innocently, but he has been bitter about the situation ever since. You learn that the other person is one of your closest friends. He is unaware of the problem.

3. Think about each of the situations in #2 where you circled No. Decide who you would talk to and write their title or name in the margin.

We will discuss your answers in your group session this week.

Day 3: Establishing Boundaries

> **Today's Objective:** You will be able to define two boundaries for a counseling relationship and explain why each is important.

When you begin to counsel someone, the counselee needs to understand the basis on which the relationship is going to proceed. These boundaries surrounding the counseling relationship need to be carefully defined. Some writers refer to this as setting up the limits. The three boundaries that need to be defined are responsibility, time, and affection.

The Boundary of Responsibility.

One of the dangers you will face in counseling is that the expectation of dependency can become a barrier to the counseling process. The counselee comes to think of you as an authority figure. You are probably active in church life, and he sees you leading a class or making presentations. He comes to feel that you are knowledgable. You will be tempted to let this go to your head. You may find yourself trying to fill that role of being the expert on life. You must remember the adage: "Admit that you don't know everything, for people will soon find it out anyway." As a wise counselor:
• Admit that you do not "know it all."
• Refuse to make decisions for other people.

Sometimes the counselee, having presented his problem, will ask you what he should do. You can say, "You remember when we began this counseling relationship, I told you I did not make other people's decisions. The best I can do is to work with and help you explore all the possibilities. Then I have to leave the decision in your hands."

When you are tempted to say, "If I were you . . ." refrain from saying it. You are presenting an impossible situation; you could never be that person. Moreover, if you persuade the person to make a decision, you will be held responsible for the outcome—good or bad.

■ 1. **In each pair of statements below, check the one in which an appropriate boundary of responsibility has been established.**

    ☐ a. **Counselor is the expert on life.**

    ☐ b. **Counselor admits he does not know it all.**

    ☐ c. **Counselee makes his own decisions.**

    ☐ d. **Counselor makes decisions for the counselee.**

    ☐ e. **Counselee assumes a dependency role.**

    ☐ f. **Counselee assumes responsibility for his life.**

    ☐ g. **Counselor refuses to make decisions for the counselee.**

    ☐ h. **Counselor gives "If-I-were-you" advice.**

    ☐ i. **Counselee is responsible for the outcome of the decisions.**

    ☐ j. **Counselor is held responsible for the outcome of the decisions.**

    ☐ k. **Counselor recommends a course of action.**

    ☐ l. **Counselor helps explore possibilities and leaves the decision in the hands of the counselee.**

2. **Define the boundary of responsibility.**

_____

_____

_____

_____

3. **Explain why you need to establish the boundary of responsibility.**

_____

_____

_____

_____

_____

_____

In the statement pairs of #1 above, you see some contrasts between a counseling relationship that has a proper boundary of responsibility and one that does not. You should have checked b, c, f, g, i, and l. Perhaps you have seen or heard counseling talk shows on which the professional counselor was very directive. He made statements like: "If I were you . . ." or "Here's what you should do." Sometimes directive counseling may be appropriate. It does require extensive knowledge about psychology, personality, human development, and spiritual values. Most lay counselors have not had adequate training for this type of counseling. Directive counseling also places more responsibility on the counselor. If the action plan does not work, the counselor is blamed. Stay with the Ten-Step Model and force your counselee to be responsible. You will compare your definition and explanation (activities 2 and 3) with other group members in your group session this week.

The Boundary of Time

Some counselors believe that many of the greatest gains come to the counselee outside the counseling hour. In my own work, I undertook some research which indicated that the twelve to fourteen hours following the counseling session were often the most significant. The session is frequently a beginning point. After the session, the counselee continues to grapple mentally with the problems discussed with the counselor. This is the reason for spacing interviews. It allows time for growth.

You should tell the counselee that you will be happy to talk with him at specific times for specific periods of time. This time arrangement does, however, depend on the circumstances. You should set time limits to suit the particular case. When the allotted time runs out, you can say, "Well, it looks as if our thirty minutes are gone. Let's meet again next week and pick up where we left off." This does not mean that you should be inflexible in concluding. A good time arrangement will help save you from long, drawn out sessions which are generally of little value. By determining a time both the counselor and the counselee use the time more wisely. You will make more progress by having three thirty-minute periods rather than one ninety-minute period.

The frequency with which you see a counselee requires much thought. I have already suggested that much of the counseling you do will only be one to three sessions. Among professionals the frequency varies from a daily interview to a once- or twice-weekly schedule. As a lay counselor conscious of your time limitations, you should not see a counselee too frequently. Your counselee needs time to gain insight.

In most cases, a weekly meeting is enough. One pastoral counselor suggests counseling sessions once every two weeks. Your counseling sessions can be fairly short. A fifteen-minute period may be quite valuable. In consideration of the length of the counseling period, each counselee is an individual and must be treated accordingly. In the early days of your counseling, you should not be too ambitious. If you determine at the end of the session that you do need to meet again, you can say to the counselee, "I suggest we meet on the next three Thursday evenings for thirty minutes. At the end of this time, we will reevaluate the situation."

Be on the alert for the chronic neurotic looking for a crutch on which to lean. Such a person can take up your valuable time and waste your energies. If you specify the number of sessions, you can evaluate the situation as it develops. At the end of three weeks, you can conclude, refer, or continue. Your time-boundary saves him from an unending and difficult relationship.

■ 1. **In light of the previous suggestions, choose the preferred time boundary for lay counseling. Circle your choice.**
   A. **Thirty-minute sessions or Ninety-minute sessions**
   B. **Daily sessions or Weekly sessions**
   C. **Three sessions and reevaluation or indefinite number of sessions**

2. **Define the boundary of time.**

   _____

   _____

   _____

   _____

3. **Explain why you need to establish the boundary of time. What are the benefits of setting this boundary?**

   _____

   _____

   _____

   _____

   _____

   _____

Keeping in mind that you need some flexibility, thirty-minute sessions would be preferred over ninety-minute sessions. Three weekly sessions with a reevaluation at the end would be preferred over daily sessions and an indefinite number of sessions. You will compare your definition and explanation (activities 2 and 3) with other group members in your group session this week.

Day 4: The Boundary of Affection

> **Today's Objective:** You will be able to define and explain the reason for establishing the boundary of affection. You will list DO's and DON'Ts for managing affection in your counseling relationships.

Transference

The boundary of affection is of particular interest for the counselor in a Christian setting. When two people come together to talk about highly personal matters, an emotional bond can develop between them. This bond is referred to as "transference."

In positive transference a strong feeling of attachment develops. The counselee may come to feel very warmly toward his or her counselor. A feeling of antagonism is described as negative transference. Feelings of hostility the counselee has toward someone else in life may be felt (or transferred) toward the counselor.

■ **In the biblical story of King Saul and David, Saul expressed transference. Read the following accounts of Saul and David's relationship. Did Saul express positive or negative transference in each case?**

1 Samuel 16:14-23 _____

1 Samuel 18:6-13 _____

Saul demonstrated a positive transference in his early relationships with David (1 Sam. 16:14-23). Later his feelings took a twist. Due to severe jealously, Saul began to blame David for his trouble. He saw that God's Spirit was with David and had left him. His feelings toward David became a negative transference that ultimately lead to attempts on David's life (1 Sam. 18:6-13).

If a counseling relationship has been productive and worthwhile, a bond will be created. Moreover, this bond will deepen with the passing of time. This makes emotional involvement even more probable. A counseling relationship involving a member of the opposite sex should be handled very carefully. An alarming number of counselors with the highest principles have found themselves drawn into a situation in which they compromised themselves and ruined their ministry.

■ **Write in your own words a definition of *transference*.**

_____

_____

_____

_____

Emotional Dynamics

The dynamics of the emotions stirred during counseling are very complex. At the risk of being simplistic, let me explain them in terms of the counselee's experience.

A woman's husband has become involved with another woman and is suing her for divorce. She spends time with a male counselor who is a Christian. He represents all that she had hoped her husband might be. She has a sensation of failure. She does not seem to be attractive as a woman. Can she reach out to this appealing man?

The counselor, in turn, can feel flattered by this attention. He believes he can be of special help. In the chain reactions that follow, the counselor's own marriage may be compromised and his status as a counselor may be jeopardized. As the counselor becomes more involved, he unwittingly sets the counselee up for another blow. When he breaks off the relationship, the counselee who came to him for help is damaged even more. Possibly the worst outcome would be for a counselor to let his own sexuality overwhelm him and then build a rationalization to justify his behavior.

■ 1. **This identifies a potential problem. To avoid it, a counselor needs to set a boundary for affection. How would you define the boundary of affection for a counseling relationship?**

_____

_____

_____

_____

2. **Explain why you need to establish the boundary of affection.**

For the counselor's benefit: _____

_____

For the counselee's benefit: _____

_____

You will compare your responses on these two activities with others in your group session this week.

Guidelines for Handling Affection

1. A Christian counselor should remain above suspicion. He should refrain from all appearances of evil (2 Thess. 5:22).
2. Counseling sessions should take place in a private setting in a semipublic place. Other people should be around but out of hearing distance.
3. The counselor should not have physical contact with the counselee.
4. He or she should counsel in the home of a person of the opposite sex ONLY when the spouse or other adults are present in the house.
5. The counselor should watch for any inappropriate feelings that may develop, and take proper actions in the relationship.
6. If emotions seem to be getting out of your control, refer the counselee to another counselor.

Handling an Overture

When verbalizations of affection come, indicate that these feelings are really toward the counseling situation. At the same time, leave the way open for the counselee to have a change of mind without feelings of disloyalty. This technique is seen in the following case.

Fredona: You know, Mr. Voyles, this counseling experience has been a great help for me. When I first came here, I felt so depressed and dispirited. I have found our talking together to be so helpful.

Mr. Voyles: Thank you Fredona. I'm so glad to know this experience has been helpful. You know that I am anxious to help you in any way I can.

Fredona: This office has become a haven, a refuge. Sometimes, when things are not going well at work, I think, "Well never mind. Next Tuesday evening I will see

Mr. Voyles. I know he will be able to help me." I just wish I could really tell you how I feel about all this. I sometimes wonder . . . if I do not feel too warmly toward you.

Mr. Voyles: Well, Fredona, I hope you realize that you do not feel this way towards me personally. It seems as if you have been helped by our counseling sessions. At the moment, you feel warmly toward the counseling situation. Now, remember, this feeling is not toward me personally but toward the situation in which you have come to know something of yourself. People sometimes go through experiences like this when they are being counseled. You may change your mind later on and feel resentful. If you do, however, don't let that worry you. I understand something of the experiences through which you're passing.

This exchange helps to clarify the issues, yet leaves the way open for a change of attitude. It also serves as a warning. Mr. Voyles has told Fredona he thinks of this as a counseling situation, and he is not going to become personally involved.

Some professional counselors refuse to see their counselees in any social setting. They do not accept invitations to visit their homes or go to the same social events. You should take the same precaution. This, of course, will be more difficult because of your relationships in church. If you become too close to your counselee, you will not be effective in your counseling. You must constantly reevaluate your relationship to your counselee. Rollo May warned that counselors are particularly prone to get into trouble in this area. It is an occupational hazard, but you are responsible for your behavior.

■ **Make for yourself a list of DO's and DON'Ts to appropriately manage affection in a counseling relationship. Glean ideas from today's lesson. Add other ideas that come to mind.**

DO's

_____

_____

_____

_____

_____

DON'Ts

_____

_____

_____

_____

_____

Prepare to share and discuss these lists in your group session this week.

Day 5: Practice the Ten-Step Model

> During today's lesson you will practice applying the Ten-Step Counseling Model to specific cases. You will evaluate your work in your group session this week.

I want you to get some practice using the Ten-Step Model. You will need a spiral bound notebook, notebook paper, or another type of blank writing paper. Use a separate sheet for each of the cases. Plan on spending thirty to sixty minutes on this assignment.

■ **In the cases below assume you have already completed stage one and decided to counsel the person. As time allows, consider some or all of the following for each case. Make a list of some:**

- **issues you would bring up**
- **alternatives you would brainstorm**
- **outcomes you might explore**
- **scriptural teachings you might examine**
- **information you might need to supply**
- **things you might say**

A. **Melinda (age 15) has been involved sexually with a boy her age. She came to talk to you out of a deep sense of guilt.**

B. **Bill has asked you to help him learn to control his temper. He was an abused child. He finds himself beating his own son when he gets mad. Thus far, the son has not been seriously injured physically. Bill thinks you can help him stop. Your state law requires persons who are aware of child abuse to report it.**

C. **You visit Benton in a nursing home. From several things he says, you believe he might attempt suicide if given the opportunity and means.**

D. **A next door neighbor talks to you about a marriage problem. Your spouse quizzes you about the subject of your conversation. You did not actually promise to keep the matter confidential.**

E. **Barry and Jill are in your youth department at church. They have been dating seriously for a year. Jill confides in you that she is pregnant. She is considering an abortion and does not want her parents to know about her condition.**

Bring your counseling plans with you to your group session this week.

UNIT 7

Counseling Sick and Grieving Persons

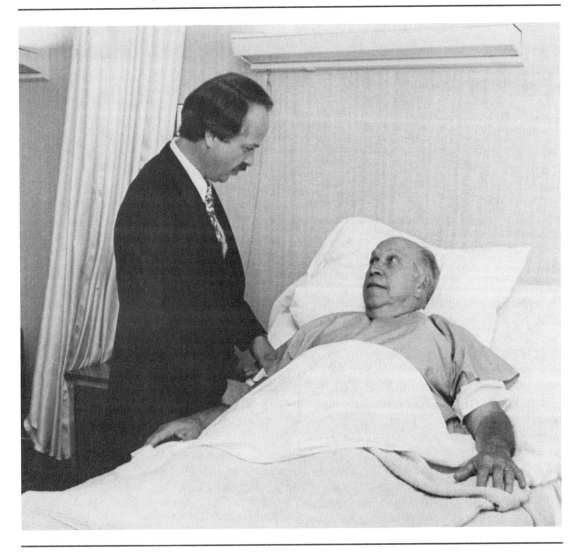

This Week's Learning Goal

After studying this unit, you will understand ways to counsel and minister to those who are sick and those who are grieving.

Why You Will Find This Study Useful

Sickness and death of loved ones and friends are very common experiences of life. In this unit, I will help you understand the psychological dynamics of illness and grief. You will discover ways to effectively minister to the sick and grieving, and you will discover many mistakes to avoid in your ministry to them.

Day 1: The Crises of Illness

> **Today's Objective:** You will be able to identify and
> describe two psychological crises that illness can cause.

One of the most important and frequent counseling opportunities you will face will be visiting and counseling people who are ill. As with your counseling in any situation, you will use the Ten-Step Counseling Model as the structure for your counseling.

As you study the coming units of WiseCounsel, mark and take notes about important facts. You will not learn all of the guidelines and information given. However, this book should become a manual you can use to prepare for each counseling experience you face. You may want to review just before making a visit. You may need to come back to it for information or ideas after a counseling experience. Only as you get real-life experiences will you really become the effective counselor you want to be. Practice and review will be vital parts of your ongoing counseling ministry.

More Harm Than Good?

Some laypersons are willing to visit sick people, but they may unwittingly do more harm than good. Many well-meaning religious workers often see the immobilized patient as either an opportunity for pushing a particular religious point of view or a captive audience for recounting personal experiences in the field of medicine, hospitals, or doctors. On the other hand, visiting the sick may be the encouragement a person needs to "hang on" to living. It could be the loving act that draws a person to consider Jesus as his or her Savior. This unit of study is being undertaken so that you will not be the cause of harm to sick persons, but will supply an effective ministry to these needy people.

Illness is not just physical. Numerous psychological reactions should be understood by the person visiting the sick. You are not expected to know all about the physical aspects of illness. Knowing something of the psychological aspects of illness, however, is of prime importance. Illness is a time of crises.

Illness Is a Social Crisis

The person who is ill is separated from his job setting. He is not able to carry on his normal work. He is away from the place where he normally spends a large portion of his waking hours. He also may have a considerable amount of anxiety as he ponders the possibility of being replaced by an ambitious person who is substituting for him. Moreover, he may have financial worries, even though he has hospital insurance.

If the sick person goes to a hospital, he is removed from his family setting. This may lead to homesickness. He has lost the security of home—spouse, children, and the routines of family life. He has even lost the pleasure of home-cooked food. He is living in another world, a world of white-gowned nurses, orderlies, dieticians, and technicians. This transfer to a strange new world may fill him with anxiety.

■ 1. Describe in your own words how illness is a social crisis. Include in your description some of the fears or concerns of the sick person who is experiencing social crisis.

_____

_____

_____

_____

_____

_____

_____

_____

Moving to a strange new world, even though temporary, creates significant social change. Anxiety and fears may abound. Think how you would feel to move to a whole new community without any time to prepare yourself psychologically for the change. You probably included in your description such concerns as job security, financial worries, homesickness, loss of the security of home, and loss of the pleasures of home life. Illness is a social crisis!

Illness Is a Personal Crisis

■ As you read the following section, underline events, activities, or feelings that tend to create a personal crisis for the sick person. I have underlined one as an example.

The sick person may have a tendency to regress to an earlier and more infantile mode of behavior. The patient in the hospital finds himself almost entirely at the mercy of other people who tell him when to eat, what to eat, how to behave. Once, when I was in a hospital, I asked the nurse who had taken my blood pressure what it was. He refused and implied that I had no right to know. I reacted, "Whose blood pressure is it?" From then on I had a feeling that nurse was very annoyed with me. In this dependent situation, it is easy to fall back into the ways and attitudes of childhood.

The patient's own body becomes the focus of the attention of the doctors, technicians, and nurses who are constantly taking his temperature, counting his pulse rate, enquiring about his bodily functions, and so on. The patient loses almost all personal privacy and must forget about modesty. Little wonder that the patient sometimes becomes obsessed with his body, and his reactions to them are almost infantile.

The experience of pain can be threatening, too. An experience with pain, particularly if it is over a long period of time, can have an undermining effect on the personality of the sick person. The threat to life and the experience of pain may unite to cause repressed emotional conflicts to flood into consciousness, giving rise to feelings of guilt.

Convalescence or recovery has been likened to growing up. In many ways it resembles adolescence. Sometimes, like the adolescent, the convalescent tries to develop too quickly, wrenching himself free from dependency and accepting responsibilities for which he is not yet ready. This is sometimes called a "plunge into health." On other occasions, he may remember the joys of being dependent as a youth and finish up "enjoying bad health."

When you visit or counsel a sick person, remember that he may be in crisis. The personality characteristics of his healthy days may be missing. He may appear to be a different individual from the one you previously knew. You are to minister to him and help him regardless of the state you find him in.

■ 1. **Look back over the events, activities, feelings that you underlined. Which two, in your opinion, would do most to create a personal crisis.**

_____

_____

2. **Describe in your own words how illness is a personal crisis. You may speak from personal experience if you like.**

_____

_____

_____

_____

_____

_____

_____

3. **Identify the following factors as contributors to either a social (S) or personal (P) crisis. Circle S or P.**

S-P A A nurse enters the room and gives the patient a complete sponge bath.

S-P B The patient must enlist a substitute to teach his Sunday School class for the next three weeks.

S-P C The patient's young children are not allowed to come to the room for a visit.

S-P D Due to the pain, the patient continues to demand pain killer more frequently than it can be given.

S-P E The patient decides he is well enough to return to work, even though the doctor said he was still too weak to work.

A sponge bath, pain, and a "plunge into health" contribute to a personal crisis. Missing the fellowship of a Sunday School class and the hug of one's young children can contribute to a social crisis.

A crisis is a turning point. It is a decisive moment or a period of change. Depending on how the patient is able to handle these crises, he will either grow from the experience or be scarred and weakened for a period of time. A sensitive counselor may be able to help the sick person cope positively with these crises. An insensitive counselor could do more harm than good. Work at becoming a sensitive counselor.

Day 2: Resources of the Christian Counselor

> **Today's Objective:** You will be able to list and explain ways to use four resources in counseling the sick.

> "Come, ye blessed of my Father, inherit the kingdom prepared for you from the foundation of the world: For I was . . . sick, and ye visited me . . . Inasmuch as ye have done it unto one of the least of these my brethren, ye have done it unto me" (Matt. 25:34-40, KJV).

A number of resources are uniquely available to you in your ministry to the sick. Although you will not have the symbolic importance the pastor may have, you still have values in your own person that can make a significant impact on people's lives.

A Caring Spirit

You represent someone who cares. The patient is often isolated and out of touch with other people. Doctors, nurses, and orderlies are hurrying about their professional duties. You say by your presence, "I have no professional stake in your case. I am interested in you personally." This may give you an advantage over a busy pastor. While the pastor's visit may be important to the patient, the patient may have a lurking suspicion that he is visiting because it is part of his job. With the lay counselor, he has no such suspicion. He knows you are there because you care.

The Christian counselor represents someone who heals. Improvement may come to the patient because of your call. Recent developments in the concept of psychosomatic medicine have helped us see the close connection of body and mind. Once again the simple technique of listening is important. A serene spirit may be of real value in the healing of the body.

The patient has been idle for so long that he often is longing to talk to someone. He often feels he is surrounded by a veil of secrecy. Now you say, in effect, "Tell me how you feel." In listening you help the patient express his hostilities and fears. This process can help clear away emotional blockages and possibly facilitate the healing process.

The Christian counselor also represents someone who needs the patient. As a representative of the church, you invite the patient to become a part of a religious community in which people are concerned about each other. If the patient already belongs to a church, you come to emphasize that others in the group are concerned about him.

■ 1. **What is one of your resources as a Christian lay counselor?**

_____

2. **In addition to showing you care by your very presence, what other way can you minister to the person's needs?**

_____

3. **What are some of the benefits of using this resource in ministry to the sick?**

_____

_____

_____

_____

_____

The first resource we have examined is your spirit of caring. Your presence and your listening are two good ways you can show you care. Your spirit of caring can calm the patient's spirit, remove emotional blockages, remind him that somebody cares, provide the growth potential of feeling needed by the church fellowship.

The Place of the Bible

Another resource peculiar to the Christian counselor is the Bible. The Bible contains the record of the struggles of men and women with the ups and downs of life. In its pages are the experiences of men and women of faith in their encounter with suffering, affliction, and adversity. Consequently, the modern sufferer can find encouragement and help in Scripture. Passages such as the twenty-third Psalm, the fourteenth chapter of John's Gospel, and the eighth chapter of Romans, have great words which have been a source of comfort through the years.

■ **Some particularly good portions of Scripture to use with sick people are:**
   ☐ **Psalm 55:22**
   ☐ **Psalm 121**
   ☐ **Matthew 6:25-34**
   ☐ **Philippians 4:6-7, 13, 19**
   ☐ **1 Peter 5:6-7**

GOD'S WC
AND WIS

Read each of these passages. Think about situations where each passage could be shared in a meaningful way with a sick person. Jot notes to yourself in the space above, or on a separate sheet of paper.

In your group session this week, you will discuss the use of the above Scriptures in counseling the sick.

When the Scriptures are read to the sick person, it is important to keep the passage short. Commit some of the great passages of Scripture to memory, so that you will be able to quote them if a crisis arises. As you stand by the bedside, you may quote such statements as "The eternal God is your refuge, and underneath are the everlasting arms," (Deut.33:27); or "Peace I leave with you; my peace I give you. . . . Do not let your hearts be troubled, and do not be afraid" (John 14:27).

GOD'S W
AND WIS

You can leave a verse of Scripture with the patient. One way of doing this is to give a "spiritual prescription"—an appropriate verse of Scripture written on a card or a piece of paper. You may say, "When you are ill, the doctor gives you a prescription for some medicine that will help you. Now I want to help you with a spiritual prescription."

■ **1. List two of the resources you have as a Christian lay counselor.**

_____   _____

2. Explain some ways you can use the Bible in counseling the sick.

_____

_____

_____

_____

_____

_____

The two resources we have examined so far are the Bible and a spirit of caring. You can read favorite passages of comfort, quote short passages, and issue a "spiritual prescription."

Using Prayer

In a survey conducted among hospital patients as to what they expected when a minister visited them, 51% said the minister should "have prayer." Prayer can have therapeutic value in a ministry to the sick.

When should you pray? You must learn to "feel the spiritual pulse" of the patient. Notice if she has a Bible or religious literature in the room. Observe her conversation. Does she indicate that she would appreciate such a ministry? You need to develop a sensitivity to the total situation. Seldom will a person refuse to allow you to pray.

A number of factors make up a satisfactory sick room prayer. You should pray in a conversational tone of voice. The prayer should be brief. Familiar verses of Scripture used in your prayer may help stimulate the patient's faith.

Your prayer should clarify the Christian attitude toward suffering. Without creating magical expectations your prayer can engender a healthy optimism. No fixed type of prayer can be memorized, since each situation will call for individual handling. An example of a sickroom prayer would be:

> "Oh Lord our God, we come to Thee, the Great Physician, to pray for thy blessing on our brother. Grant to him that he will know that thou hast said, 'Lo, I am with you always.' Grant that in this experience, he can know that 'all things work together for good to them that love God.' Give thy guidance to nurses and doctors. Give the sense of thy presence to our brother and healing to his body and spirit. Through Jesus Christ our Lord, we pray. Amen."

■ 1. **List three of the resources you have as a Christian lay counselor.**

_____   _____

_____

2. **Explain some things you can include in your prayer with the sick.**

_____

_____

_____

_____

_____

_____

We have examined a caring spirit, the Bible, and prayer. In your prayers you may want to include familiar verses of Scripture to stimulate faith, clarify the Christian attitude toward suffering, and develop a healthy optimism.

Good Literature

Good literature for the patient is also helpful. You can leave it with him and it will serve to remind him of the visit. It will provide something for him to turn to in his lonely hours. Although many materials have been prepared for this purpose, you should select carefully. The reading material should be on good paper, contain a message of comfort and encouragement, be attractive in format, and of light weight so that it will not be too difficult to hold in weakened hands.

■ 1. **List the four resources we have discussed for use by the Christian lay counselor.**

A _____   C _____
B _____   D _____

2. **Explain at least one way you can use each of these resources in counseling the sick.**

A _____
B _____
C _____
D _____

Day 3: Guidelines for Visiting the Sick

> **Today's Objective:** You will be able to identify violations of hospital visitation guidelines and describe things you should do in given circumstances.

In pastoral counseling the concept of the healing team is emphasized. The pastor is part of a team of professional people who are ministering to the patient. You should see yourself as a part of this healing team, even if there is no formal recognition of the fact. Since visiting the sick is often carried on in an institutional setting, you must respect the essential procedures within the institution. When you enter a hospital's doors, make sure that you respect the rules that are a vital part of its functioning. Here are a number of guidelines to keep in mind when you make a hospital visit:

Guidelines for a Hospital Visit

1. When you approach a room, if the door is closed, knock before you enter.
2. Obey such signs as "No Visitors" or "isolation." If you have any uncertainty, check at the nurse's station.
3. As you enter, look over the room (inconspicuously) and size up the situation. Watch for circumstances that may make your visit an inconvenience.
4. Let the patient take the initiative in shaking hands.
5. Be careful where you position yourself. Watch out for tubes and containers attached to the patient. Seat yourself in a place that will not require the patient to move around to keep eye contact.
6. Remember that the patient's condition is personal.
7. Do not visit when you are ill.
8. Resist the temptation to turn the visit into a conference on medical problems.
9. Identify yourself as you enter the room. Remember that the sick person may be disoriented or have a temporary memory loss.
10. Keep your visit brief.

■ **The following are violations of the above guidelines. In the blank write the number of the guideline that has been violated.**

_____ A. Dorothy wants to make sure she can report accurately on Michelle's condition tonight at prayer meeting. She asks detailed questions about the doctors, the tests, the medications, other treatments, the causes of the problem, and so forth. She leaves with a full report.

_____ B. Rhonda drove thirty miles to visit Amy. They are in the same WMU group. The door is closed and has a "No Visitors" sign on it. Rhonda knows that is just so Amy can rest. Surely Amy would not want her to go back home without first coming in for a visit. Rhonda goes in to visit.

_____ C. Luther is proud of his record of visiting every member who goes to the hospital. Kathryn had a baby early yesterday morning. She goes home tomorrow. Surely this little cold should not stand in the way of Luther's untarnished record.

_____ D. Jimmy is visiting Barry. He discovers that they have a common interest in baseball. After two hours of lively discussion, Jimmy has prayer and leaves.

_____ E. Paige has just returned to her room from gall bladder surgery. Every movement hurts. Gordon arrives for a visit. He moves to the bedside, gives a strong handshake, and says, "Hi, Friend."

_____ F. Mildred and Ruby visit the hospital together each Tuesday. They are in a hurry today to get to a luncheon for the Young at Heart Club. Mr. Sandlin has just been admitted for tests. They find his room, open the door, and walk in. They walk back out red-faced. The doctor was examining Mr. Sandlin.

_____ G. Wayne just had back surgery. Glenn does not want to appear to be in a hurry, so he sits down in a chair by the head of Wayne's bed.

_____ H. Herbert has been undergoing chemotherapy for a common form of cancer. Chester is a new deacon. He knows he may face this same disease with others in his deacon flock. He spends most of the visit learning all he can about the disease—the symptoms, the prognosis, the treatment options, and so forth.

_____ I. Karen stops by to visit Rita. She finds that some of Rita's relatives have come from out of town to visit. Karen sees this as an excellent opportunity to get acquainted with Rita's family, so she stays for a visit.

Well, as far as we can tell, no one introduced himself or herself (#9). That may not always be necessary. Just be sure not to leave the patient guessing who you are. Here are the violations: A-6; B-2; C-7; D-10; E-4; F-1; G-5; H-8; I-3.

■ Using the guidelines for a hospital visit, write what you would do in each of the following situations.
   1. Your pastor calls and asks you to visit one of his close friends. You have had a low grade fever but feel up to the visit. What would you do?

   _____

   2. The sign on the door says "Immediate Family Only."

   _____

   3. Doug asks you to have a seat. You realize that he will not be able to see you without straining his head. What would you do?

   _____

   4. You have just walked in to visit Edith when the nurse delivers supper.

   _____

Each hospital visit will be a little different from the others. You must be flexible. You should follow the basic guidelines, however. (1) Even if you want to please your pastor, do not visit if you are sick. Remember your immune system may be weak also. Protect yourself and others. (2) When the sign on the door tells you to keep out, write a note and leave it at the nurse's desk. The nurse can explain when you might be able to visit.

(3) Doug is trying to think of your comfort. Your job is to think more about his. If your sitting down is difficult for him, stand up. If you can sit down and talk comfortably with the patient, he will sense that you came for a relaxed, friendly visit. Sometimes standing communicates, "I only have a little time, so let's get this over with quickly." (4) Yes, this is an inconvenient time to visit. Edith will try to be polite and ask you to stay. Excuse yourself anyway. If you must visit on this trip, spend thirty minutes in the coffee shop and then come back.

Helping the Convalescent and the Chronically Ill

Hospital stays have been dramatically shortened across the years. The patient often finds himself facing an awkward situation when he returns home. He may be weakened, fearful, or apprehensive. His problems with returning home are frequently more psychological than physical.

Similar to the convalescent is the chronically ill individual. The sudden illness, drama of hospitalization, and surgery all attract attention. As illness drags on into weeks, months, or even years, people seem to forget. Though more prolonged, in many ways ministry to these individuals will be similar to that of the convalescent. We noted previously that convalescence is like growing up all over again.

You can be of great help during this period. Your objective must be to help the person move from dependency to accepting life's responsibilities. The chronically ill must be helped through the lonely isolated hours when no one seems to care. Even with a healthy philosophy of life, a person can feel threatened by the anticipation of future pain or a crippling disease.

Particular assistance may be rendered by helping to interest this person in hobbies or activities that will fill the lonely hours and foster her creative capacities. If she has an interest in reading, for instance, you may be able to help her by suggesting materials or by providing literature.

During long periods of enforced idleness, both the convalescent and the chronically ill often do much thinking. A listening ear and an understanding heart may give the lay counselor a supreme opportunity for meaningful ministry.

■ **Describe two practical things you can do to minister to the convalescent or chronically ill person.**

_____

_____

Day 4: The Stages of a Grief Experience

> **Today's Objective:** You will be able to identify stages of the grief process in given cases.

In ministering to the sick, you will find that your wider ministry includes the patient's family as well. The family often has special needs during this time that call for a caring ministry. A ministry to family is more prominent when bereavement over the death of a loved one is involved.

The funeral may seem to be the all-important part of this ministry. The pastor may believe that one follow-up visit is all he has time or needs to make. Studies have shown, however, that grief lasts for a long period after the loss of a loved one. Dr. Lindemann, a noted psychiatrist, has concluded that five or six interviews may be necessary to help a person through an experience of grief.

In his book *Good Grief,* Granger Westberg has identified ten stages a person may go through in a grief experience. The individual does not master one stage and then move on to the next. The person may periodically lapse back to one of the earlier stages. Not everyone passes through all of these stages, but they can be anticipated in many people. Knowing and understanding these stages will give you an excellent tool for helping those caught in the grieving process. Many people are helped and relieved to know that their experience of grief is not abnormal or unusual.

We will think about grief primarily from the standpoint of a person who has suffered the death of a loved one. Grief, however, can arise from any significant loss. These mini-grief experiences can be as varied as children leaving home, loss of a job, moving from one city to another, or a financial set-back. As a counselor, you should make an effort to understand the grieving process so you can help those with whom you work.

■ **As you read the following stages of grief, think about persons you have observed in grief. See if you can think of an example of each stage. If you do, write a brief description on the given line. If no example comes readily to mind, move to the next stage.**

Stage One: We Are in a State of Shock

The first stage is a period of shock in which the grief stricken person refuses to believe that the loss has been experienced. A characteristic statement would be, "That cannot be true." This mechanism gives the griever some space within which he/she can come to terms with reality.

■ **Example:** _____

Stage Two: We Express Emotion

Once the reality of the loss is realized, crying is a normal reaction. This is less true of men who have been taught that "men don't cry." However, emotional release is healthy and appropriate.

■ **Example:** _____

Stage Three: We Feel Depressed and Very Lonely

Depression is a universal feeling in grief. The griever has a sense of hopelessness and isolation. He may feel totally deserted by everyone, even God.

■ **Example:** _____

Stage Four: We May Experience Physical Symptoms of Distress

The stresses of the grief process may cause physical symptoms that do not respond well to medication. These may result from a person who has stalled in the grief process and is bottling up hurt, guilt, or frustration. Working through the grief process may help significantly in relieving the physical symptoms.

■ **Example:** _____

Stage Five: We May Become Panicky

Fear of the unknown can cause a person to panic. The person may be unable to concentrate in order to work. He may constantly think about the loss. He may even believe he is losing his mind. Helping him see this as a normal part of the process can alleviate his fears.

■ **Example:** _____

Stage Six: We Feel a Sense of Guilt About the Loss

No person ever did all he or she could to help the person who has died. Now the griever looks back and sees all the missed opportunities. This often leaves the person with a haunting sense of regret and failure.

Two types of guilt may be experienced. Normal guilt results from memory about actual failures or wrongs committed. Neurotic guilt is a feeling based on unrealistic expectations or events beyond the control or responsibility of the person. Suppose a woman's husband died of a heart attack in the night. She expresses guilt because she did not wake up and get him medical attention in time. This is neurotic guilt. She should not hold herself responsible for something she really had no control over.

■ **Example:** _____

Stage Seven: We Are Filled with Hostility and Resentment

The individual may sense that a terrible injustice has been perpetrated on him. Anger or resentment may be expressed toward a physician, a friend, a relative, the individual who died, or even God. A typical statement would be, "Why did this happen to me." One particularly difficult aspect of this stage is the accusation, "After all these years of serving God, He has turned on me and taken my loved one."

■ **Example:** _____

Stage Eight: We Are Unable to Return to Usual Activities

Our society has taught people that grief is appropriate immediately following the loss. Then one must get on with life. We have taught ourselves that we should not grieve openly after a brief time of mourning. This is not always possible. Experiences with friends, places, or events may bring back memories that reopen the wound. Consequently, the person finds great difficulty in returning to his or her normal routine.

■ **Example:** _____

Stage Nine: Gradually Hope Comes Through

Finally a moment comes when the individual accepts the situation and is able to say, "I lost my job," "I have retired," "My husband has gone to be with the Lord." The cloud of depression begins to break up. The person begins to feel relief that the grieving is coming to an end.

■ **Example:** _____

Stage Ten: We Struggle to Readjust to Reality[1]

Persons face grief in different ways. Those with mature Christian faith often grow stronger in their faith and ability to help others through similar trials. Those with immature faith may continue to struggle with grief issues for some time. One never comes out of the grief process the same as he was before. All grievers must struggle with the adjustment to the new reality of their lives.

■ **Example:** _____

Below are some common statements or questions you might hear from a grieving person. See if you can determine what stage of grief each statement or question represents. Write the number of the stage beside each. Assume that Jean has just lost her husband Ron by death.

_____ 1. "I just can't go back to Sunday School. I would feel so awkward being the only woman without a husband present."

_____ 2. "I think I'm going crazy. I just can't get my mind off of Ron lying in that casket."

_____ 3. "Why did God let this happen? I hate Him for doing this to me!"

_____ 4. "The doctor must be wrong. Ron can't be dead."

_____ 5. "I've had these bad headaches almost constantly for the past month. The doctor says he can't find anything wrong."

_____ 6. "If only I had made Ron keep his weight down, he would not have had the heart attack."

I did not give you examples from each step. I left out steps 2, 3, 9, and 10. Remember that you will always find overlap between stages. A person may experience guilt, hostility, depression, and emotion all at the same time. You will not always be able to clearly define a single stage of grief that a person is in. However, you should be able to help him see that his experiences are quite normal. You may not have the same answers as I do, but I have identified the statements and questions this way: 1—Stage Eight; 2—Stage Five; 3—Stage Seven; 4—Stage One; 5—Stage Four; 6—Stage Six.

Do you remember my mention of bibliotherapy (a counseling technique in which you loan or give books to the counselee to read)? *Good Grief* is a good example of the kind of book you could give or loan to a counselee. It is inexpensive and only fifty-seven pages. Giving a book like this to the counselee allows him to spend time with an authoritative counselor studying the subject of grief. After he has had time to read the book, you could schedule some time to get back together for a discussion of content that especially relates to the counselee.

Bibliotherapy is one way you can help a person who is going through a grief process. Tomorrow we will examine several other ways you can help.

Day 5: Helping a Grieving Person

> **Today's Objective:** You will be able to describe six ways to help a grieving person.

> "Pure religion and undefiled before God and the Father is this, To visit the fatherless and widows in their affliction, and to keep himself unspotted from the world" (Jas. 1:27, KJV).

Three Tasks

Three tasks that need to be accomplished as you work with a grief stricken person are:
1. Help the grieving person break loose from bondage to the deceased person.
2. Assist the grieving person to readjust to an environment in which the deceased person is missing.
3. Motivate the griever to form new relationships.

Six Ways to Help

Here are six ways that you can help a grieving person and accomplish the three tasks.

1. Agree that the experience will be painful and trying. Glib assurance is of little value. Many Christian workers have a tendency to be too reassuring as they try to help grief stricken people. They so emphasize Christian hope that the grieving person feels guilty for the pain and sorrow that he feels. Better help is provided when you help the person accept the fact of sorrow.

■ **Many do's and don'ts need to be considered in helping a grieving person. From the paragraph above, describe one do and one don't.**

DO: _____

DON'T: _____

2. **Allow the person to face the reality of the loss.** Do not try to divert the sorrowing person. A pastor was given the responsibility of sharing some bad news with a student in his church. Her father had been killed accidentally. He spoke later with the students who helped the young lady prepare for the journey home. He asked them what they had done to help her. They responded that every time the girl began to cry, they immediately introduced another subject so that she would not have time to think about her loss.

Grief is a painful process not only for the individual, but also for those who witness her suffering. We sometimes try to alleviate her pain, so that we will feel better ourselves. This reaction is fairly typical. One writer has called this "trying to camouflage death." The reality of death must be faced. Do not divert the person from facing the reality or pain of death.

■ **Describe another do and don't to follow in helping a grieving person.**

DO: _____

DON'T: _____

3. **Help the grieving person talk about the deceased.** Many would-be helpers feel that the deceased person should never be mentioned. This is a false perception. "Do not be afraid to mention the dead person to the griever. To avoid doing this will only isolate the griever in his own grief, possibly fostering denial or other unhealthy reactions."[2]

In the course of your talking with the bereaved person, you should incorporate the name of the deceased and personalize the conversation. In many cases the griever will be gratified to hear the name of their loved one spoken aloud.

Questions You Can Use

★ "Can you tell me a little about his death? What happened?"
★ "What has been happening since her death?"
★ "How have things been with you and your family and friends?"
★ "Have you been through any other bad times like this?"
★ "What is your favorite memory of him?"
★ "Can you tell me about her? What kind of person was she?"
★ "How did the two of you meet?"

■ **Describe another do and don't to follow in helping a grieving person.**

DO: _____

DON'T: _____

4. Support the person during the grief process. Grief work will be painful. This work involves not only grieving for the person who has passed, but also for the hopes, dreams, fantasies, and expectations the griever loses when a loved one dies. The counselor's function is to stand by, watch, and try to support them as they work through the pain. This is not an easy task. Do not leave the person to complete this work alone. Assure the person that you will stand by to support him or her during this trying time. Your presence and listening ear may be the most valuable way you can demonstrate this support. Comforting Scripture can also be supportive during this time. Consider using some of the following passages:

- Psalm 23
- John 14:1-4
- 1 Corinthians 15:55-57
- Philippians 1:21

OD'S WORD

ND WISDOM

■ 1. **Read these Scriptures and think about ways you could share them with a grieving person. Write in the margin any other Scriptures you think would be helpful.**

2. **Describe another do and don't to follow in helping a grieving person.**

DO: _____

DON'T: _____

5. Help the person deal with guilt. Guilt is an important factor in grief. Yesterday, we looked at two types of guilt—normal and neurotic guilt. Guilt often manifests itself in depression. It leaves the subject isolated and overwhelmed with a sense of hopelessness. Guilt that is not dealt with can become a major obstacle to completing the grieving process. The person can stall in the process and have great difficulty returning to healthy living.

Several stages are involved in handling normal guilt. The person must accept responsibility and confess the wrong. The Christian has the advantage of being able to seek God's forgiveness and cleansing. If some form of restitution can be made, this too will help. Do not try to help the person rationalize away responsibility for normal guilt just in order to feel better. You should help the grieving person through this process. You should help the person with neurotic guilt (guilt way out of proportion to one's responsibility) understand that he or she was not responsible in that particular way.

■ **Describe another do and don't to follow in helping a grieving person.**

DO: _____

DON'T: _____

6. Help the person establish new relationships. Sooner or later the person must break loose from the image of the lost one and begin to establish new relationships. Some withdrawal and isolation are normal and needed. However, do not allow the grieving person to abandon relationships with others.

One of the tragedies of grief is seen in the person whose spouse has died. Because of all the common associations the two had at church, he or she finds the church has too many memories. Consequently, the person withdraws from its fellowship. He or she must be helped to overcome these initial painful experiences. The church is actually a wonderful resource for anyone working through a grief experience. It provides a unique opportunity for establishing new and meaningful relationships.

■ **Describe another do and don't to follow in helping a grieving person.**

  DO: _____

  DON'T: _____

Here is a summary of DO's and DON'Ts for helping a grieving person.

DO's
- Agree that the experience will be painful and trying.
- Allow the person to face the reality of the loss.
- Help the grieving person talk about the deceased.
- Assure the person that you will stand by to support him or her during this trying time.
- Help the person deal with normal guilt.
- Help the person with neurotic guilt understand that he or she was not responsible in that particular way.
- Help the person establish new relationships.

DON'Ts
- Don't give glib assurance that everything will be okay.
- Don't divert the person from facing the reality or pain of death.
- Don't avoid talking about the dead person to the griever.
- Don't leave the person to complete the grief work alone.
- Don't try to help the person rationalize away responsibility for genuine guilt.
- Don't allow the grieving person to abandon relationships with others.

For Further Study
  Equipping Deacons in Caring Skills, Vol. 1 by Homer D. Carter.
  Nashville: Convention Press, 1980. (0-7673-2056-5)
  Equipping Deacons in Caring Skills, Vol 2 by Robert Sheffield.
  (0-7673-1943-5)
  Resources for Ministry in Death and Dying by Larry A.
  Platt and Roger G. Branch. Nashville: Broadman Press, 1988.
   (0-8054-6945-1)
  On Death and Dying by Elisabeth Kubler-Ross. New York:
  The Macmillan Company, 1969.
The following DeaconCare booklets are available in
  multiples of 10 by calling 1-800-458-2772:
  When You Have Someone in the Hospital (0-9999-6955-2)
  While You're in the Hospital (0-9999-6977-3)

UNIT 8

Marriage and Family Counseling

This Week's Learning Goal

After studying this unit, you will understand ways to help couples and families through your counseling.

Why You Will Find This Study Useful

Marriages and families are breaking apart at an alarming rate. Lay counselors may frequently find themselves on the front line of defense in helping troubled homes. You will learn some guidelines for effective counseling. Then you will gain a better understanding of ways families can function more effectively and positively.

Day 1: Guidelines for Marriage and Family Counseling

Today's Objective: In a given list of good and
poor guidelines for marriage and family counseling,
you will be able to identify the good guidelines.

Without seeing yourself as a professional marriage counselor, you will still encounter
situations that have to do with marriage and family life. Keep in mind throughout this
unit that you will use the Ten-Step Counseling Model in most, if not all, of your
counseling. The content in this unit will be of use primarily during steps 7, 8, and 9. As
you *review alternatives, explore outcomes,* and *supply information,* you will be able to
use the information you study this week in your counseling. Let's consider some
guidelines for you to follow in this type of counseling.

Involve the Interaction of Two or More Personalities

In individual personal counseling the aim is to help one person know himself and come
to terms with his life situation. Marriage and family counseling seeks to facilitate the
relationship of two or more people with each other.

Each individual may have relatively good emotional health, but the interpersonal
relationships between spouses or in the family may have deteriorated. Because many of
their problems arise from an inability to discuss their problems, these people have to
learn to communicate with each other. If you spend too much time on the mental health
of the individual, you may not succeed. You must focus on the relationships and help the
members learn to compromise so that a mutually beneficial relationship may be realized.
This can be accomplished best by counseling all the involved family members together.

■ **Check each of the following situations where this guideline is followed.**

☐ a.   **You counsel with Valerie about communication problems she has with her
husband.**
☐ b.   **You help Hugh and Irene discover ways for their family to cope with their
oldest son's drug problem.**
☐ c.   **You counsel with Kristen and Carl about ways to handle anger and
disagreements in their marriage.**
☐ d.   **You counsel with parents, Beverly and Rick, and child Tim about Tim's
antisocial behavior.**

Neither a nor b follows the guideline. Valerie's husband should be invited to the
counseling, as should Hugh and Irene's children. If the other involved persons refuse to
come, do the best you can with those who will. However, you will be most effective when
all involved persons are present. In both c and d you followed the guideline.

Conduct Joint Interviews with Caution

Joint interviews should not be prematurely undertaken by the lay counselor. A joint interview is difficult to handle. If it seems to be getting out of hand you might say to an aggressive husband, "Well thank you, Mr. Jones, I wonder if you would mind waiting in the next room for a few minutes while I talk with Mrs. Jones?" Later you could talk to Mr. Jones separately.

You do need to see them interact. Therefore, you do not want to avoid joint interviews just because they are difficult. You must develop a sensitivity to the family's interactions and determine when it is going well or becoming nonproductive.

Maintain Strict Neutrality

- Members of a family often will form alliances within the unit.
- Sometimes a husband and wife will be antagonistic toward each other.
- Sometimes one parent and a child will team up against the other parent.
- Sometimes the parents see the child as the cause of all the problems.

In any of these or similar situations people will try to win you over to their side. You must avoid being manipulated or maneuvered into such a position. If one or more of your counselees think of you as their ally against one or more other family members, the counseling may break down. Those you appear to be "against" may refuse to cooperate, or they may just refuse to participate altogether.

The marriage counselor must never allow himself to become judge, jury, or prosecuting attorney. Often you will need to be very specific and state that you are committed to remaining completely neutral. Taking care not to indicate an absence of concern, you may have to say you are concerned for all of them and want to act accordingly.

■ **You are counseling with the Harrisons, Andrew and Bonita. Andrew is an alcoholic. Bonita identifies his drinking as the chief problem of their marriage. What should you do? Check the item below that illustrates a counselor trying to maintain strict neutrality.**

  □ **a. Begin to talk with Andrew about the damaging effects of alcohol, and try to get him to agree to enter a treatment facility.**
  □ **b. Ask Andrew to explain why he drinks, what he feels about his marriage and job, and how he feels about his drinking.**

In the above situation, "a" may well be one of the things you will do in reviewing the alternatives, exploring outcomes, and supplying information. Without further investigation, however, you may give Andrew the impression that you have teamed up with Bonita against him.

Maintain strict neutrality and try something like option "b." You may discover that he resorted to drinking when he found he could not talk over problems with Bonita without being condemned. This certainly does not justify his drinking. However, even if you were to get him into a treatment program, he might return to the same home environment and start drinking all over again. In that case you would really have two problems to deal with. You need to help Andrew and Bonita learn to communicate in a more satisfying way, and you need to help Andrew deal with his alcoholism.

Clearly Define the Situations

An effective counselor helps define situations. Marriage and family counseling situations are often filled with confusion. In the midst of a series of accusations and counter accusations, a steady mind is needed to help the emotional family members gain a correct perspective as to what is going on. The counselor with an understanding attitude tries to:
• pinpoint difficulties,
• help explore alternatives, and
• give oversight to setting up goals.

■ **Study the previous activity (p. 129) and the feedback. By using the "b" option, what did you (the counselor) do to define the situation?**

_____

Bonita came to counseling with her mind made up that Andrew's drinking was THE PROBLEM. As a perceptive counselor, you pinpointed another difficulty. You helped Bonita discover that she too is responsible. She must then deal with her condemning ways of communicating, while Andrew deals with his alcoholism.

Help the Family Members Negotiate Differences

Negotiation is very important in labor relations, national concerns, and other aspects of life. It is also significant in family life.

In marriage counseling you would begin with both the husband and the wife. Ask each spouse to list responses to the question, "What do you want from your marriage?" Then ask them to list responses to the question, "What are you willing to contribute to your marriage?" You need to coach your counselees in answering the question in behavioral language. Experience has shown that many women will say they want "respect," or a man may say he is willing to give "consideration." These statements are too vague. They need to be stated in terms of actions that can be observed. She will need to say she wants him to call when he is delayed at work, or consult with her before making a major purchase. He will need to say he will not bring someone home for supper without consulting with her. Once the lists of "What I Want from This Marriage" and "What I Am Willing to Contribute to This Marriage" have been completed, take one item at a time and negotiate these behaviors.

For family counseling follow a similar pattern. Find out what each member of the family feels like he or she needs from the relationship (in behavior terms). Then discover the contributions they are willing to make to the family. Once you have uncovered this information, help the family negotiate behaviors that will lead to mutually satisfying relationships.

You may want to focus on only a few behaviors in any given interview. Then the couple or family can take a week to practice the new behaviors before they look at another concern.

Leave Decisions in the Hands of Your Counselees

Remember that you are not the judge and jury. You are not responsible for the success of the marriage or the family. The couple or the family is responsible for its decisions and behaviors. If you make decisions for your counselees, you assume a responsibility that is not yours to take. Therefore, leave decisions in the hands of your counselees. Help them consider alternatives and explore probable outcomes of each alternative. But, in the final analysis, they must decide what to do. They must assume responsibility for their own actions and decisions.

■ **In the following list of guidelines, mark the good guidelines we have dealt with today with a G. Mark the poor guidelines with a P.**

_____ 1. **Tell confused counselees what to do.**
_____ 2. **Involve the interaction of two or more personalities.**
_____ 3. **Leave decisions in the hands of your counselees.**
_____ 4. **Avoid arguments by counseling spouses separately.**
_____ 5. **Clearly define the situations.**
_____ 6. **Identify the problem person and then work on him.**
_____ 7. **Help the family members negotiate differences.**
_____ 8. **Conduct joint interviews with caution.**
_____ 9. **Maintain strict neutrality.**
_____10. **Help family members set one day each week to negotiate differences.**

Look back over this lesson and check your own work. Prepare to discuss in your group session the reasons you marked some of the above guidelines with a P (Poor).

Days 2 and 3: Describing the Ideal Family

> **Objective:** You will be able to describe some of the traits of an ideal Christian family.

The family was the first institution established by God (Gen. 2:20-24). He created marriage for companionship, sexual fulfillment, and procreation (having children). One role of the family is to "train a child in the way he should go, and when he is old he will not turn from it" (Prov. 22:6). Marriage and the family are important parts of God's plan for the world and the way people relate to each other. However, many modern families and marriages are sick. They reproduce children who continue the learned behaviors that lead to their own sick families and marriages. If you, as a Christian counselor, are to have a significant impact on this tragic state of affairs, you must be prepared to guide couples and families to function the way God intended.

We will not be able to cover in one day or even in one unit all that the Scriptures can teach us about marriage and families. I do, however, want you to begin studying passages that provide guidelines for family living. In units 10 and 11 you will examine biblical teachings about marriage, divorce, and remarriage. In this lesson, I want you to begin to study what the Bible has to say about relationships within the family. This should help you better understand the biblical ideal for family living. When you counsel couples and families you should be prepared to lift up the ideal, and help less-than-ideal families seek God's will for their relationships.

The last assignment in today's lesson will take some time and thought. For this reason, I have allowed two days for this lesson. Divide it in any way you like. I would suggest, however, that you at least get started on the description of the ideal family.

Husbands and Wives

■ Read the following Scriptures related to the relationship between husbands and wives. Under "Husband" and "Wife" write brief summaries of the roles of each in a marriage relationship. Use extra paper if you want to include more details.

    ☐ Ephesians 5:21-33
    ☐ Colossians 3:18-19
    ☐ 1 Peter 3:1-7

GOD'S W
AND WIS

Husband	Wife
_____	_____
_____	_____
_____	_____
_____	_____
_____	_____
_____	_____
_____	_____
_____	_____
_____	_____

Parents and Children

■ Read the following Scriptures related to the relationship between parents and children. Under "Parents" and "Children" write brief summaries of the roles of each in family relationships. Use extra paper if you want to include more details.

    ☐ Deuteronomy 6:6-9
    ☐ Proverbs 22:6
    ☐ Proverbs 23:22
    ☐ 2 Corinthians 12:14
    ☐ Ephesians 6:1-4
    ☐ 1 Timothy 5:8

GOD'S V
AND W

Parents	Children
_____	_____
_____	_____
_____	_____
_____	_____
_____	_____

An Ideal Family

The Scriptures are filled with teachings that apply directly and indirectly to family life. Family members who are faithfully living under the lordship of Christ are the key ingredients to a successful Christian family. I want you to begin forming a description of the ideal Christian family.

■ **On a separate sheet of paper begin writing a description of the ideal Christian family. Use the Scriptures about family relationships you have already studied, your previous convictions about the family, other Scriptures you are familiar with, and any other resources you may have available. Give some time and thought to this project. Identify related Scriptures in your description for later reference. You may want to consider answers to some or all of the following questions:**
  - **What are the key ingredients in a Christian family?**
  - **What character traits will members of the family exhibit?**
  - **How should husband and wife relate to each other?**
  - **How should children relate to each other?**
  - **How should parents and children relate to each other?**
  - **How should the family make decisions?**
  - **What is communication like in the ideal family?**
  - **How does the ideal family relate to the church?**
  - **How does the ideal family relate to others outside the family unit?**

Please do not take this writing assignment lightly. This is certainly no easy task. You do need to think through exactly what an ideal family should look like. Then you will be better able to lift up the ideal as you counsel families that have fallen short of God's plan. Bring your description to your group session this week. Add to your description as you continue your study this week.

Day 4: Five Needs of a Family

> **Today's Objective:** You will be able to recognize needs that family members have and identify ways the family can help meet some of these needs.

In today's study we will focus on family needs, their nature, and the way in which the family should fulfill these needs. We will focus on five need areas Abraham Maslow identified for the individual. As a counselor, you may need to educate the family members about the kinds of needs they should be sensitive to. You will sometimes need to help them understand ways they can help meet needs or avoid frustrating the meeting of the needs of individual members.

Physiological Needs

These needs are the basics of survival. Examples include food and drink, shelter, and for the parents, sex needs. The task of the family would be to provide shelter in the form of adequate accommodation. Though often plentiful in an affluent society like ours, food becomes a need when people have inadequate nutrition in their diets. The type of food fed to the children will help lay the foundations for their eating patterns in later life.

Sexual needs call for open channels of communication between husband and wife. As the children grow, they need an adequate sex education. Probably the best way to do this initially will be for the father and mother to make loving gestures to each other. When one counselee was asked to describe his father and mother's love life, he responded, "Love life—that's a joke. I never remember seeing my father kiss my mother." Appropriate loving gestures between father and mother are an essential factor in adequate sex education.

■ 1. **List some of the physiological needs a family member might have.**

_____

_____

_____

2. **What way(s) can the family help meet some of these needs?**

_____

_____

_____

Safety Needs

We have a need to live in an orderly world. Within the family, this translates into a harmonious atmosphere. The family is no place for physical violence or verbal abuse. Parents need to be vividly aware that such activity is threatening to the children.

Differences of some sort will always exist between parents. When these are mild, they will teach children that life is never lived without problems. Intense arguments, however, have no place in family life. Strong differences should be dealt with away from the living room and out of the hearing range of other family members.

Another aspect of this need is seen in the foolish threats sometimes made within a family. For a mother to threaten a disobedient child, "I'll be gone when you come home from school," is plain foolish. Ease of divorce has given rise to the threat "Why don't you divorce me?" Once again the child is threatened. We must provide homes that give children a sense of security.

■ 1. **List some of the safety needs a family member might have.**

_____

_____

_____

2. **What way(s) can the family help meet some of these needs?**

_____

_____

_____

Love Needs

Every individual has a need for a sense of being loved. The family is the first and most significant provider of love for the child. Parents must demonstrate love to each other and to the children. Gestures alone and words alone are not enough. We need to regularly verbalize love by saying, "I love you." We also need to demonstrate love through our actions.

This love is also demonstrated by physical contact between family members. The bumper sticker "Have you hugged your child today?" carries a message we need to hear.

■ 1. **List some of the love needs a family member might have.**

_____

_____

_____

2. **What way(s) can the family help meet some of these needs?**

_____

_____

_____

Esteem Needs

Everybody needs to feel important. Husbands and wives should avoid downgrading and criticizing each other. They also should avoid making belittling comparisons to other husbands and wives. They should regularly commend each other, particularly in the presence of others.

Downgrading, criticizing, and belittling comparisons should also be avoided with regard to the children. In group psychotherapy we use a technique called "praise bombardment." The shy, reserved person is placed in the center of the group and all the members make praise statements about him. Without formally setting it up, the family should engage in praise bombardment. They can help build the family member's self-esteem. Husbands and wives, mothers, fathers, and children should be careful not to take each other for granted.

■ 1. **List some of the esteem needs a family member might have.**

_____

_____

_____

_____

   2. **What way(s) can the family help meet some of these needs?**

_____

_____

_____

_____

Self-Actualization Needs

At the highest level of needs, stands those of finding fulfillment of our potentialities. Children should be given ever increasing responsibilities. One educator put it well when he said that the main task of parents is to prepare their children to get along without them.

Both husband and wife need to have opportunities to develop their potentialities. Wives particularly are often frustrated as their children grow to independence and all their parenting skills suddenly become useless. Family members need to help each other find opportunities for challenge and self-fulfillment.

■ 1. **List some of the self-actualization needs a family member might have.**

_____

_____

_____

_____

   2. **What way(s) can the family help meet some of these needs?**

_____

_____

_____

_____

You should have been able to extract answers to today's activities from the content materials. If you had any difficulty, you may want to compare your answers with others in your group. This has not been a complete list of needs by any means. It will, however, give you some idea of the kinds of needs a family ought to be sensitive to.

The family unit provides an ideal place for the needs of the family members to be met. Providing for each other's needs should be conscious and intentional. This is hard work, but it is vital work for maintaining a healthy family.

Day 5: Seven Marks of a Viable Family

> **Today's Objective:** You will be able to list and describe seven marks of a viable family.

Our plane had taken off for Florida and the flight attendant was demonstrating the way to put on the life preserver in case of an emergency while over water. Unfortunately, the young lady was new and did not know how to do it. Trying desperately to follow the instructions coming over the public address system, she managed to put her head through the wrong place and wound the straps around herself. Strapped, struggling, and frustrated, the unfortunate girl burst into tears and had to be rescued by a fellow stewardess who quickly and efficiently went through the procedure. Pity the poor airplane passengers should the plane come down in the ocean!

Many members of families today seem to be in a similar predicament. The condition of modern family life is often deplorable. Many people would not know a good family if they saw one. They have never seen a demonstration of a viable family. Like the passengers on the airplane, all they have seen are families in a tangled mess.

Let's not overstate the case. Many successful families exist, though they may not receive the attention of the community at large. By observing good families in action, I have identified seven indicators of a viable (practical, workable, successful) family. Together with your description of the ideal family and these seven indicators, you will be able to use your influence in evaluating families and pointing them in the right direction. You will be able to help families work toward mutually satisfying relationships.

> **Viable Families**
>
> 1. Have a Foundation of Faith.
> 2. Have a Variety of Leadership Patterns.
> 3. Have a Story to Tell and a Storyteller.
> 4. Express Their Affection.
> 5. Practice Hospitality.
> 6. Prize Their Rituals.
> 7. Accept and Cope With Eccentrics.

1. Viable Families Have a Foundation of Faith.

In a survey conducted by a leading magazine, the respondents were asked how significant was their belief in God. To the astonishment of the magazine 60% of the respondents considered such a belief to be "very important." Letters sent in with the questionnaires expressed convictions like these: "Believing in God and worshiping Him is a vital part of our family life." "Our religion holds our marriage together. Without it we would be just another number in the divorce records." "When spiritual and religious foundations are strong, many other threats to family life can be surmounted."[2]

Jesus told a parable of two men who built houses. One built his house on the sand, while the other built his house on the rock. When the storms came, the house on the sand collapsed. The house on the rock stood firm. Families need foundations. A foundation of faith in Jesus Christ will be the basic factor in viable family living.

■ **List and briefly explain the first mark of a viable family. Viable families:**

1. _____

_____

_____

_____

2. Viable Families Have a Variety of Leadership Patterns.

Families have leaders, and leadership functions within the family frequently change. When asked who is leader of any given family, the answer might be in the form of another question, "When and under what circumstances?"

The Bible portrays the father as the leader of the family. No one can deny the value of the presence of a strong masculine figure in a family. However, an abusive dictator is of questionable value.

Women have often moved into positions of leadership within the family out of necessity. With our high divorce rate, the number of single parent families is increasing. Feminine leadership in some homes is inevitable. Single parent families are not the ideal, but some of them turn out remarkably well.

You probably have seen a family where the children may have become the leaders. As the years pass the children may become increasingly important in their leadership role. This role is expressed in the conference title, "Parenting Our Parents." Leadership roles are never rigid within a dynamic family unit. They are dependent on time and circumstances.

■ **List and briefly explain the second mark of a viable family. Viable families:**

1. **Have a Foundation of Faith.**

2. _____

_____   _____

_____

_____

3. Viable Families Have a Story to Tell and a Storyteller.

Any family gathering is likely to include the sharing of recent or past experiences. Then comes a moment when the family storyteller is called to perform. Mother or Father is often placed center stage as they recall, "When you were children. . . ." The story is often historical. The great popularity of the book and TV special *Roots* may be an indication of the way we enjoy a look into the past, particularly our own past.

My cousin was our storyteller. She lived in Australia. When a friend in another part of the country wrote a letter inquiring about some long lost relatives, Helen looked up the information and sent it back. Through this experience she developed an obsessive interest in her own roots. She began a search of old newspapers, books, death certificates, marriages, and old cemeteries. In a letter to me she explained, "I want to share with you the trials and tribulations and the happy times of ancestors we never knew, and can only know now in our imaginations."

Blessed indeed is the family that has a historical library—photo album or shoe box—with the wedding licenses, birth certificates, snapshots, and diplomas that tell the story of the family enterprise. Every family needs a historian—one of those souls who likes to collect, hoard, research the family tree, and write down the story for the generations that follow.

■ **List and briefly explain the third mark of a viable family. Viable families:**

1. **Have a Foundation of Faith.**

2. **Have a Variety of Leadership Patterns.**

3. _____

_____

_____

_____

4. Viable Families Express Their Affection.

Many authorities are lamenting the ways some institutions are impacting the family. Some sociologists are saying the family is obsolete, because society has provided all the services formerly the responsibility of the family. This assessment carries some truth. However, families can and ought to perform functions available no where else. Certainly others exist, but one of the needed contributions of the family is the affection members express toward one another. We discussed this need for love in day 4. Family members need to express their affections for one another.

■ **List and briefly explain the fourth mark of a viable family. Viable families:**

4. _____

_____

_____

_____

5. Viable Families Practice Hospitality.

I have noticed a strange thing about families. The larger they are, the greater their capacity for expansion. My wife and I come from two different types of families. I am an only child; she is one of seven. At my home, inviting someone for a meal was an ordeal. My mother almost threw a fit in her anxiety to do everything perfectly.

How different the situation was with the mother of seven. Church on Sunday was a gathering time. Every visitor who wandered into the church service received an invitation to go home and eat with the Bailie's. Through their home, an unending succession of visitors were welcomed, fed, entertained, and inspired before going on their way.

The Bible speaks about hospitality. Twice it states that the leader of a church must be hospitable (1 Tim. 3:2; Titus 1:8). Paul told the Roman Christians to "Share with God's people who are in need. Practice hospitality" (Rom. 12:13).

In practicing hospitality we are twice blessed. We help people, and our family is strengthened in the process.

■ **List and briefly explain the fifth mark of a viable family. Viable families:**

    4. **Express Their Affection.**

    5. _____

       _____

       _____

       _____

       _____

6. Viable Families Prize Their Rituals.

An 88-year-old man lay dying. A friend reached over and moistened his lips with a damp cloth. The aged man's lips moved, "We thank thee, O Lord, for these and all thy mercies." He had customarily offered this prayer before each meal. Rituals such as these live on across the years.

A family ritual is an oft repeated little ceremony. Of it we can later say, "We always did it this way in our family." Of course, our finest rituals have to do with our faith: asking the blessing before the meal, reading the Bible, and praying together.

■ **List and briefly explain the sixth mark of a viable family. Viable families:**

    4. **Express Their Affection.**

    5. **Practice Hospitality.**

    6. _____

       _____

       _____

       _____

7. Viable Families Accept and Cope with Eccentrics.

Engineers sometimes use a piece of machinery known as an eccentric wheel. Quite different from the other gears and cogs, the eccentric wheel makes it possible for a machine to perform some unusual functions. Families have eccentrics, too. These family eccentrics are members that are different, perhaps a little off center, or odd. The viable family not only copes with them, but they discover a variety and zest eccentrics can bring to the family experience. In caring for them and interpreting them to outsiders, solidarity and a sense of parental love is communicated to the less fortunate member of the family unit.

■ **List and briefly explain the seventh mark of a viable family. Viable families:**

   4. **Express Their Affection.**

   5. **Practice Hospitality.**

   6. **Prize Their Rituals.**

   7. _____

   _____

   _____

   _____

   _____

Using a separate sheet of paper, see if you can list all seven marks of a viable family. For any you do not recall, go back and review the content on that particular mark.

Check your work with the list on page 137.

The Christian church with its emphasis on the sacredness of the marriage bond and the value of the family unit has found itself faced with new obligations. To stem the tide of divorce and family disintegration, we must enlist a great force of lay counselors who approach counseling with Christian values and commitments. Keep on developing your skills and knowledge of marriage and family counseling. You are one of our best possibilities for preserving godly families. Studying any or all of the books below will help you more effectively provide marriage and family counseling based on Christian values and biblical principles.

For Further Study
Marriage Mentors by Bob and Yvonne Turnbull. Nashville: LifeWay Press. (0-8054-9852-4)
Counsel for the Nearly and Newly Married Couple's Guide by Ernest White and James E. White. Nashville: Convention Press, 1992. (0-8054-9610-6)
Counsel for the Nearly and Newly Married Leader's Guide by Ernest White and James E. White. Nashville: Convention Press, 1992. (0-7673-2051-4)
Building Relationships: A Discipleship Guide for Married Couples by Gary D. Chapman. Nashville: LifeWay Press, 1995. (0-8054-9855-9)
The Five Love Languages by Gary Chapman. Chicago: Northfield Publishing, 1992, 1995. (1-881273-15-6)

UNIT 9

Providing Guidance for Behavior Change

This Week's Learning Goal

After studying this unit, you will understand six techniques to use in guiding behavior change.

Why You Will Find This Study Useful

Some behavior requires external help in removing an unsatisfactory behavior and replacing it with a desired behavior. This is especially true for parents who are seeking to guide their children in desirable behavior. The six techniques you learn this week will help you guide behavior change effectively. These techniques will help your own relationships and will be helpful to parents as you teach them to use the techniques as well.

Day 1: Behavior Change and Pinpointing

> **Today's Objective:** You will be able to describe a principle for bringing about changes in thoughts and feelings, and you will be able to apply the pinpointing technique in specific cases.

As you counsel, you will encounter occasions when you will want to help a counselee bring about a change in behavior. Growth experiences and values can help motivate changes in behavior. The Ten-Step Model emphasizes this approach to behavior change. You assist the counselee in reviewing the alternatives. Then he applies values as he explores the outcomes and makes a decision about what action to take.

Sometimes, an individual's internal motivation is not sufficient to bring about a change in behavior. For instance a person who smokes, drinks alcohol, or takes drugs may need some external motivation to help change his or her behavior. In such cases, external motivation may help the counselee establish the desired behavior. Then, the success of the new behavior will help him develop a value for the behavior that can replace the need for the external motivation.

One Principle for Behavior Change

In many forms of counseling the focus of attention is on thinking and feelings. Our emphasis focuses more on "behavior" than thinking or feelings. Thinking and feelings affect behavior, but a change in behavior can change thinking and feelings. This approach to counseling says that if we want to bring about cognitive (thinking) and affective (feeling) changes, we should start with a change of behavior.

■ **A basic principle is involved in this approach to counseling. Study the following three statements. See if you can identify the principle these statements describe.**

A. **"Actions seem to follow feeling, but really actions and feeling go together, and by regulating the action which is more under the more direct power of the will, we can indirectly regulate the feeling which is not."[1]—William James**

B. **"It is much easier to act yourself into a new way of feeling than to feel yourself into a new way of acting."—E. Stanley Jones**

C. **"Commit thy works unto the Lord, and thy thoughts shall be established."— Proverbs 16:3, KJV**

In your own words, write a summary statement of this principle.

_____

_____

_____

_____

_____

_____

The principle might work something like this: You decide to get up before the crack of dawn to go fishing. When the alarm goes off your body says, "I don't *feel* like getting up." By an *act* of your will you roll out and jump into the shower. Soon you are awake enough to start dreaming about reeling in a big fish, several big fish. Now only an emergency could keep you from going fishing. Your mind and body agree: "We feel like going fishing." Notice that the action to get up preceded the feeling that getting up was a good idea. The principle is this: To establish new patterns of thinking and feeling, bring about a change in behavior first.

Techniques for Guiding Behavior Change

We are going to focus on the skill of guiding behavior change. In the process, we will consider six techniques. Some of these techniques will be useful in your counseling with adults. Some of them are most useful to parents who are guiding the behavior of their children. You can use all of these techniques to teach parents better ways of developing acceptable behaviors in their children.

Techniques for Behavior Change

1. Pinpointing
2. Praising
3. Behavior Shaping
4. Pairing
5. Timing
6. Time Out

Pinpointing

Pinpointing is one of the techniques that is helpful in guiding behavior change with adults and children.

Pinpointing: is describing the desired behavior in clear detail.

Winston Churchill had a unique gift for communicating his ideas to people. Part of his skill lay in his capacity to pinpoint. His secretary tells of an occasion when, in the course of a trip, he decided the party would enjoy a picnic lunch. He called the headwaiter to the table and proceeded to give instructions, "I want some substantial sandwiches, get hold of a large loaf, and don't cut the slices too thin-or too thick, either. Trim the crust off the edges, and put plenty of butter on the bread. Please see to it there's enough beef for us to know it's a beef sandwich. And make certain that the beef comes to the edge of the bread. I don't like to bite into a sandwich before I can tell what's inside of it." Mr. Churchill continued to emphasize his point by asking for a piece of paper and a pencil. He produced a sketch of a sandwich just the way he wanted it made. In behavior language, Mr. Churchill was "pinpointing."

■ In each of the following pairs, identify the one that is a "pinpointing" statement? Place an X in the box beside your choice.

☐ A. Be in at a decent hour.
☐ B. I want you to be home by 11 PM.

☐ C. He's immature.
☐ D. As soon as something annoys him, he yells.

☐ E. When her husband is talking, she interrupts.
☐ F. She has no depth.

☐ G. On three occasions when I have introduced him to a group of people, he has just lapsed into silence and made no effort to enter into the conversation.

☐ H. He doesn't give himself.

You will always be tempted to lapse into generalization with statements like: Be in at a decent hour; He's so immature; She has no depth; and He doesn't give himself. What do these statements mean? They don't mean very much. They are too general, too indefinite. If you hope to guide changes in behavior, you must first describe what you want to change and spell it out clearly and precisely. Statements B, D, E, and G do a better job of pinpointing or describing a behavior.

■ 1. Suppose you are counseling a couple. Sue says, "Mike doesn't love me any more." This is a general statement that is too vague to be helpful. What could you say to get Sue to pinpoint the behavior Mike does not display?

_____

_____

_____

_____

_____

_____

_____

Which of the following statements would more clearly pinpoint Mike's behavior? Check all the pinpointing statements.

☐ a. Mike doesn't touch me or hug me anymore.
☐ b. Mike doesn't bring me flowers like he did when we were dating.
☐ c. Mike is always thinking about meeting his own needs. He doesn't pay any attention to my unmet needs.
☐ d. Mike spends all his spare time with our children. He and I never have time to be alone except late at night. By that time we are too tired to take time for leisurely conversation.

2. Assume that a mother wants her son, Johnny, to develop better table manners. Change this general description of behavior to a "pinpointing" description. General statement: "Johnny, mind your manners while you are at the table."

Pinpointing statement: _____

_____

If you are learning to pinpoint, you will have written statements like: "Don't talk with food in your mouth." "Say please when you ask for food to be passed to you." "Eat your peas with your fork, not your knife." These clear statements help Johnny know exactly what you want him to do. Minding his manners will be difficult unless he has been taught exactly what manners are.

In counseling people like Sue and Mike, you will need to stop a counselee who makes general statements that are too vague. This is a part of step 3 in the Ten-Step Model— Clarify the Situation. You could say, "Sue, that is pretty vague. Could you tell me exactly what Mike does not do that makes you believe he no longer loves you?" or simply, "Sue, be more specific." All four of the statements—a, b, c, and d—are more specific. In counseling however, you would probably even want to follow up on "c" and ask about the specific needs she is talking about.

Day 2: Praising

> **Today's Objective:** You will be able to apply
> four methods to improve one's praise capacity.

If our behavior has good consequences, we tend to repeat it. If it has bad consequences, we do not repeat it. This is true, provided we have good common sense. In guiding behavior change you reward good behavior and punish undesirable behavior.

A Powerful Reward

What do people want *most* in life? Beautiful home? High salary? Fancy automobile? Trip around the world? I am sure the answer to that question would vary between people. However, one of the greatest rewards for desirable behavior is ATTENTION. Many business managers are discovering the power that attention carries. They are using attention as a motivational influence on their subordinate workers. This technique was popularized in the little book, *The One Minute Manager*.

Attention's power as a reward can also be seen in many classrooms and homes. When a child misbehaves, he receives attention from the teacher or parent. Even though a reprimand is intended to reduce the bad behavior, it sometimes has the opposite affect. The bad behavior increases and the reprimands increase accordingly. Because attention is such a powerful reward, some children will endure reprimands and embarrassment in order to get attention from a significant adult. The child may learn that bad behavior is more likely to get attention than good behavior is. I want you to focus with me on one of the greatest rewards one individual can give to another—attention.

Attention can be broken down into five levels: Looking, Listening, Concerned Questioning, Touching, and Praising. The first four levels have been discussed in previous units. Today, we will concentrate on praising. I want to help you upgrade your praise capacity. This program of reinforcement will involve looking for something to praise rather than criticize, making praise descriptive, preparing for the task, and undertaking a training program.

Once you improve your own praise capacity, you will recognize the value of praise in giving attention. Then you can teach this technique to counselees for their own benefit. Adults, in general, and parents, in particular, can benefit from the use of praise.

Praising

1. Look for something to praise rather than criticize. Our little poodle had grown old but not gracefully. He was arthritic, dragged one leg painfully, had one eye damaged in a fight, and had ragged hair. He looked like a worn, untidy mop. Ginger Hazelton, eleven years old, was visiting our home. On her best behavior, she was commending everything in our house. When she faced the poodle, her capacity to commend met its supreme test as I asked, "How do you like my poodle?"

The little girl looked at that matted mop of a dog, and she responded, "He certainly knows how to wag his tail."

If you look long and carefully enough you will find something to commend in everyone. In this way, you will help your counselee do something about developing his potential.

■ **During this week, I want you to practice praising. Without talking to anyone about what you are doing, I want you to improve your praise capacity through practice. Select one member of your immediate family, a work associate, or someone else that you relate to many times during the week. Target your increased praise toward that one person. Write the name of the person on this line:**

_____

You have studied one way to increase your praise capacity: Look for something to praise rather than criticize. Make a list of some things you can praise in the life or work of the person you just named.

_____

_____

_____

_____

_____

_____

_____

_____

2. Make Your Praise Descriptive. Dr. Harrison Jones is a successful neurosurgeon. He is enormously popular with the staffs of the hospital where he works. This comes not only because of his surgical skills, but also because of his unusual capacity to commend with descriptive praise. When examining the X-rays, he addresses the technician, "These are wonderful pictures. You know how to get the exact position that I need." Looking at the patient swathed in bandages he tells the nurse, "If an ancient Egyptian pharaoh had ever heard about you, he certainly would have employed you as a bandager of the royal mummies." Sitting for hours looking at his neighbor's slides, he remarks, "That picture from the Star Ferry in Hong Kong shows the way a good shot can be framed and made to be very attractive." Learn from Dr. Jones. Make your praise descriptive. (This is one place where the pinpointing technique is valuable.)

■ **In the following pairs, mark the descriptive phrases with a D. Leave the nondescriptive phrases blank.**

_____ A. "Phil, I appreciate the good work you do."

_____ B. "Phil, your report was thorough and well-researched. Your good work will really help me in my meeting with the Board."

_____ C. "Jenny, you were a good girl in church today."

_____ D. "Jenny, I like the way you sat quietly and listened to the preacher at church today."

_____ E. "Mark, that flower arrangement you sent to me at work was a total surprise. I was so proud. I really felt loved."

_____ F. "Mark, Thank you for being such a loving husband."

Descriptive statements are not too hard to pick out when contrasted with nondescriptive ones, are they? You probably noticed that B, D, and E are longer, more specific, and more descriptive than are A, C, and F.

■ **Write one descriptive statement you can use to praise the person you selected earlier. Then look for an opportunity to use this statement this week.**

_____

_____

_____

3. Keep Some Praise Statements in Mind. Unless you have a very good vocabulary, you may have difficulty coming up with the right word of praise at the right time. Learn some basic forms of praise and use them at appropriate times. The following statements, for instance, would be appropriate to use with children in rewarding and strengthening their behavior.

You really pay attention	Thank you	That's right
I'm pleased with that	Great	Excellent
That's clever	Good thinking	Good
That's interesting	I like that	Good job
That was very kind of you	You are special	Exactly
Show Grandma your picture		

■ **Prepare a list of your own praise statements. If some in the list above are appropriate, circle them. Write other statements below, and in the margin if necessary.**

_____

_____

_____

_____

Having prepared your statements look for an opportunity and watch the magical effect of praise in establishing a new behavior.

4. Practice to Upgrade Your Praise Quotient. You might get an idea from Kenneth Weeks who realized he always seemed to be criticizing his employees. He decided to use his date book as a means of recording and evaluating his "praise quotient." In one corner of each day's segment, he puts "PR" which reminds him to use praise as a way of improving his public relations. By the end of the first week, his book looked like this:

At the end of the week Kenneth knows what has happened. He did well on Monday, slipped a little on Tuesday, but by Friday he was doing a good job. Looking back at his week, he recalled Friday was a good day. Ten praise statements a day looked like a good target for him.

In learning to praise, you are acquiring a means of helping to change people. Best of all, you develop an entirely new attitude toward life itself. You discover the optimism that comes to people who look for the best in others. You become a positive model to those around you as well.

■ **Using an index card, your date book, or a piece of paper, keep a "praise diary" for the remainder of this week. At the end of the week you will evaluate your PQ— Praise Quotient in your group session.**

Day 3: Behavior Shaping and Pairing

> **Today's Objective:** You will be able to apply the techniques of behavior shaping and pairing to change behavior of children in a given situation.

Today, you will learn two more principles for guiding behavior change. Though these may be used in other circumstances, they primarily are for use with children. Therefore, you will want to be able to teach these two principles to parents for use in guiding their children.

Behavior Shaping Principle: Reduce complex behavior to small, logical, elementary steps that will be reinforced.

Mrs. Swain began to despair of Margaret, her eleven-year-old, who had never learned to be tidy. Margaret's room generally looked as if it had just been hit by a tornado. Mrs. Swain decided to use the shaping technique to change Margaret's behavior.

First, she described the desired behavior: "Margaret will keep her room neat and clean."

Next, she broke the desired behavior into a series of small tasks for Margaret to perform each day. She sat down and wrote a plan to increase the small tasks until Margaret reached the objective—keep her room neat and clean. Here is Mrs. Swain's plan for Margaret:

DAY   1: Pick up dolls, books, and stuffed animals.
DAY   4: In addition to the above, hang up clothes.
DAY   7: In addition to the above tasks, make bed.
DAY 10: In addition, vacuum floor and dust.
DAY 13: In addition to completing all the preceding tasks, straighten shelves and desk.
DAY 16: Report when room is ready without prompting.

Notice the way in which Mrs. Swain described the behavior she expected from her daughter. She described the behavior clearly. More importantly, she broke down the behavior into a series of small, achievable steps. This made each step of the end behavior easily within Margaret's capabilities.

■ **Assume that you plan to use behavior shaping in the following situation: Billy is now old enough to take care of the yard work for the family, but he has never done any of the work so far.**

  1. **Define the ultimate behavior desired.**

  _____

  2. **Break the behavior down into a series of small, achievable steps.**

  _____

  _____

  _____

  _____

  _____

  3. **In the margin beside #2 above, decide on a weekly schedule for implementing each step.**

You will check your work this week in your group session.

The Pairing Principle: Behavior is reinforced more effectively as a second reinforcer is added.

Two men known as the "Potty Psychologists" attracted enough attention to cause hundreds of mothers to write letters seeking their help. Toilet training is undoubtedly a difficult task for all parents. The two psychologists came to their client's home equipped with two potty chairs, potato chips, candy, soda, and a large doll. Their mission—to toilet train a three-year-old boy.

After giving the small boy as much soda as he could drink, he was placed on a specially designed potty. When the child urinated the reinforcements began.
• He was rewarded with potato chips.
• The specially designed potty played, "Mary Had a Little Lamb."
• The two psychologists hugged the boy.
• They told him they were going to contact his grandfather and tell about his clever grandson.

Theoretically they could have just given potato chips, praised the child, promised to tell grandfather, or just let the potty play "Mary Had a Little Lamb." They multiplied the effect of the reinforcement by "pairing" the rewards.

■ **Briefly explain the pairing principle in your own words.**

_____

_____

_____

_____

_____

_____

_____

Social Reinforcers

A special class of reinforcers exists that has social impact on a person. They are known as social reinforcers. The commendation of the child by the "potty psychologists" and their mention of granddaddy gives us an example of the use of social reinforcers. These may be divided into three categories: gestures, proximity, and physical contact.

1. Gestures. Mr. Dalton does not get to PTA very often, but his wife tries to encourage him in every way she can. She is president this year. Mr. Dalton makes a special effort to be at the first meeting, but arrives ten minutes late. As he takes his seat, he looks over to his wife who holds up her circled finger and thumb in a gesture that obviously said, "Thanks, honey, I knew you'd make it." Reinforcing gestures include such actions as:
• Smiling
• Laughing
• Looking intensely interested
• Winking
• Clapping

2. Proximity. The Love Axiom may be stated as, "The emotional closeness of two human beings is manifested by the physical proximity of their bodies." Proximity reinforcers include such actions as:

- Walking together
- Eating together
- Playing games
- Sitting on the child's bed
- Talking and listening to each other

3. Physical Contacts. A psychologist once said, "Large numbers of people are virtually untouched and out of touch. Others are touched, but only with the intent of sexual arousal. This contact can be unaffectionate and even hostile. What people need—both children and adults—are warm handshakes, pats, and hugs that indicate that the other person is giving attention and esteem." I couldn't agree more. Physical contacts include such actions as:

- Touching
- Hugging
- Stroking arm
- Holding hands
- Patting head, shoulder, or hand
- Holding on lap
- Stroking hand

■ **Review your schedule for shaping Billy's behavior to perform the yard work on page 150. What are some social reinforcers you could pair together to reinforce Billy's good behavior?**

_____

_____

_____

_____

_____

_____

Preeminent among the social reinforcers are commendation and praise (day 1). However, the skill of the reinforcer will be tested as he tries to decide which reinforcer will bring him the best results. In Billy's case you could reinforce his work in some ways like the following:

- Give him an "okay" gesture while he is mowing.
- Smile.
- Brag (in Billy's presence) to the neighbors, relatives, or other family members about his progress.
- Walk with Billy around the yard commenting on the good work you see.
- Pat him on the back and say, "Good job."
- Make a photograph of his first complete job (including the mowing, trimming, raking, and so forth) and display it on the refrigerator.
- Get a small trophy engraved "Lawn Keeper of the Year" and award it at the next family get together. Better yet, plan a cookout and make the event extra special.

Some of you may think this much fanfare is a little fanatic for such a simple task as yard work. Maybe so. However, think of Billy. If he develops a real satisfaction in doing a good job on the yard, you will get a neat yard. You will save your own time, since you will not have to do it yourself. You may even avoid the experience of many parents who must beg, plead, threaten, and discipline a child before he will do the yard work. Try shaping and pairing sometime soon on a simple task of behavior change and see if it works for you.

Day 4: Timing

> **Today's Objective:** You will be able to describe three principles related to timing of reinforcement.

Timing is at the heart of guiding behavior change. Timing of reinforcement is important for any age person. However, we will give our attention to planned behavior change that a parent might use with a child. Three vital aspects of timing must constantly be remembered if a parent is going to reduce unsatisfactory behaviors, teach new behaviors, and make these behaviors an integral part of a child's life.

> **Three Timing Principles**
>
> 1. The Immediacy Principle,
> 2. The Sequential Principle,
> 3. The Intermittent Principle.

Immediacy Principle: Rewards have their greatest effect when they are given immediately upon performance of the desired behavior.

The closer the giving of the reinforcement to the behavior being reinforced, the more certain the behavior will be established. Experimenters with both animals and humans have discovered the principal of immediacy. The very moment an animal makes a move in the direction of the desired behavior, a buzzer sounds and food is given. The little boy being taught to wear his glasses is placed in a room where the glasses are laying on a table. The moment he moves toward the glasses, a clicker sounds; and he is given a piece of candy.

■ 1. **Place a check beside the action below that is an appropriate application of the immediacy principle. Billy mowed the grass and trimmed around the house and sidewalk on Saturday.**
   - ☐ A. **On Monday you give him some extra spending money for doing such a good job on the yard.**
   - ☐ B. **As Billy puts up the yard equipment, you praise him and decide to go out for pizza to celebrate.**

   2. **Describe the Immediacy Principle in your own words.**

   _____

   _____

   _____

Certainly Billy's reinforcement is much more immediate on Saturday than it is on Monday. You should have checked B.

Sequential Principle: If the reinforcer is to be effective, the right sequence must be followed. First perform the task. Then receive the reward.

Not only is immediate reinforcement important, but the sequential principle makes a difference too. Examine this encounter between Mrs. Simmons and her son Paul.

Paul offered to rake the leaves in their large yard if his mother would give him $5.00. When his mother agreed, he asked for the money and said he would rake the lawn Monday afternoon. Mrs. Simmons responded, "No way, first you rake the lawn. Then I will give you $5.00."

This perceptive mother is applying the "first-then" principle, "Require the less preferred activity to come before the more preferred activities."

■ **Describe in your own words the Sequential Principle.**

_____

_____

_____

Intermittent Principle: To motivate a new behavior, reward every time.
To maintain a learned behavior, reward regularly, but gradually reduce the frequency.

One of the strongest objections to programs of changing behavior comes from people who object to the idea of rewarding people for doing anything. They further develop the idea that the subject (employee, child, or spouse) easily gets the idea that he should be continually rewarded. The process has no end. This understandable attitude comes from a failure to understand the principle of scheduling or intermittent reinforcing.

Observers have long noted that human behavior develops a certain momentum. Activities commenced or learned with difficulty, once mastered and repeated a number of times, are carried on with ease. To keep performances going, rewards should be gradually reduced in frequency. This is sometimes called partial scheduling and may be done on the following scale.

Scheduling Rewards	
Activity	**Rewards**
To Establish behavior	Reward each time without delay
To Maintain behavior	Use a reducing schedule: Reward 80% (4 of 5 times) Reward 50% (1 of 2 times) Reward 30% (1 of 3 times) Reward Occasionally

■ 1. **Describe the Intermittent Principle in your own words.**

_____

_____

_____

Day 5: Time Out

> **Today's Objective:** You will be able to write three guidelines for using Time Out in your disciplining.

Time Out

Earlier this week, I described attention as one of the greatest rewards. I pointed out that attention, even if it comes in the form of punishment, can still be a reward. I would like to suggest that one of the greatest punishments is the withdrawal of attention. This leads me to suggest a very practical technique in disciplining children—Time Out or simply T. O. As a family counselor, you will have opportunities where you can teach this technique to parents. They in turn can develop skill in using this technique as a method of discipline.

Mrs. Lindeman is completely frustrated with her son Stan who has an annoying habit of punching his sister Wilma on the arm. She says, "I'm tired of the way you keep on teasing your sister, and I have decided to do something about it by using T.O with you. Every time you tease your sister I am going to put you in the bathroom for 3 minutes."

When she tells her friend Mrs. Knox about her plan, the lady smiles benevolently and says, "You're wasting your time. I tried that with my Jimmy. I got so tired of threatening him, I sent him to his bedroom. When I finally let him come out, he let me know he quite enjoyed the experience."

■ **Before I discuss the details of Time Out, what do you think made the difference between what Mrs. Lindeman did and what Mrs. Knox did?**

_____

_____

_____

_____

How did I say you would use T. O. in counseling?

_____

I suggested that you will use Time Out in your counseling as you teach parents this alternate technique for discipline of their children. Let's examine the differences between Mrs. Knox and Mrs. Lindeman's application of T. O. As you read, try to identify some guidelines for Time Out.

1️⃣ Mrs. Knox chose the wrong place for T. O. If it is to be effective, the child must be placed in the least stimulating environment possible. His room is not the place. A completely bare room would be best of all—no people, no toys, no television, and no books.

■ **Write one guideline for effectively using T. O.**

_____

_____

2 When Mrs. Knox was completely frustrated after interminable threats she sent Jimmy to his room. T. O. calls for consistency. The child must be sent to the room "every time" he misbehaves.

■ **Write a second guideline for effectively using T. O.**

_____

_____

3 Mrs. Knox did not have specific time arrangements. T. O. does not need to be long. Periods of time from one to five minutes can be very effective. This makes a kitchen timer important in the process. The parent sets the timer for a specific period. When the bell sounds, both parent and child know the punishment is over.

■ **Write a third guideline for effectively using T. O.**

_____

_____

T. O. is an application of the concept that withdrawal of attention is the greatest punishment you can inflict on an unruly child. Keep in mind that T. O. is primarily for use with children. You should have derived three guidelines for using Time Out effectively.

Guidelines for Time Out

1. Select the least stimulating environment possible.
2. Be consistent. Apply T. O. every time the child misbehaves.
3. Make the T. O. periods brief (one to five minutes).

■ 1. **How is your PQ? On day 2, I asked you to keep a diary this week to evaluate your Praise Quotient. Rate yourself on the following scale.**

_____   **0—Did not keep a diary.**
_____   **50—Not too praiseworthy (One praise statement a day or less).**
_____   **75—Averaged two to three praise statements a day.**
_____   **90—Averaged three to five praise statements a day.**
_____ **100—Averaged five to eight praise statements a day.**
_____ **110—Averaged eight or more praise statements a day.**

2. **On a separate sheet of paper, write about how praise affected your relationships this week. Bring your report to your group session.**

In this week's study you have been introduced to techniques that a person can use to bring about a change in behavior. This set of techniques has many different applications. You will find them particularly valuable in working with problems of family discipline.

UNIT 10
Counseling Youth

This Week's Learning Goal

After studying this unit you will understand principles to use in a counseling ministry with youth.

Why You Will Find This Study Useful

The youth years are times of significant change. Youth must cope with changing bodies, changing relationships, and increasing demands. They frequently need someone to listen and guide them as they try to cope with life. You will discover biblical and psychological principles that will help you guide youth to make wise choices. You will also identify ways to develop better communication between a youth and his parents.

Day 1: Master and Mission

> **Today's Objective:** You will be able to relate Scriptures and principles to two key decisions youth must make as they prepare for adulthood.

The Book of Proverbs is a collection of the counsel given by the wise men of Israel. In the first seven chapters it emphasizes the period of life we call adolescence or youth. In these chapters the writer spells out a series of problem areas and issues youth often face.

■ **Read the following Scriptures and make a list of some of the problems the writer addresses.**

☐ Proverbs 1:7   ☐ Proverbs 1:10-15   ☐ Proverbs 2:16-19

☐ Proverbs 3:9-10   ☐ Proverbs 3:27-28   ☐ Proverbs 4:24

☐ Proverbs 5:1-6   ☐ Proverbs 6:1-5   ☐ Proverbs 6:6-11

☐ Proverbs 6:16-19   ☐ Proverbs 7:6-27

GOD'S WORD AND WISDOM

_____

_____

_____

_____

_____

The proverbs you just read include such problems or issues as fear of the Lord, responding to discipline, peer pressure to do wrong, adultery, seductive people, money management, responding to wealth, helping the needy, corrupt talk, prostitution, and work ethics. These sound strangely modern. Solomon wanted to give, "Knowledge and discretion to the young" (Prov. 1:4). This is a challenging task you will face as a counselor.

This week we will examine some of the problem areas youth face. I will help you discover how to deal with youth who seek your help in relation to some of these issues. Youth must make at least three important decisions as they prepare for adulthood. We want to look at two of these decisions today. We will examine the third tomorrow. These important decisions are:
• Who is my Master?
• What is my mission?
• Who will be my mate?

Who is My Master?

All of your counseling should be done in consciousness of settling the all important question, "Who is my Master?" Youth may serve one of many masters: money, material things, peers, worldly values, Satan, self, or others. "No one can serve two masters. Either he will hate the one and love the other, or he will be devoted to the one and despise the other. You cannot serve both God and Money" (Matt. 6:24).

■ **Read the following Scriptures. For each passage, list at least one reason a youth should make Christ Lord and Master of his or her life.**

GOD'S WORD
AND WISDOM

Psalm 119:9-11 _____

1 Corinthians 10:13 _____

John 10:10 _____

Acts 1:8 _____

2 Corinthians 5:17 _____

Without Christ as Master, a youth has the disadvantage of trying to live his or her life without:
• the Spirit's help in overcoming sin and temptation
• guidance for godly living
• the abundant life Jesus wants to give
• the power for godly living and Christian witness
• the benefits of a new nature

As you counsel youth and others, you should constantly be on the lookout for the person whose most basic need is for a saving relationship with the Lord Jesus Christ. Sometimes the person may be open to your sharing the gospel in your first encounter. More frequently, you will want to build a relationship first. As you help meet some of the person's perceived needs, he or she will be more open to your concern for spiritual matters. Sharing the value of knowing Christ demonstrates your concern for the youth's total well-being.

If you do not have the ability to share your faith in Christ effectively, you will want to find and develop a way to share the gospel clearly. You may want to focus your method on using your personal testimony, a marked New Testament, a gospel tract, a learned presentation of the gospel, or some other approach. Helping a youth decide to make Jesus Christ his Savior and Lord (Master) is a significant way you can help him get a handle on living.

What is My Mission?

Career choice has a significant impact in every person's life. Discovering a direction for life and work is a challenge for every youth. When counseling a youth concerning career, you will need to become familiar with his abilities and requirements for positions in the workplace. This information will help you as you brainstorm alternatives and explore the outcomes.

Youth also need to understand that work should be seen as a calling from God. Martin Luther was a monk. In his monastery days he believed that, as a monk, he had a "vocation," a calling from God to spend his days in prayer and worship away from the temptations of the world. After his conversion experience, he began to view all this in a different way. He preached that a man's work was a calling from God. He said the girl who milked the cows and the man who shoveled the manure were doing a greater service to God than the monk who was singing psalms in the monastery.

This emphasis has led to the use of the word *vocation* to refer to a person's career. We must counsel youth to make their career decision in the light of it being a calling from God. Youth will then see their work as a part of their overall mission in life.

■ **Read each of the following Scriptures. Write a brief statement of how each passage could be used to help a youth understand his or her mission in life.**

Proverbs 3:5-6 _____

_____

Ecclesiastes 9:10 _____

_____

GOD'S WOR

AND WISDC

Matthew 6:33 _____

_____

Ephesians 4:1 _____

_____

Ephesians 4:28 _____

_____

Colossians 3:20-24 _____

_____

You will discuss these Scriptures in your group session this week.

Day 2: Who Will Be My Mate?

> **Today's Objective:** You will be able to relate Scriptures and principles to one more key decision youth often make as they prepare for adulthood.

As youth consider dating and eventually marriage, four questions need to be answered. Let's examine them today.

Do Opposites Attract?

One of the notions accepted by many youth is that opposites attract. Some speculate that people may be drawn toward each other because of "complimentary needs" that each may supply to the other. Evidence indicates, however, that "like attracts like" is a better principle. Similarity of social background, attitudes, values, and philosophy of life contribute to better relationships. This suggests that a youth will probably be much happier married to someone with many similarities.

You need to help youth make good choices and not to be fooled by a popular myth that moves toward a marriage with someone who is altogether different. An "opposite" may be attractive and entrancing while dating but altogether irritating within marriage.

■ **In the marriages described below, write an M in front of the ones more likely to result in a satisfying relationship and an L in front of those less likely to result in a satisfying relationship.**

_____ 1. Wife is outgoing and enjoys being around people.
           Husband is quiet and reserved.
_____ 2. Wife is pessimistic about the world situation.
           Husband always looks for the best in a given situation.
_____ 3. Wife's father is machinist in an automobile plant.
           Husband's father is a plumber.
_____ 4. Wife is a high school drop-out.
           Husband has a masters degree in accounting.

Which principle below is more likely to result in a satisfying marriage relationship? Check your choice.

☐ **A. Opposites attract.**
☐ **B. Like attracts like.**

Many other factors are involved in a happy marriage, but normally the "like attracts like" principle will result in happier relationships. In numbers 1, 2, and 4 above, the husband and wife of each combination have very different dispositions or backgrounds. These marriages are not unworkable. They are, however, less likely to result in a satisfying relationship. Similar backgrounds are more likely to produce satisfying relationships. In #3 both persons come from a "blue-collar" family background. This similar background is more likely to result in a happy marriage than if one spouse were from a family with inherited wealth, for instance.

Is Religion Important?

The most important single commonality is a bond of faith. Youth should be helped to see the importance of marrying a Christian. Marriage should be more than a partnership between two individuals. It should be a triangular relationship between a husband and wife and their common Lord.

■ **Write a summary of this principle found in 2 Corinthians 6:14.**

_____

_____

Although many young people lightly view the role of religion in interpersonal relationships, research has shown that religion plays an important role in marriage stability. Studies have shown that prospects for a marriage are better if the couple:
• belongs to a church
• are married by a pastor or priest
• attend Sunday School
• attend church at least two to four times a month.
These religious practices provide a foundation for a healthy relationship.

Spouses need common and shared interests in certain things they do together. Being a Christian and attending Sunday School and worship together helps. A strong faith will always be an important consideration in the development of a strong husband-wife relationship. Second Corinthians 6:14 teaches that Christians should not marry those who are not Christians. The best way to avoid marrying an unbeliever is to never date one.

GOD'S WORD
AND WISDOM

Do Attitudes of Relatives and Friends Matter?

One sociologist visiting the Orient sympathized, "Isn't it a shame that your parents should choose your future spouse instead of the way we do it in America?" The girl responded, "Do your marriages turn out better than ours?" The sociologist reluctantly admitted that our divorce rate told its own tale. The attitudes of family and friends do make a difference in many marriages.

A student once said, "I want to make it quite clear, I am not marrying Bonnie's family."

A lecturer responded, "I am sorry to tell you this; you *are* marrying her family. They will be psychologically present in your home. There's a good chance they will be physically present. And, if you can't stand them now, just wait until you are married."

Despite all our freedom in America, the opinion of parents and friends is still important in making a marriage choice. The approval of parents and friends is a factor in helping to establish a good marriage relationship. If anything like a sizable group of relatives and friends oppose a marriage, the participants should sit down and rethink the situation.

■ **See if you can state a principle for youth to consider concerning the attitude of family and friends toward a potential marriage partner. Write the principle here:**

_____

_____

You will discuss this principle in your group session this week.

How Important Is Age?

Love is a growth experience. The chronological age of the partners in a marriage will be an important factor in assuring the development of a good relationship. A marriage prospect who is a good risk will be at an age characterized by both stability and flexibility. Stability is evidenced by habits and attitudes that will guide and direct life on a well-defined course. This must be tempered by a flexibility seen in the individual's capacity to change. Both of these traits have a relationship to age.

A girl who is eighteen may have much flexibility but little stability. On the other hand, the man of thirty ought to have plenty of stability, but he may not be very flexible. So, marriage should come at a time when there is a happy medium between the two extremes of flexibility and stability.

■ **State this principle concerning age in your own words.**

_____

_____

Adolescence is one of the most significant periods of change in all of life. The youth's body is changing. His relationships with his parents are changing. School is a new and different type. Vocational plans are in a state of fluctuation. This time, when everything is changing, is not the best time to be making the permanent, lifelong commitment that marriage calls for.

Studies made of the relationship between age and success in marriage suggest that early marriage is a major cause of divorce and unhappiness in marriage. Early marriage was defined as before twenty for females and before twenty-five for males. The conclusion from the research was:

> The longer marriage is delayed into the twenties or even early thirties, the greater the possibility of a successful relationship.

■ **Suppose a youth came to you and asked, "What is the best age to get married?" What would you answer and why?**

_____

_____

_____

_____

_____

_____

_____

_____

_____

Day 3: Coping with Sexual Desires

> **Today's Objective:** You will be able to identify some ways for youth to appropriately cope with sexual desires.

Adolescence is a time when romantic love and the sex drive are powerful emotions. How a youth controls and guides these emotions can lead to meaningful relationships or to heart-rending tragedy. In trying to help youth with the multitude of problems that arise in their love life we will build on this assumption: Many of life's problems arise from loving the wrong object, at the wrong time, with the wrong type of love.

Loving the Wrong Object

Any discussion of love faces difficulties of definition. People speak of loving such dissimilar objects as God, pecan pies, cats, old shoes, money, and mother. One definition by a psychiatrist gets to the heart of the problem, "Love is an intense positive interest in an object."[1] Problems arise when people choose to love the wrong objects.

■ **Read the following Scriptures. Make a list of some of the wrong "objects" people tend to love and some of the "objects" people are encouraged to love.**

Titus 2:4	1 Timothy 6:10	Proverbs 20:13	Micah 6:8
Psalm 4:2	Proverbs 6:27-32	Ephesians 5:25	John 13:34
1 John 2:15	Matthew 22:37	Matthew 5:44	Mark 12:31

GOD'S WORD AND WISDOM

WRONG "OBJECTS"   RIGHT "OBJECTS"

_____   _____
_____   _____
_____   _____
_____   _____
_____   _____

Add to the list other right and wrong objects youth might love.

The Wrong Type of Love

Even the word *love* raises problems of semantics. The English word must cover so many different ideas. Three Greek words—*eros, philia,* and *agape*—can give us a basis for a better understanding of "love."

Eros is selfish, emotional, and sexual love. It is basically the physical attraction between the sexes. In the writings of the Greeks, *eros* was the "love of desire." As a consequence, once the object of desire has been possessed, *eros* may lose interest or die away. Although the New Testament was written in Greek, the word *eros* was not used.

Philia may be thought of as the mental level of love. This is the love of friendship or brotherly love. It represents the attraction of similar intellectual and cultural interests. Some of the most unusual love affairs of history have had very little of the erotic type of love about them. The *philia*-type of love contributes to a long lasting marriage relationship.

Agape is the unselfish level of love. It is the word most frequently used to describe the love of God. It is used to describe the love Christians are to have for each other. This is a love that desires the best for another, no matter what sacrifice may be required to attain it. The classic exposition of this type of love is set forth in 1 Corinthians 13.

■ **Draw a line from the type of love on the left to its definition on the right.**

1. *eros*   a. Friendship, brotherly love

2. *philia*   b. Unselfish, God-like love

3. *agape*   c. Sexual, erotic love

Many of the problems youth face regarding love arise when *eros* is the dominant type of love expressed. Outside of marriage, this is the wrong kind of love. Answers to the activity above are 1-c, 2-a, 3-b.

Loving at the Wrong Time

The writer of Ecclesiastes states, "There is a time to love." In the stages of human growth and development, appropriate love experiences come at different times. During adolescence, youth are vulnerable to their sexual drives. This is a period of hormonal surge that is filled with emotional upheavals. Youth need to learn ways to control their sexual desires until marriage.

S WORD

WISDOM

■ 1. **Read the following Scriptures and write some ways a youth can find help to control his or her sexual desires. Psalm 119:11; 1 Corinthians 10:13; Romans 6:13; Ephesians 6:10-18.**

_____

_____

_____

_____

_____

2. **Read the example of Joseph as he resisted the temptation to yield to sexual desires—Genesis 39:7-23. Write a brief summary of how he resisted.**

_____

_____

_____

_____

_____

_____

3. **How did God respond to Joseph's faithfulness? (vv. 21-23)** _____

_____

Youth may need you to give them suggestions about specific ways they can resist temptation. Staying spiritually close to the Lord through prayer, reading His Word, and memorizing Scripture are good starting places. Youth need to depend on the help and strength only God can give. Staying away from tempting situations, just saying no, and fleeing when temptation comes are some practical ways to remain faithful.

Joseph set a good example for youth to follow. He responded to the temptations of Potiphar's wife by
• refusing to give in (v. 8)
• recognizing his responsibility to others (vv. 8-9)
• recognizing this as a sin against God (v. 9)
• just saying no (v. 10)
• running away from the temptation (v. 12)

God rewarded Joseph for his faithfulness. He was with Joseph and caused all that he did to prosper.

Day 4: Helping Parents Communicate

> **Today's Objective:** You will be able to identify guidelines of negotiating that help improve communication between a youth and his parents.

Communication

In adolescence, children who were formerly open and communicative all too frequently become secretive. They build a wall between themselves and the other members of the family. A major task of the counselor will be to help parents establish or improve communication with their children.

The communication theme runs through Proverbs as it emphasizes listening. Listening is the most important aspect of communication in family life, "My son, pay attention to what I say; listen closely to my words" (Prov. 4:20). "My sons, listen to me" (Prov. 7:24). "Listen to my instruction" (Prov. 8:33). Wisdom is portrayed as saying, "Listen for I have worthy things to say" (Prov. 8:6).

When the United States put a man on the moon, we sat and wondered at the technological miracle. Neil Armstrong said, "That's one small step for a man, one giant leap for mankind." One father said, "That man on the moon can communicate with me, and I can't get in touch with Jimmy sitting in the next room."

One major task of the wise counselor will be to teach communication skills to parents and youth. Parents are frequently frustrated by youth who reject their voice of experience and advice. If this impasse is to be overcome, the parent must work at the task of communication. One way of doing this is to use a negotiating technique. Here are seven guidelines you could teach parents to follow to improve communication.

> **Guidelines for Negotiating**
>
> 1. Maintain self-control.
> 2. Acknowledge your own failures.
> 3. Refuse to compromise in some situations.
> 4. Take time to listen.
> 5. Acknowledge his ability to reason.
> 6. Start a new train of thought.
> 7. Attack wrong actions, not the person.

■ Below the explanation of each of the following guidelines, describe the kind of behavior that would be a *violation* of the guideline. In other words what is the opposite of the guideline.

1. Maintain self-control. Much talk by the teenager will sound unreasonable if not downright impertinent. Make allowances for the brashness of immature youth. If he loses his temper, do not descend to his level by losing yours.

■ Opposite: _____

If you wrote something like lose my temper, get mad, storm out of the room and refuse to talk further, slap, or something similar, then you have the idea about opposites to the first guideline.

2. Acknowledge your own failures. Adults make plenty of mistakes. If you acknowledge them, your teenager is often more open to dialogue. Do not be afraid to say you are sorry.

■ Opposite: _____

3. Refuse to compromise in some situations. We cannot negotiate whether or not to obey the law. The teenager *must* do this. Choose very carefully where you will draw other lines or boundaries. Make sure that the situation cannot be negotiated before you refuse to compromise.

■ Opposite: _____

4. Take time to listen. Remember how much your teenager glorifies talking. Fight every impulse to interrupt. Listen, listen, listen. Just give a response of "Oh," "I see," or "You may have a point there." You may even be surprised some day when he talks himself out of some of the ideas he previously held.

■ Opposite: _____

5. Acknowledge youth's ability to reason. When he asks why, simply saying, "Because I say so," is not enough. Do not downgrade his weak arguments or make sarcastic comments. Use good-natured questions that will help him face his own inconsistencies. Ask him for recommendations.

■ Opposite: _____

6. Start a new train of thought. Consider a new approach or alternative. Say, "Have you thought of this?" "What will you do if this arises?" Sometimes an illustration will help, "I once knew a fellow . . ."

■ Opposite: _____

7. Attack wrong actions, not the person. When Junior does something foolish, don't say, "You're so stupid; that's not the way to go about things." The better way would be, "I love and respect you, but I think that action was wrong. Even if I don't like your behavior, I still love you."

■ Opposite: _____

■ **Below are seven behaviors that would violate the guidelines for negotiating. Write the correct guideline on the line below each violation.**

A. The parent continues to ask questions and make accusations without waiting to hear an explanation.

Guideline #_____ : _____

B. The parent's answer is, "You don't have to understand it; you just do what I say."

Guideline #_____ : _____

C. Mother gets into a shouting match with her daughter.

Guideline #_____ : _____

D. Father says, "I can't believe you're so immature. You are old enough to know better."

Guideline #_____ : _____

E. Youth says, "Dad, you always act like you're perfect and never make a mistake."

Guideline #_____ : _____

F. Mother says, "Okay. Okay. You know I believe (activity) is wrong, but I don't want you to hate me the rest of your life. You can go to the party, but you behave yourself."

Guideline #_____ : _____

G. Father disagrees with the youth's proposal. They get locked into an argument rehashing the same old issues, but they make no progress toward a solution.

Guideline #_____ : _____

In the cases above A did not take time to listen. B did not acknowledge the youth's ability to reason. C lost her self-control. D attacked the person rather than the behavior. E seems to have problems admitting he is ever in the wrong. F compromised on a moral issue that should have been a firm boundary. G failed to get out of a rut by using a new train of thought. The guideline numbers are A-4; B-5; C-1; D-7; E-2; F-3; G-6.

As parents learn to negotiate with teenagers, they will discover time, patience, and understanding are required. Family unity will be part of the rewards. Parents will be grateful to you for helping them develop this skill.

Day 5: Other Problems and Principles

> **Today's Objective:** You will identify additional problem areas youth encounter, and you will practice your preparation for counseling one significant problem.

This week in your group session you will discuss problem areas you will likely face in counseling with youth. Complete the following assignments in preparation for your group session.

■ 1. **Make a list of problems or issues youth may need help with. I have given you a few to get you started.**

Problems and Issues Youth Face

| Physical Appearance | Depression | Parents Are Divorcing |
| Physical Abuse | Suicide | Friend Is Pregnant |

_____

_____

_____

_____

_____

_____

_____

_____

_____

_____

2. **For more responses, talk to two or more youth. Use separate sheets of paper and write down their responses to the following questions:**
   - **"In your opinion, what problems and issues do youth face that are difficult for them to handle?"**
   - **"What decisions do youth often need help in making?"**
   - **"If you had to identify the single most difficult problem youth face in your school, what would it be?"**
   Bring these responses with you to your group session this week.

3. **From all the problems, issues, and decisions you have identified, select the one that you believe is the most troublesome for youth in your community. Write it on this line:**

   _____

4. **Assume that you are in a counseling session with a youth who is facing the problem you identified in #3. Move to step 7 in the Ten-Step Model—Review the Alternatives—and make a list of alternatives you would identify with the youth. Write them on the following page.**

_____

_____

_____

_____

_____

_____

5. **Think through each of the alternatives you just identified. Think about the outcomes of each alternative and how you would go about exploring them with the counselee. You do not need to write a response for this item, but you do need to think through step 8 of the Ten-Step Model—Explore the Outcomes. You will discuss some of these during your group session this week.**

6. **Read the following Scripture passages. Write a brief statement of the principle for Christian living you find in each verse.**

   a. **Leviticus 19:3** _____

   _____

   b. **Proverbs 23:20-21** _____

   _____

   c. **1 Corinthians 6:19** _____

   _____

   d. **Ephesians 6:1** _____

   _____

   e. **Colossians 3:5** _____

   _____

   f. **1 Timothy 4:12** _____

   _____

   g. **1 Timothy 5:1-2** _____

   _____

   h. **Titus 2:6-7** _____

   _____

GOD'S WOR
AND WISDO

For Further Study

☐ *Before You Marry* by Daniel G. Bagby. Nashville: Convention Press, 1983.

☐ *The 24-Hour Counselor, Volume I* and *II* compiled by Richard Ross. Nashville: Broadman Press, 1988. These cassette tapes provide biblically based and clinically sound suggestions for youth who are struggling with a variety of contemporary problems.

☐ *Today's Youth* by Wade Rowatt. Nashville: Convention Press, 1993.

☐ *Ministry with Youth in Crisis* compiled by Richard Ross and Judi Hayes. Nashville: Convention Press, 1993.

UNIT 11
Counseling Singles and Senior Adults

This Week's Learning Goal

After studying this unit, you will understand some of the unique needs of singles and senior adults and ways to provide counsel and ministry to help meet these needs.

Why You Will Find This Study Useful

Singles and senior adults are growing in numbers in our communities and churches. Each group has life situations that create unique needs. You will identify some of these unique needs and explore ways to provide wise counsel and ministry to help meet these needs. Your ministry may help reach some of these individuals for Christ or help restore them to active church membership.

Days 1 and 2: Counseling Singles

> **Objective:** You will be able to identify unique needs of three types of singles and discuss biblical teachings that speak to some of the issues singles encounter.

An estimate reveals that 63 million adult Americans are single. Singles are people. Many of their needs and problems are similar to those of youth and married adults. The Ten-Step Counseling Model will serve as your counseling process regardless of age or marital status.

As you counsel singles, you will encounter problems and decisions that are unique to this group. Today and tomorrow we will examine some of these. Many of the issues will have no easy answers, so prepare to work hard in developing a biblical approach to the issues that arise in counseling singles.

Singles provide a variety of ministry opportunities. They also are one of the most responsive age groups to the outreach efforts of the church today. Singles cannot be treated as a single group, though. This category consists of three broad groups of people.

Never Married Singles   **Divorced Singles**   **Widowed Singles**

Some needs of singles are common to each of these groups. Yet, each group has some unique needs and life situations that you need to recognize and understand.

■ **As you read about the three types of singles, underline specific problems or needs that singles may encounter. These should help you begin to focus your attention on the kinds of help singles may call for from a counselor.**

Never-Married Singles

Those who have never been married are generally the younger segment of singles. Some may be contemplating marriage. Others may be focusing on their chosen career path. Still others may be searching for some direction in their lives, because they did not resolve that issue as youth.

For a variety of reasons, people are choosing to marry later in life than was true twenty years ago. Singles usually must balance career demands with relationship demands. This tension creates a need for wise counsel as they make life-changing decisions. Singles contemplating marriage sometimes have a rather naive view of the type of relationship they will have with someone of the opposite sex. Some are disillusioned by the type of experiences they observe in their peer group or on television. Your role as counselor may focus primarily on the need of singles to make wise decisions as they approach new life situations.

■ From the previous section, make a list of some of the problem areas never-married singles may encounter. Think of other types of problems and add them to the list.

_____

_____

_____

_____

_____

_____

_____

_____

_____

_____

_____

_____

Some of the areas you listed may include contemplating marriage, career development, direction in life, balance between career and relationship demands, relationships with the opposite sex, and disillusionment with modern-day models for singles and for marriage.

Many of the issues you studied for youth are also issues for never-married singles. Singles also must determine who their master is and find fulfillment in life through their mission and career. They must apply biblical principles if they consider selecting a mate. They must control their sexual desires.

■ A decision some never-married singles consider is: "Should I marry at all, or should I remain single?" The Bible gives counsel concerning marriage and whether a person should marry or remain single. Read the following Scriptures and write a one-sentence summary of the teaching for each passage. You will compare your summaries with the members of your triad in the group session.

A. Genesis 1:27-28 _____

_____

B. Genesis 2:18,23,24 _____

_____

GOD'S WORD
AND WISDOM

C. Matthew 19:10-12 _____

_____

D. 1 Corinthians 7:1-2,7-9,25-28 _____

_____

E. 1 Corinthians 7:36-38 _____

_____

F. 1 Timothy 4:1-3 _____

_____

God created male and female and assigned them the task of filling the earth with their offspring. He also created woman because man needed a companion. God's plan for marriage from the beginning was one man and one woman for life. Jesus strongly upheld God's original ideal for marriage (Matt. 19:3-9). Jesus was then asked if a person should marry at all. He did not forbid marriage. He said, however, that some have "renounced marriage because of the kingdom of heaven." Remaining single for the Kingdom's sake was an acceptable option.

Paul recommended that a person would be better off not married so he could devote himself to serving the Lord. Remaining single was a desirable option for Paul. He did, however, encourage marriage for those who could not control their passions. He later wrote Timothy and warned him to beware of those who forbade marriage. It is a good thing from God.

■ **Continue your search for unique needs in the following section and underline them.**

Divorced Singles

A second group of singles are the divorced. The most obvious of these are the parents with children. Single parents struggle with the problems of rearing a family, maintaining a career, and facing all the problems of the single life. Divorced singles may struggle with grief (over the loss of a significant relationship), bitterness, resentment, or guilt.

Because the Bible condemns divorce as contrary to God's plan for marriage, many Christians have been less than tactful in the way they have related and ministered to the divorcee. The divorcee may feel discouraged and repelled by Christianity. These singles are a difficult challenge to both church and counselor. Because of their significant need, they also constitute one of the great opportunities for ministry.

Although a divorced person's first marriage may have been a bad experience, most are willing to try married life again. Too often divorced persons do not take time to evaluate his/her own behavior and attitude. This often leads to a second marriage that has the same or similar problems to the first. As a result, some divorced people will go through a string of failed marriages hoping to eventually find the "right" partner.

■ **From the above content, make a list of some of the problem areas divorced singles may encounter. Think of other types of problems and add them to the list.**

_____

_____

_____

_____

_____

_____

_____

_____

_____

Divorced singles often face the problems of rearing children alone; maintaining a career; coping with grief, bitterness, resentment, and guilt; coping with financial problems; and evaluating behavior or attitude problems that create relationship problems. Others face problems as they consider remarriage.

As a counselor, you may be able to help the divorced evaluate their behaviors and attitudes that may cause problems in relationships. You should be able to help them with decision making related to child rearing, career, and financial concerns. Using the Ten-Step Model, help the person identify the problem and determine an action plan.

This is a good stopping point in this two-day assignment. I suggest you stop for today and pick up here tomorrow.

****

Remarriage for Divorced Singles?

Remarriage is an issue you are likely to face if you counsel with many divorced people. Christians do not agree about what the Bible teaches regarding remarriage of divorced people. You need to study the Scriptures for yourself and understand the issues involved. Then, as you work with divorced people, you can provide information for them as they study for themselves to know and obey God's will.

Three basic positions are taken:
1. *All divorced persons who marry again are living in adultery.* (See Mark 10:11-12; Luke 16:18; Rom. 7:3; and 1 Cor. 7:10-11.)
2. *Divorced persons who had grounds for their divorce may remarry. Others should not.* (See "except for fornication" in Matt. 5:31-32 and 19:9. This view identifies fornication as the grounds for divorce.)
3. *Divorced persons are permitted to marry again.* (This view identifies the principles of forgiveness and renewal as a basis for remarriage. It points to Jesus' treatment of sinful people as a model—Luke 19:1-10; John 4:1-42; and John 8:2-11. It believes Paul's statement in 1 Cor. 7:12-16 implies the possibility of divorce and remarriage. This view still holds that God's ideal for marriage is a permanent relationship between one man and one woman for life.)

Here are some questions that you must seek to answer:
1. Is remarriage after divorce ever permitted?
2. Is remarriage after divorce permitted, but only in certain circumstances? If so, what are the circumstances where remarriage is permitted?
3. Is remarriage permitted in all cases after divorce?
4. If remarriage is permitted, what principles should a divorced Christian follow in selecting a mate?

■ 1. With these questions in mind, read the following Scriptures. Make notes to yourself about what each Scripture teaches. You may want to use a separate sheet of paper and make more detailed notes.

Matthew 5:31-32 _____

_____

Matthew 19:8-9 _____

_____

Mark 10:11-12 _____

_____

Romans 7:1-3 _____

_____

1 Corinthians 7:10-15 _____

_____

1 Corinthians 7:39-40 _____

_____

If you want to further research teachings on divorce, these are some related passages in addition to the ones above:
☐ Genesis 2:18-25
☐ Leviticus 21:1,7,13-15
☐ Deuteronomy 24:1-4
☐ Malachi 2:13-16
☐ Matthew 19:3-9
☐ Mark 10:2-12
☐ Luke 16:18

2. What other biblical principles do you believe must be considered when addressing the issue of remarriage (if any)? Write them here. Provide a Scripture reference if you can.

_____

_____

_____

3. From your study, what conclusions would you draw about remarriage?

_____

_____

_____

4. What concerns or unanswered questions do you still have with regard to remarriage of divorced persons?

_____

_____

_____

This is a very emotional issue with some Christians. As a counselor you should always uphold God's ideal of marriage as a permanent relationship. You should also be available to minister to those who have sinned by failing to measure up to the ideal. Remember that we are all sinners in need of God's love and grace.

For those who are considering remarriage:
- help them identify and study relevant biblical teachings
- use the Ten-Step Model to identify problems, review alternatives, and explore outcomes
- provide appropriate information and literature
- encourage them to diligently seek the leadership of the Holy Spirit in making their decisions
- as always, leave the decision making in the hands of your counselee
- continue to minister to persons even if they make what appears to be a poor decision

Widowed Singles

The third segment of the singles population consists of people who have been married and have lost their spouses through death. Because women generally live longer than men, women will be in the majority in this group. Widowed singles face the needs discussed earlier related to processing grief. They also have to deal with such problems as loneliness, changed relationships to friends, additional home responsibilities, financial pressures, and sometimes getting a job and single parenting.

■ 1. **From the above content, make a list of some of the problem areas widowed singles may encounter. Think of other types of problems and add them to the list.**

_____

_____

_____

_____

_____

_____

2. **The Bible counsels widows in the following passages. Read each one and summarize its application to widows.**

Romans 7:1-3 _____

_____

1 Corinthians 7:8-9, 39-40 _____

_____

1 Timothy 5:3-16 _____

_____

Though remarriage for divorcees is debated, the Bible clearly gives widowed singles permission to remarry. You will discuss these summaries in your group session this week.

The differences between some of these groups, particularly the divorced and the widowed, was highlighted in a discussion group of singles. A recently widowed man listened to the sometimes bitter statements of some of the divorced. Then he addressed himself to the group, "I have listened carefully to all your complaints about your former mates, and it becomes clear you wanted to get out of your marriage. I dearly loved my wife and did not want to lose her. I obviously don't belong here."

This reminds us that, though the word *single* calls to mind a whole sub-culture, singles are not all the same. Trying to help them is not going to be easy. Singles are, however, a ripe field for Christian ministry and witness. Singles can also provide valuable leadership and ministry.

A Successful Single Is a Possibility

One successful single belonged in turn to each of the three groups of singles we have examined. He was a never-married single into middle age. After his marriage he was separated from his wife (and for all practical purposes divorced), and later widowed. His name was John Wesley, the great evangelist of the eighteenth century.

Dedicated to his ministry and concerned as to whether a man could love God and a woman, he remained single until he was forty-eight years of age. These years were highly productive. He had a courting relationship with Grace Murray that lasted for ten years. She, however, left him to marry one of Wesley's preacher friends, John Bennet.

One winter day, Wesley fell on the ice and injured his ankle. He was carried to the home of a widow named Molly Vazeille. He came to this experience with the wounds of a broken relationship with Grace. Considering his forty-eight years of being single, many were amazed that he married this widow after having known her for one week. The marriage was a disaster. They finally separated. Though divorce was out of the question, Wesley lived like a divorcee, separated from his wife. Later the news came that Molly had died, and Wesley became a widower.

Having been in each of these singles categories—bachelor, the equivalent of divorced, and a widower—Wesley demonstrated an amazing capacity to overcome all the debits of the single life. He was able to use his singleness to advantage by living an itinerant life. He established three centers of ministry in different parts of England. His constant moving around the Methodist societies would have been next to impossible if he had been married and rearing a family.

Wesley stands astride the eighteenth century as a human instrument in the great movement of God known as the evangelical revival. As a single, Wesley made significant contributions to God's kingdom. He stands as a demonstration that singleness need not be a handicap. It can be an asset in victorious living and service for the glory of God.

■ **The Bible includes some notable singles. Test your Bible knowledge and check the singles in the list below.**
   ☐ a. **Noah**
   ☐ b. **Moses**
   ☐ c. **David**
   ☐ d. **Jeremiah**
   ☐ e. **Jesus**
   ☐ f. **Paul**

We know that Noah, Moses, and David were all married and had children. Jeremiah, Jesus, and Paul were singles. We are not sure whether Paul had ever been married. Some suggest that he had been married at one time. However, when he wrote 1 Corinthians 7, he was single and commended that status to others. Jeremiah, Jesus, and Paul were successful singles who each made very significant contributions to the Kingdom. Yes, successful singles are a possibility in God's kingdom.

Day 3: Helping Senior Adults Make Decisions

> **Today's Objective:** You will be able to apply the Ten-Step Counseling Model to a case study to identify alternatives for a senior adult.

While many important decisions are made during the youth years, one can generally recoup from a bad decision and start again. The decisions of the senior adult are often much more final. One decision can determine the way she is going to spend the rest of her life. As a counselor, you will have opportunities to help senior adults get in touch with their present circumstances and make wise decisions.

Help Identify Additional Alternatives

Like the youth, the senior adult is not always aware of the various options available to him or her. Following a devastating experience like the death of a spouse, a senior adult may think he has only one way to go. You will use the Ten-Step Counseling Model to help senior adults make decisions.

■ **I want to test your knowledge of the Ten-Step Counseling Model. On a separate sheet of paper, write the following items of the Ten-Step Model (no peeking).**
   ☐ **two stages**
   ☐ **ten steps**
   ☐ **twelve questions**
   ☐ **two decisions**
   ☐ **three sources of assistance (referral)**

Check your work with the course map.

Mr. Sutcliffe's wife died after a short illness. Friends knew just how much he had depended on her. They immediately began to suggest that she would have wanted him to remarry. They convinced him that this was the only way he would be able to survive. The result was a quick marriage that collapsed after a relatively short period of time. It left both him and his second spouse disillusioned.

■ **What was wrong with the counsel Mr. Sutcliffe received?**

_____

_____

_____

Mr. Sutcliffe's friends had good intentions, but they failed to provide wise counsel. First, they identified only one alternative. Second, they essentially made the decision for him—he had to remarry to survive. Third, they expressed urgency and made him rush into a decision to marry.

One of the tasks of the counselor is to help his elderly counselee face a series of alternatives and ponder these possibilities carefully. Since some decisions are so important and often final, senior adults should not be forced to rush a decision. Remember to allow the counselee to make his own decisions. Though these are not new, pay special attention to these guidelines as you counsel senior adults.

> 1. Challenge the senior adult to consider a variety of alternatives.
> 2. Encourage the senior adult to take sufficient time to explore the outcomes before making a decision.
> 3. Do not make a decision for your counselee.

Case Study

Jim Simpson sat down with **Harriet Bailie** and talked with her about the future. Harriet is a widowed senior adult who owns a very nice house. She wonders what would happen if she were to become ill. Harriet's daughter and her family expressed a willingness to move in with her. She is afraid this would not be best for her daughter's family. However, she believes this is her only alternative.

■ **Assume that you are in Jim Simpson's spot, counseling Harriet. What alternatives would you suggest Harriet consider? What could she do?**

_____

_____

_____

_____

_____

_____

_____

Compare your answers with Jim's on the following page.

Jim responded, "Well, Harriet let's see if we can think about some other options you may want to consider.

1. You could continue to live in your house. It is your home and has many associations. Maybe you could find a compatible companion to share the house with you. You could always provide hospitality for your family or friends. The rental income would help you financially.
2. You mentioned that your daughter had expressed an interest in bringing her family and moving in with you. Make sure that you, your daughter, and her family will be happy with such an arrangement.
3. You might sell your house and move into a retirement village where a variety of services are provided. You will have the association of people your own age.
4. If you are interested in supporting a Christian institution, you could investigate plans whereby you can give them your home while you continue to live in it for the rest of your life. They will care for the maintenance and other aspects of the house."

Many decisions that senior adults face have no simple or easy solutions. Take time and help them process the decision carefully. When faced with helping a senior adult with a decision, your response might be, "There is probably no simple answer to this. Why don't we spend some time looking at the pros and cons? Have you considered these possibilities?"

Days 4 and 5: Life Review Techniques

> **Objective:** You will be able to explain two techniques for ministering to senior adults through Life Review.

Life Review is a counseling method that is particularly helpful to senior adults. Life Review helps senior adults get in touch with their past and find some meaning and purpose for their living. One of the needs of a senior adult is to find a sense that his or her life has made some lasting contribution to others. One nursing home incorporated the Life Review process into every aspect of its activities stating, "creating an accepting climate for Life Review and reminiscence is perhaps the most important way we can further the home's therapeutic milieu." Life Review is much more than escape into the past. It holds tremendous potential for the senior adults who are looking for some meaning for their existence.

■ **In your own words, what is the value of the Life Review Technique?**

_____

_____

_____

_____

_____

Life Review: Autobiography Technique

For some time writing has been recognized as having certain psychological values. Writing one's life story is a valuable experience for a senior adult, but getting around to this task is not as easy as it seems. Napoleon Bonaparte used to say that every French soldier had a marshal's baton in his knapsack. I am equally convinced that a good proportion of the literate population have a book in their heads. Unless a person gets her book written down, it will be of little value to anyone.

One ministry you can have to senior adults is to move their potential book into reality, all the time remembering there may not be much time left. This book may deal with almost any subject you can imagine. For the purpose of finding meaning in the life they have lived, however, senior adults are most likely to benefit from writing an autobiography—their life story.

Provide the basic resources needed for writing. I like an 8½x11 writing pad with holes punched down the left side so the completed pages can be placed in a three-ring binder. You need a writing instrument—pencil, pen, typewriter, or a computer with a word processor. Make sure the senior adult knows how to handle the equipment. Time may be needed to help the person master these skills.

"Where will I begin?" is the common question. Developing an outline is an excellent starting point. Help the person think through all the things he or she wants to include in his/her life story. This will help the senior adult think about many of the topics and events he or she wants to include. It will also help him remember to include the key events in the places they belong.

The following topics are simply suggestions and do not have to be rigidly adhered to. Use them as "pump primers." The senior adult may want to take a separate page for each main point in the outline and list people and events that he or she wants to include. Help them prepare a personalized outline for their autobiography.

Autobiography Outline

1. My ancestors as I remember them.
2. My educational experiences.
3. My childhood friends and playmates.
4. The turning points in my life.
5. My spiritual development.
6. My love and hate history.
7. My family (spouse, children, grandchildren).
8. My career history.
9. My health history.
10. My experiences with death.
11. My crisis history.
12. Accomplishments I am proud of.

These subjects may serve to provide a broad framework for the senior adult. Some may prefer to take a chronological approach. That is okay. Others may need more specific questions to deal with the spiritual dimensions. Here are a few thought provoking questions you may want to ask. These will help the senior adult focus on some specific subjects, he may not have considered otherwise.

Questions for the Life Reviewer

★ Do you feel you have had a calling in the particular occupation you have been in or still are pursuing?

★ How do your Christian convictions influence the way you treat your body?

★ How do you find meaning in illness, suffering, and death?

★ Are you comforted by the idea of life after death, or does it bother you?

★ How does your faith effect the way you deal with money?

★ Can you give some examples of how you've seen God at work in your life?

★ Have you ever had a crisis of faith, a spiritual crisis? How did you deal with it? What was the outcome?

★ Have you had problems in sharing your faith? Can you recall any particularly satisfying experiences?

■ **Briefly describe the autobiography technique for Life Review.**

_____

_____

_____

_____

_____

Just for practice, develop a partial outline of your own life story. Write your outline on a separate sheet of paper.
- **Select three topics from the Autobiography Outline.**
- **Make an outline of your own life story for these three points.**
- **Bring your outline to your group session to share with your triad.**

This is a good place to stop in this two-day lesson. Pick up with the oral history technique tomorrow.

****

Life Review: Oral History Technique

With the realization that older people often have experiences that can be of value for future generations, a new breed of historians has arisen and introduced the concept of "oral history." The historian records on audio tapes the recollections of a particular person about his earlier days. Methods used by these people can be of value in using Life Review Therapy.

To use the oral history technique, you must have a tape recorder with which you are familiar and a supply of cassette tapes. You should begin by building a good relationship with the interviewee. Explain the types of questions you are going to ask. Use the following "Life Review Questions" as an outline for the oral history. Remember that

LIFE REVIEW QUESTIONS[1]

Memories of Family Life and Neighborhoods
1. Would you begin by telling about your earliest memories?
2. What are your favorite memories of your childhood?
3. Could you talk about what life was like when you were young?
4. Can you tell me about your grandparents?
5. Did they or your parents pass on any ideas or teachings which were especially important in your life?
6. Was there a person or group that strongly influenced your life?
7. Would you tell me about it?
8. Could you discuss major turning points in your life?
9. From what events or periods in your life did you learn the most?
10. What can you tell me about changes you've seen in the neighborhoods you've lived in? The city?

The Larger World
1. In your opinion, what period in our history was most interesting?
2. What was life like during major historical events (such as World Wars or the Great Depression)?
3. During your lifetime, you've seen many changes in the world and in the ways people live. What are the most striking changes to you? How do you feel about these changes?
4. What things do you think do not change through time?
5. In your experience, is life more or less difficult now than it was 25 or 50 years ago?
6. What do you think are the major problems we face today? How can young people help solve them? How can older people help solve them?

Personal Philosophy or Spiritual Outlook
1. When you were younger, did you ever have a dream or an aspiration to do or be something special?
2. Would you tell me about it?
3. Do you have any dreams now?
4. How do you feel about growing older?
5. What were your feelings about aging when you were young?
6. How is it different from what you expected?
7. How would you describe the situation of older people in our society today?
8. What role do you think older people should play in society?
9. What advice would you pass on to younger people?
10. Is there anything you have not gotten out of life that you really want?
11. What are your hopes for the future?
12. What has it been like to review your life?

these are just types of questions that could be useful in your work. In the actual interview itself, the questions would be tailored to the individual whom you were interviewing. Interviewing is not easy, but one secret is to learn how to use questions effectively. I hope you have already made some progress in your ability to ask questions since your study of unit 1.

■ **Briefly describe the oral history technique for Life Review.**

_____

_____

_____

_____

_____

Once you get the interview on tape, the major task is accomplished. Consider some of the following uses of the tape:
1. Provide a tape player and the tape for the senior adult to listen to.
2. Make one copy and circulate it to family members of the senior adult.
3. Transcribe the tape, edit it, and put it in a book format.

Even if they are never read or heard by another person, an autobiography or an oral history will have been a highlight experience for the senior adult.

■ **Optional Activity: Use one of the Life Review techniques to help a senior adult review his or her own life. You may want to consider one of your own relatives, so you can find out more about your own "roots." Another person would be one of the senior adults in your church. This technique would be even more meaningful for those who are homebound or in a nursing home. Try it out and report on the results to your WiseCounsel group.**

For Further Study
The following resources may be helpful as you identify ways to help single and senior adults with many of the problems they face.
- *Enduring Triumphantly: Finding Victory Over Chronic Illness* by Ron Goble and Kathy Goble. (0-6330-1857-0)
- *Forward Together: A New Vision for Senior Adult Ministry* compiled by John G. Johnston. (0-7673-3115-X)
- *Grandparenting by Grace* by Irene M. Endicott and C. Ferris Jordan. Nashville: LifeWay Press: 1994. (Member 0-8054-9897-4; Leader 0-8054-9882-6)
- *Recovering from the Losses of Life* by H. Norman Wright. (Member 0-8054-9874-5; Facilitator Guide 0-8054-9873-7)
- *The Single-Adult Ministry Solution* compiled by Tim Cleary. (0-8054-9835-4)
- *Start a Revolution: Nine World-Changing Strategies for Single Adults* by Stephen Felts. (0-8054-9823-0)
- *Strength for the Journey: A Biblical Perspective on Discouragement and Depression* by James P. Porowski and Paul B. Carlisle. (0-7673-9105-5)
- *A Time for Healing: Coming to Terms with Your Divorce* by Harold Ivan Smith (Member 0-8054-9875-3; Facilitator Guide 0-8054-9876-1)
See Page 224 for order information.

UNIT 12

Resentment, Guilt, and Suicide

This Week's Learning Goal

After studying this unit, you will understand ways to counsel people who struggle with resentment, guilt, and thoughts of suicide.

Why You Will Find This Study Useful

The subjects in this unit can be devastating to human personality if not dealt with appropriately. You will learn to help people learn to handle resentment and guilt. As a Christian counselor, you can provide a scriptural remedy to help also. In the last two day's lessons, you will learn to identify and counsel potential suicides.

Day 1: The Resentment Syndrome

> **Today's Objective:** You will be able to identify three reactions of the Resentment Syndrome.

When a professional in the field of family life appears before a lay audience, one question is inevitable: "What is the most important problem faced by people today?" The audience awaits the answer. Is it sex, finances, in-law difficulties, management of children? If I were compelled to answer this question, I would take the plunge and say unhesitatingly: The most important problem faced by people today is resentment.

Resentment is seldom talked about. Virtually no books have been written on the subject. An examination of the indexes of books on marriage counseling show they, too, are strangely silent. The one group of workers with a lot to say on the subject is the leaders of self-help groups. These nonprofessionals working very effectively with some of the most stubborn personality problems like alcoholism, drug addiction, and criminal propensities, see resentment as a vital factor in the personalities of these people.

One of the reasons professionals have said so little about resentment is that it is not easily described. It is not just a single entity but rather a whole group of related reactions that could more accurately be described as a syndrome. The Resentment Syndrome is a combination of reactions representing some of the most destructive forces seen in human personality today. Let's examine three of those reactions today.

The Invisible Wall

In the city of Berlin, a wall divides East Berlin from West Berlin. It was built by the East Germans, not to keep the enemy out, but to keep the people in. At Checkpoint Charlie, the entrance to the city of East Berlin, that wall snakes its way between the artificially divided cities separating houses, neighbors, and families.

The wall of resentment, though not visible to the eye, is just as effective a barrier in human relations. Two people can live in the same house, walk the same carpets, and even sleep in the same bed. Yet, they can have an invisible wall between them. The wall has been built a block at a time by resentments until it has become a primary obstruction to communication.

■ **Read the principle stated by Jesus in Luke 11:17. If you apply this principle to the invisible wall resentment builds, what does it say about the results of resentment in a relationship?**

_____

_____

_____

GD'S WORD

D WISDOM

Looking the Wrong Way

Angel Sparkman was vividly aware of the past. Her husband Al was the eternal optimist—particularly at the card table. Gambling always held a strange fascination for him. When his company sent him to a convention in Las Vegas, he took with him the $5,000 he and Angel had saved toward remodeling their house. Of course he had not bothered to mention the matter to Angel. Like so many other wooers of Lady Luck, after a good beginning, he finally lost it all. He didn't tell Angel for some weeks. When she finally saw the bank statement and demanded to know the whereabouts of the money, he tried to excuse his behavior by saying he might have easily doubled their money.

As much as they tried they could never accumulate that much money again. As Angel watched her friends moving into their new houses or remodeling their old homes, she became more frustrated. Angel described her reactions, "Whenever we have a difference and start arguing, I immediately think of Al's irresponsibility at Las Vegas."

Backward looks in life, particularly in the marriage relationship, can be dangerous. They are examples of resentment. The word resentment comes from two Latin words and literally means "to feel back." It ushers in a crippling condition in the sphere of relationships.

■ **Paul gave some counsel to Christians that could be applied to the Resentment Syndrome. Read Philippians 3:13-14 and write a summary of his counsel.**

GOD'S WOR
AND WISDC

_____

_____

You must help your counselee see what is happening in resentment and learn to put the past behind him and look to the future.

Imprisoned

Let's face it, resentment is self-defeating. The Seven Steppers, an organization founded to help rehabilitate convicts, certainly understand this self-defeating aspect of resentment. Appropriately for convicts, their program of action is stated in the form of an acrostic using the word FREEDOM. Each word in the acrostic represents one of the seven steps the group uses.

In many ways the crux of the problem is contained in the fifth step: "Deciding our freedom is worth more than our resentments, we are using that Power to help us free ourselves from these resentments." Resentment presents a major problem for the convict. Leaving prison with a chip on his shoulder, he is vulnerable, overreacts, makes an impulsive move, gets into trouble with the law, and finishes up back in the penitentiary once again.

Married or single, the person who nurses a resentment is just as much a prisoner as the inhabitant of the penitentiary. The main difference is the nature of the prison. Rather than bricks and mortar, resentment is an emotional wall that just as effectively incarcerates the resentful person.

■ **In Ephesians 4:31-32 Paul gives a command to Christians. What is that command?**

_____

GOD'S WORD
AND WISDOM

Using the three pictures as clues, list the three reactions I described in the Resentment Syndrome.

_____   _____   _____

Day 2: Handling Resentment

> **Today's Objective:** You will be able to describe a way to help a counselee overcome resentment.

> "The discretion of a man deferreth his anger;
> and it is his glory to pass over a transgression."
> —Proverbs 19:11, KJV

Continuing on yesterday's discussion of resentment we will notice two more considerations, along with a plan of action for handling the difficult Resentment Syndrome.

Reactive or Proactive?

Possibly the most frustrating single aspect of resentment is that life seems to be out of our own hands and under the control of someone else. We then react with resentment toward that person. Gordon Allport, one of America's leading psychologists, has charged his fellow psychologists with being forever preoccupied with the "re" words—reflex, reaction, response. These words indicate a passive condition. Allport suggests the time has come for an emphasis on the "pro" words—programming, proceeding, promise. Resentment is life lived at the reactive level. To help with the Resentment Syndrome you need to emphasize:

NOT: Reflex, Reaction, or Response
BUT: Programming, Proceeding, Promise

With a reactive approach to life, a person allows the actions of others to greatly influence his or her own feelings and actions. The individual reacts or responds to another's actions.

June, for example, has a reactive approach to life. When her coworkers tease about her weight she laughs, but inside she boils with anger. She hates her work because of the resentment she carries for those coworkers. Her reactive approach to living allows her coworkers to "control" her feelings about her work.

Doctors have long noted the way our emotions affect our bodies. The manner in which we react to others can be an action of self-destruction. The noted eighteenth century Scottish physician, John Hunter, who suffered with angina pectoris, once remarked, "My life is in the hands of any rascal who chooses to annoy or tease me." Ironically he predicted the precise circumstances of his own death. At a medical board meeting Hunter got into an argument with a colleague who contradicted him. He was so enraged that he stormed out of the room and dropped dead.

But why should we put ourselves into someone else's hands? We must learn to take control of our own lives. We need to be proactive rather than reactive.

We must act instead of react.

With a proactive approach to life, a person does not allow his or her feelings to be dictated or controlled by others. The individual decides to initiate a positive action that avoids or overcomes the destructive or hurtful actions of others.

■ **How do you think June (in the example above) could use a proactive approach to cope more effectively with the teasing of her coworkers?**

_____

_____

_____

_____

June cannot afford to live with resentment forty hours a week. She would be using a proactive approach if she decided to lose weight and take away the object of their teasing. She could decide that she is satisfied with her weight and just ignore their teasing. She could apply for a transfer or look for a new job. She could approach her coworkers one at a time, explain her sensitivity about her weight, and ask each one politely not to tease her any more. By taking action to avoid or overcome a problem, June, not her coworkers, is in control of her life. This is a proactive approach to life.

■ **Summarize the approach a counselee should take in dealing with resentment by describing these two options:**

REACTIVE: _____

_____

PROACTIVE: _____

_____

Case Study: Carla's parents died and left their estate to their two children. Carla's brother Ralph received a much larger share of the estate. He was given all the household furnishings in addition to one half of the estate. After a legal bout, Ralph's inheritance was upheld.

Label Carla's possible approaches to her feelings of resentment as either reactive or proactive.

_____ a. **Carla decides that family relationships are far more valuable than material possessions. She plans a family reunion so she can demonstrate to Ralph that she is not going to hold a grudge.**

_____ b. **Carla snubs her brother and, for all practical purposes, breaks off any relationship with him. By avoiding him, she does not have to think about her ill feelings very often.**

Carla can choose to be reactive or proactive in dealing with her feelings of resentment. Her reactive approach in *b* does not resolve the problem; it merely hides it temporarily. In *a* Carla takes a proactive approach. She will struggle at the reunion to overcome her resentment. The positive demonstration of her love and acceptance of Ralph will help her begin to cope with her feelings of resentment.

Practice Forgiveness

One action a person can take against the Resentment Syndrome is to intentionally practice forgiveness. This action is imperative for a healing of a broken relationship.

■ **Read each of the following Scriptures. Write a statement summarizing what the verses say to a person suffering from the Resentment Syndrome.**

GOD'S WORD AND WISDOM

Matthew 5:23, 24 _____

Matthew 7:1-5 _____

Matthew 18:21-35 _____

Luke 17:3-4 _____

Colossians 3:12-13 _____

Forget

You have probably heard the instruction, "Forgive and forget." The two go together. Some would suggest that continuing to remember a wrong may be an indication that the forgiveness was not genuine.

The philosopher Kant discovered that his trusted servant Lampe had systematically robbed him over a period of years. Although he needed Lampe desperately, he discharged his servant and wrote in his journal, "Remember to forget Lampe." Handling the Resentment Syndrome calls for decisiveness!

Clara Barton, the founder of the American Red Cross, also learned this lesson. A friend of Miss Barton asked her about a particularly traumatic event in her life. Miss Barton seemed perplexed.

"Can't you remember?"

Miss Barton replied, "I distinctly remember forgetting it."

Case Study

Althia Murray was expecting her second child. At thirty-nine years of age, she was justly apprehensive. Just three weeks from the anticipated delivery date, her husband Harry came home with the news that the boss wanted him to take some clients to their hunting lodge in Canada for a few days. Harry kept assuring her that the baby would not come early. Althia reluctantly agreed for him to go. The day after his departure, she went into a hard and difficult labor. Just at the moment when she needed him most, Harry was hunting in Canada.

Althia could not forget those terrible days. As she related, "I know all the reasons why I should forget this incident. I'm aware that any mention of it will hurt my relationship with my husband. But some foolish little thing will spark my memory—a word, a name, a sound and my head becomes like a movie, one scene after another. Then, before you can turn around, I am pouring out my hostility and reminding him of all the details of the things we desperately need to forget."

Stop and Think Technique

Althia talked her problems over with a counselor. They decided to use the "Stop and Think" technique. She secured a card headed "Resentment Reducer." On this card she filled in the statement of her problem. "Harry was hunting when I needed him most." She then entered six good points about Harry.

Resentment Reducer

Problem: Harry was hunting when I needed him most

━━━━ STOP ━━━━

THINK: 1. Harry provides for our financial needs.

2. Harry is a die-hard romantic.

3. Harry is gentle and kind.

4. Harry is adventurous – fun to be with.

5. Harry has a great sense of humor.

6. Harry likes my family.

Althia carries the card in her pocketbook. The moment the thought of Harry and his hunting comes into her mind she goes into action. She:

a. Removes the card and looks at it.
b. Concentrates on "STOP"—says it out loud.
c. Reads and concentrates on the six good points about Harry.

The counselor has introduced Althia to an effective way of handling resentment. By using this technique, she breaks the resentment cycle and mentally shifts gears. The chain of negative thinking is deliberately broken by injecting positive ideas. These positive ideas are incompatible with an anxious state of mind and help to extinguish the undesirable response.

'S WORD

WISDOM

■ 1. **Paul encouraged the Philippians with a similar technique. Read Philippians 4:8 and list the things Paul suggests that we think on.**

_____

_____

_____

2. **We have discussed several ways to handle resentment. Using the following words as reminders, describe a way for a person to overcome the Resentment Syndrome. Reminders: Proactive, Forgive, Forget, Stop and Think.**

_____

_____

_____

_____

_____

_____

_____

_____

_____

Day 3: Handling Guilt

> **Today's Objective:** You will be able to list actions for a counselee to take in handling a guilty conscience.

Covering Violations Brings Discomfort

Guilt can goad us on to becoming the best we can be; or it can drain us of mental, emotional, and physical energy. In the experience of David, we see the way in which this blackmailer works: "When I kept silent my bones wasted away through my groaning all day long," Psalm 32:3. The natural, but self-defeating, behavior of people who violate their values is to cover up their failures. These secrets frequently have a destructive effect as the secretive person not only conceals the matter from others but also from himself. David's penitent thirty-second Psalm lays down some specific principles for dealing successfully with guilt.

■ **Read Psalm 32.**

■ ■ ■ ■ ■

GOD'S WORD

AND WISDOM

Keep your Bible open as we examine David's remedy.

1. Accept Responsibility—Confess the Sin

"I acknowledged my sin to you and did not cover up my iniquity" (Ps. 32:5).

David could have spent time excusing or justifying his behavior. When David spoke about the situation, however, he did not engage in blaming Bathsheba or rationalizing his behavior. When Nathan said, "You are the man," David immediately responded, "I have sinned," (2 Sam. 12:7-13). Accepting responsibility is the first big step in handling guilt.

■ **Which step in the Ten-Step Counseling Model relates to this action?**

   Step #_____: _____

Openness about our sins, failures, and shortcomings is the way back to wholeness. Just as hiding violations of our values brings on difficulties, so openness is the way back. This experience may be called self-disclosure, openness, or even confession. It is a biblical concept.

■ 1. **Read and summarize the following Scriptures.**

   Matthew 5:23-24 _____

   _____

   James 5:16 _____

   _____

   1 John 1:9 _____

   _____

GOD'S W

AND WIS

   2. **Write the first action one should take in handling guilt.**

   _____

In step 5 of the Ten-Step Model, you challenge the counselee to assume responsibility for his own actions. This is one place in counseling where confession of wrong may be dealt with. Sin against God must be confessed to Him, and He promises forgiveness (1 John 1:9). When we sin against our fellow man we must seek his forgiveness as well (Matt. 5:23-24). The first action one should take in handling guilt is to assume responsibility and confess the sin.

2. Restitution Is a Vital Step in Responsible Living

David's response to the story told by Nathan contains an interesting statement. He blazed with indignation at the action of the rich man taking his neighbor's ewe lamb. David said, "The man who did this thing deserves to die! He must pay for that lamb four times over" (2 Sam. 12:5-6). David was making reference to the principle of restitution. In its application to animals the principle said, "If a man steals an ox or a sheep and slaughters it or sells it, he must pay back five head of cattle for the ox and four sheep for the sheep," (Ex. 22:1).

The application to humans is, "When a man or woman wrongs another in any way, and so is unfaithful to the Lord, that person is guilty and must confess the sin for his wrong, add one fifth to it and give it all to the person he has wronged," (Num. 5:6-7).

Most of us have not paid very much attention to this important principle, although Alcoholics Anonymous certainly has. AA asks individuals to list all the persons he or she has harmed. Then the individual is challenged to become willing to make amends to them. Whenever possible, the alcoholic is to make direct amends to these people.

Of course we do not undertake an act of restitution to obtain forgiveness. Forgiveness of sin comes only through faith in Christ. However, many people maintain, "I don't feel forgiven." The reason for this could be that they may need to make restitution. We all need to go through an experience of "putting back," that shows the reality of our experience of forgiveness.

Although restitution is mentioned more frequently in the Old Testament than in the New Testament, the New Testament contains a beautiful example of the application of the restitution principle. Zacchaeus the covetous tax collector had met Jesus and committed himself to become a disciple.

■ **Read Luke 19:1-9. What restitution did Zacchaeus promise to make?**

_____

_____

Zacchaeus was not going to add just the one fifth of the ill-gotten gains to his victims as the law demanded. He was restoring the money fourfold. Zacchaeus realized he would be unable to trace many of the people he had cheated. He promised to give half his goods to the poor. He knew he could never live a satisfactory life as a follower of Jesus if he did not do something to repay the people he had hurt.

In a sense, making restitution is a positive confession. It can be a significant step in abundant living. If restitution is not possible, an individual needs to seek and accept God's forgiveness. Individuals also need to understand that restitution alone cannot get rid of guilt. Restitution must be accompanied by forgiveness.

■ **Write two actions to take in dealing with guilt.**

  1. _____

  2. _____

An Experience of Well-Being Emerges

In response to the accusation, "Thou art the man," David made his statement; "I have sinned." Then he heard the words of the prophet declaring, "The Lord has taken away your sin," (2 Sam. 12:13). David could then speak from experience: "Blessed is he whose transgressions are forgiven" (Ps. 32:1).

One of the outcomes of accepting responsibility, becoming open, and making restitution is a feeling of well-being. What makes a person feel good? Honesty, for one thing. With nothing to hide, he looks his fellows in the eye and has a warm sense of well-being.

The thirty-second Psalm begins on a sad introspective note as David recounts the agony of a guilty conscience. As the psalm progresses to the last verse, David's spirit begins to lift; and it ends in a shout of joy!

■ **In summary describe each of the following from today's study:**

   1. **The problem of guilt:** _____

   _____

   _____

   _____

   2. **Two actions to take in handling guilt:**

      a. _____

      b. _____

   3. **The results of experiencing forgiveness:** _____

   _____

   _____

   _____

As you counsel, watch for the symptoms of a guilty conscience. Then work with the counselee to accept responsibility for his actions, confess his sin, and decide to make restitution where possible. A clear conscience truly is a blessing.

Day 4: Identifying Suicidal Individuals

> **Today's Objective:** You will be able to list the warning signs of a potential suicide.

The whole idea of suicide seems to be a glaring contradiction to the fundamental drive of human personality. The basic human drive is toward survival. However, we must remember that unfortunate forces are running against these concepts of the value of life. As Christian counselors committed to the idea of the worth and value of each individual, we must stand ready to help people who, for a variety of reasons, may be contemplating suicide.

Who Are the Potential Suicides?

Statistics show that the people who are most likely to commit suicide are in the following order:

1. elderly white males
2. American Indians
3. physicians
4. dentists
5. adolescents
6. college students
7. alcoholics
8. drug addicts
9. homosexuals

You may be surprised to know that the typical successful suicide victim is an older white male eighty-five years of age or older. To help meet the challenge of this situation we will need to mobilize an army of helpers, particularly peers of the potential suicide. Never have we needed to be more aware that we are our brother's keeper. To accomplish this you will have to be sensitive to signals that might be indicators of suicide.

Indicators of a Potential Suicide

You should be aware of the following indicators in deciding if your counselee is contemplating suicide:

1. A previous attempt. Of all the people who complete an act of suicide, 45% have previously attempted suicide. As a counselor, you should investigate whether your counselee has tried this before. If he has, you will be alert to any of the signs of a new attempt.

2. Preparing for death. The subject may begin to spend a disproportionate amount of time "putting things in order." Adolescents have been known to distribute their most precious possessions when they are contemplating suicide. Any action that could be interpreted as a preparation for death should be carefully noted.

■ **List two indicators of a potential suicide.**

1. _____

2. _____

3. Acquiring a means for a possible suicide attempt. The individual who has never owned a gun may purchase a weapon, a large number of sleeping pills, or other materials that could be used in a suicide attempt. These acquisitions may be indicators of some of the ideas in his mind.

4. Isolation and withdrawal. The subject begins to isolate himself and withdraw from the circles in which he previously moved.

■ **List four indicators of a potential suicide.**

1. _____
2. _____
3. _____
4. _____

5. Composes a suicide note. A person may put together a note in which he explains why he decided on the act. Apparently this is important for many people who feel that once the true facts about his circumstances are revealed, others will be filled with remorse or admiration for the victim. He may write a couple of versions which may be left around. If someone finds this note, the subject may joke about it and say he never really meant it. Discount this levity. Remember that if a person went to the trouble of writing this down, he should be observed carefully.

■ **List five indicators of a potential suicide.**

1. _____
2. _____
3. _____
4. _____
5. _____

6. Big changes in behavior patterns. Any sudden or dramatic changes in behavior may be an indicator of an underlying difficulty that may lead to suicide.

■ **List six indicators of a potential suicide.**

1. _____
2. _____
3. _____
4. _____
5. _____
6. _____

7. Verbal Clues. As the individual talks, he may make statements such as, "I've had it." "I'm through." "I have sometimes wondered about ending it all." Although these statements may be stated as "kidding" or "only joking," take them seriously and encourage him to keep on talking. You might even say, "I wonder why you said that?"

> No one of these seven clues may be enough in itself to indicate an impending suicide. The moment several of these emerge, you should interpret this as a warning.

■ **List all seven indicators of a potential suicide.**

1. _____

2. _____

3. _____

4. _____

5. _____

6. _____

7. _____

Day 5: Counseling a Suicidal Individual

> **Today's Objective:** You will be able to apply the steps to take in counseling a suicidal individual.

Fred Harris belonged to the same Keen Agers group at the church as Gene Simpson. Gene was an enthusiastic participant in most of the activities but has not been to any of their meetings lately. Noticing this absence, Fred decided to call on Gene and arrived at the house to be met by Gene's daughter Marjorie. Marjorie, obviously pleased to see one of her father's friends coming by, told Fred how glad she was to see him. She confided that she was worried about her father. He just sat and looked at television all the time.

As Fred talked with Gene he noticed a big change in his friend's attitudes. Gene made statements like, "My daughter and her family don't really understand me. I don't think anybody would miss me if I weren't here. I sometimes wonder if life is worth living."

Gene continued, "I had forgotten about my dues to the Keen Agers, would you mind taking them? Would you be able to take me by the bank? I need to check on my insurance policy."

What should Fred do? A plan for action would include some of the following steps:

1. Turn the Conversation to a Focus on the Subject of Suicide.

We immediately notice one of the differences between social conversation and counseling. In social conversation you follow the lead of your friend. If he just wants to hint then leave the topic, you let them out. But in counseling you are trying to help. Once the subject of suicide has been hinted or raised, it is open for discussion. This discussion deals with the matter of life and death.

■ **If you were Fred trying to counsel Gene, how would you turn the conversation to focus on the subject of suicide? Write a description of what you would do.**

_____

_____

_____

_____

_____

Fred might say, "I'm concerned about you Gene. You know I really do enjoy fellowship with you and so do the people at the Keen Agers. Many of them wanted to be remembered to you. I was surprised and concerned when you spoke about life not being worth living. Why don't you tell me more."

2. Try a Modeling Technique.

I once listened to a presentation by a fine minister of the gospel. He described an experience he had when he was returning from admitting his wife to a psychiatric ward at the hospital. As he drove past a lake, he began to wonder about ending his life by driving his car into the lake. He rebuked himself, "No, that wouldn't be right and it would hurt a great number of people." The response of the group to this brave man was terrific. Sharing an experience of your own sense of inadequacy can be a very effective way of helping people. Your counselee realizes others have had a struggle with similar ideas.

■ **Has the thought of suicide ever crossed your mind, even briefly? If so, write a brief description of your experience and how you handled those thoughts.**

_____

_____

_____

_____

_____

If you do not have an experience of your own where you can model the role (step 6 in the Ten-Step Model), you can use the story of one of the biblical characters below who struggled with thoughts about death. Select one of these men. Read the passage that describes his struggle. Then write a brief summary of his struggles.

- Elijah—1 Kings 19:1-8   • Jonah—Jonah 3:10—4:11
- Moses—Numbers 11:10-35   • Job—Job 7

_____

_____

_____

_____

_____

3. Explain That Most People Experience Some Periods of Depression.

People can work through periods of depression and remain creative and productive people. You can relate the story of Rubenstein, a Russian pianist and composer, who died at 95 after a brilliant career. When he was 20 years old he tried to hang himself but failed. He then went on to his greatest accomplishment. Who knows what the future might hold.

■ **Write a brief explanation about depression for Fred to use in counseling Gene.**

_____
_____
_____
_____
_____

4. Listen Carefully to All the Individual Has to Say.

As we have discussed in other units, talking through one's problems has a therapeutic affect. Give your counselee a chance to verbalize his fears and hurts. Listen actively.

5. Help Him Build a New Network of Relationships.

You will not be able to stay with this person all the time. He or she needs new or renewed relationships that provide a support system for the person. The church is a fine resource for us to use. Sunday School classes and other smaller groups associated with the church can help form this network.

■ **Make a list of the kinds of new or renewed relationships Fred could help Gene develop.**

_____
_____
_____
_____
_____

6. Confront the Illusionary Notion of Death.

Somehow some strange ideas have developed across the years about the nature of death. A picture has been painted that is often far from the reality of the situation. Consider:
• Snow White, so beautifully laid out and awaiting a kiss from a handsome prince
• the heroic figure Socrates drinking his hemlock
• the modern mortician emphasizing that death is a restful sleep

While there is life, changes can be made. Death is irreversible. One pertinent comment is: "Suicide is a permanent solution to a temporary problem."

As you talk with a potential suicide, tear down the notion of death as sweet restful sleep. Lead the person to face the reality, finality, and harshness of death.

■ **Write a description of death that points out the reality, finality, and harshness of death.**

_____

_____

_____

_____

_____

_____

Keep in mind that the Bible does talk about the glories of heaven, about death as sleep or rest, and about the coming resurrection of the dead. However, God does not intend for persons to take their own lives (Ex. 20:13). Suicide is not a justifiable way to get away from a problem. People may need your help to see other alternatives.

7. Involve Others in the Situation.

The suicidal person may try to swear you to secrecy—don't do it. Grave questions have been raised about the counselor making commitments to never tell anything about what is said to him or her. Confidentiality is not the same sacred cow as we formerly made it out to be. If your suicidal friend says, "If I tell you, will you promise not to tell anyone?" One answer might be, "I am sorry but I cannot commit myself. If it is necessary for your own good to share something with some other person, I'm afraid I will have to tell."

You may need to discreetly involve some other friends or family members in the situation so that there are a number of concerned individuals watching and ready to help.

■ **Think about the counseling situation between Fred and Gene. Place a check beside those people you would involve in the situation.**
   ☐ **Marjorie, Gene's daughter**
   ☐ **Marjorie's husband**
   ☐ **Others in Marjorie's family**
   ☐ **Gene's pastor**
   ☐ **Close friends in the Keen Agers group**
   ☐ **Gene's Sunday School Teacher**

   How would you go about involving them. Write out an action plan on a separate sheet of paper and bring it to your group session.

Any of the people listed would be appropriate to involve in given situations. You most certainly would want to include Marjorie, her husband, and perhaps even her family. They live with Gene day in and day out. Remember the approach I recommended for family counseling? Get the whole family, including Gene, together to tackle the problems. Lead them to take specific actions that can improve Gene's sense of being needed and loved.

8. Make a Verbal Contract with the Person.

Bill Blackburn, in his excellent book, *What You Should Know About Suicide,* points out that the suicidal person can sometimes be very convincing in stating that he now feels better and is abandoning his ideas about suicide. Blackburn suggests the person commit himself not to make any attempt without first contacting you or someone else. He suggests this form of the contract:

"I will contact you or _____, if I begin thinking about taking my life. Even if I have trouble reaching you, I will keep on until I have talked to one of you about these thoughts of suicide."[1]

■ **How frequently do you think you should use this technique of making a contract with suicidal persons. Check your opinion.**
  ☐ **In every case.**
  ☐ **In almost every case.**
  ☐ **In some cases.**
  ☐ **Never. It is not important.**

I asked for your opinion. Now, I want to give you mine. I would encourage you to use this contract in every case of a potential suicide. Even if the person jokes about it and claims that he did not seriously consider suicide, make him agree to the contract. You do not want to take any chances.

9. Try a Thought Stopping Technique.

Refer back to day 2 (p. 192) where you learned about the Stop and Think Technique. This technique is equally effective with the suicidal person.

■ **Describe one way Fred could use this technique with Gene.**

_____

_____

_____

_____

_____

_____

Review the nine steps for counseling a suicidal person. You will discuss your responses to today's activities in your small-group session this week. Then you will apply them to another case study.

> **For Further Study**
> ☐ *What You Should Know About Suicide* by Bill Blackburn. Waco: Word, Incorporated 1982.
> ☐ *Fatal Choice: The Teenage Suicide Crisis* by John Baucom. Chicago: Moody Press, 1986.

UNIT 13
Counseling Through Group Experiences

This Week's Learning Goal

After studying this unit, you will understand ways to use counseling and support groups to minister to human needs.

Why You Will Find This Study Useful

You can multiply your ministry by working with a group of people who share a common need. Many people need the fellowship and accountability a support group can provide. You will discover ways to start counseling and support groups in your church to minister to a wide variety of common human needs.

Day 1: Spectators or Participators?

> **Today's Objective:** You will be able to select appropriate guidelines that foster growth in group experiences.

Developing Participators

Contemporary Christianity is beset by a serious problem. We have turned into a generation of spectator Christians. One of the ways we can reverse this undesirable trend is to involve people in group experiences. Notice the value the writer of Hebrews placed on Christians working and meeting together:

> "Let us consider how we may spur one another on toward love and good deeds. Let us not give up meeting together, as some are in the habit of doing, but let us encourage one another" (Heb. 10:24-25).

GOD'S WORD AND WISDOM

■ **Read Hebrews 10:24-25 again. How can we help each other?**

_____

_____

We can encourage one another. We can stimulate or spur each other toward love for others and love for God. We can challenge each other to do good deeds. We need each other for mature Christian discipleship. Group settings can work to bring out the best in people. That is one reason the church is so important. The writer of Hebrews told his readers not to neglect meeting together.

■ **Think about the past thirteen weeks you have met with your WiseCounsel group. What are some of the ways the group sessions have helped you most?**

_____

_____

_____

_____

I do hope your group experience has been a very positive and growing experience. Group experiences can have a powerful impact on people's lives. These experiences can help a person change his or her attitudes, values, and behaviors. Often you can accomplish in a group things you cannot do through individual counseling. Self-help groups like Weight Watchers accomplish significant changes in peoples lives (and bodies). When you add the activity of God into a church-related group experience, life-changing power is present. This week we will focus on the idea of using groups in counseling.

Many people are apprehensive about getting involved in group techniques, so we will approach cautiously an area in which you are already partially familiar. You will learn to use group processes in counseling. You will learn to use Bible study experiences to help people determine biblically based action plans to address their problems.

Group Experiences Can Be Life-Changing

When John Wesley, the founder of Methodism, began his spiritual quest, he tried the solitary way. He found that way did not achieve his spiritual objective. At one stage of his quest, he heard about a godly man named Rev. Hoyle. Wesley went to this man's home and poured out the story of his unsatisfactory solitary spiritual quest. The minister heard him out and then responded, "Sir, you are to serve God and go to heaven. Remember you cannot serve Him alone; you must, therefore, find companions or make them; the Bible knows nothing of solitary religion."[1]

When Wesley's much sought after spiritual experience finally came, it took place while he was with a group of people meeting on Aldersgate Street. He said, "I felt my heart was strangely warmed, I felt I did trust in Christ alone for my salvation." When Wesley began to lead converts to mature spiritually, he developed a group process to assist their development. A number of valuable features of group life become clear after examining the procedures of the groups in the early Wesleyan movement.

Distinctives of Early Wesleyan Group Life

1. They Recognized the Importance of Individual Differences. They provided group experiences at various levels of maturity. Churches need to consciously realize people need a variety of experience opportunities. One way is to provide group counseling experiences for those who can benefit most from such an approach.

- ■ **Check the guideline that best applies this lesson from Wesleyan groups.**
  - ☐ A. **Decide on one good group process and encourage everyone to become involved.**
  - ☐ B. **Provide a variety of group opportunities so people can participate in one that best meets their needs and preferences.**

2. They Utilized Different Patterns of Leadership. At the one level the group functioned under his unquestioned control of the leader. The leader used the lecture method as he addressed himself to the group as a whole. He aimed at information and inspiration. Very little interchange took place. These groups were called "Societies."

The leader of the "Class Meeting" talked to members concerning their behavior. Periodically the leader would be moved to different groups so that a greater number of individuals would be influenced by the gifted leader. In the "Band" the leader was called on to exercise special skills. He had to lead the group by speaking of his own spiritual state first of all. He modeled confession and openness for the group to follow. His capacity to be open was of primary importance. The leader was to be both a model and a facilitator.

At the level of the "Select Society," the leader was more of a moderator. Apparently a leader was not really necessary as the group members interacted with each other.

■ Check the guideline that best applies this lesson from Wesleyan groups.
　□ A.　All group leaders should use the same approach to group leadership.
　□ B.　Group leaders should adjust their leadership style to the needs and maturity of the group.

A good leader must be versatile. We cannot do all our work with one single skill. In different situations the leader goes about his work by using different techniques.

3. Self-disclosure Was Important. Members were encouraged to talk openly and honestly about their own spiritual lives. Wesley suffered much criticism because of his commitment to confession. Despite the problems it brought, Wesley continued to insist on the procedure and answered all the complaints with convincing arguments.

■ Check the guideline that best applies this lesson from Wesleyan groups.
　□ A.　Encourage members to talk about application of a truth to their personal lives.
　□ B.　In your discussions, deal with facts not personal feelings.

4. Laypeople Gained Importance. Though an Anglican clergyman, Wesley gradually gave a larger place to laypeople and used them in his groups. As radical as it seemed in his day, he also used women as leaders in his groups.

■ Check the guideline that best applies this lesson from Wesleyan groups.
　□ A.　Use laypeople as group leaders.
　□ B.　Use only professional counselors and seminary-trained staff members as group leaders.

5. Wesley Trained the Leaders. Since most group leaders were laypersons, Wesley provided regular opportunities for the training and updating of his leaders. He knew the groups could not achieve their purposes without leaders who knew what to do and how to do it.

■ Check the guideline that best applies this lesson from Wesleyan groups.
　□ A.　Give your leaders a book and put them to work immediately.
　□ B.　Provide adequate training programs to equip group leaders for their jobs.

6. Some Groups Became Stagnant and Spiritually Sterile. This should serve as a warning to us. Like an individual, a group may have an agonizing struggle to come to birth. After a precarious infancy it grows into vigorous youth. During youth, it may make many mistakes and act impulsively, but it eventually functions at the peak of its capacity. By middle age, it settles down to enjoy the comforts of its achievements. The settling continues, often leading to a lingering senility and finally death. Groups must go through a constant process of reorganization, or they will stagnate and become a liability to your church rather than an asset.

■ Check the guideline that best applies this lesson from Wesleyan groups.
　□ A.　Help groups to begin, mature, end, and begin again.
　□ B.　Do everything possible to keep groups going indefinitely.

The guidelines you should have identified are 1-B; 2-B; 3-A; 4-A; 5-B; 6-A. Here is a summary of guidelines that apply the lessons learned from a study of the successful Wesleyan groups.

Guidelines for Groups

1. Provide a variety of group opportunities so people can participate in one that best meets their needs and preferences.
2. Group leaders should adjust their leadership style to the needs and maturity of the group.
3. Encourage members to talk about application of a truth to their personal lives.
4. Use laypeople as group leaders.
5. Provide adequate training programs to equip group leaders for their jobs.
6. Help groups to begin, mature, end, and begin again.

Day 2: Counseling and Support Groups in the Church

Today's Objective: You will be able to outline and describe a plan for starting a support group in your church.

Your counseling ministry can be multiplied many times over by your involvement in group counseling experiences. Your church might even want to use groups as an outreach ministry of the church. Let's look at ways you can start counseling and support groups in your church.

Identify the Needs

In the secular world, groups form based on a common need. People who want to lose weight join Weight Watchers or Overeaters Anonymous. Alcoholics join Alcoholics Anonymous and their families join Al-Anon. An Alzheimer's Disease Support Group provides group counseling and support for families where one member has Alzheimer's Disease. Needy people join a support group because of a need in their lives.

Your pastor, church council, or other church leaders may want to survey the needs of the congregation. If a number of people have common needs, consider forming a short-term support group. Needs may be related to a common problem like coping with cancer treatment. A common need might also be more positive like singles who are preparing for marriage. The common need might also be job related like nurses trying to live their faith on the job. The deciding factor would be: Would the people with this common need benefit by getting together regularly to discuss their common concerns?

■ Read through this list and circle the kinds of people in your church for which a counseling and support group might be helpful.

Cancer Patients	College Students
Diabetics	Divorced Persons
Expectant Mothers	Foster Parents
Homemakers	International Students
New Baptists	New Christians
New Church Members	New Parents
Newcomers to the Community	Nurses
Parents	Parents Who Have Lost Children by Death
Parents with Gifted Children	Parents with Retarded Children
Retired Citizens	School Teachers
Single Parents	Singles Preparing for Marriage
Step Families	Step Parents
Unemployed Persons	Widows
Working Women	Youth with Divorced Parents

What other groups of people can you think of that might benefit from a counseling or support group?

_____

_____

_____

_____

_____

What person, committee, or group would be responsible for deciding what kinds of support groups your church might consider?

_____

Select and Train a Leader

Once the need for a counseling and support group is established, search for a leader or leaders for the group. Where possible, choose a leader who has been successful in living with or through the problems on which the group will focus. The leader needs to have basic counseling skills like you have received in your study of WiseCounsel. Therefore, WiseCounsel graduates would be a good place to start looking for a leader. The leader also needs to feel comfortable serving as a facilitator of group discussions.

Depending on the type of group, the leader may need to do some specialized study before getting started. This special study might include a study of group dynamics or Scriptures related to moral or ethical issues involved. Books and resource people related to the subject area may also prove to be invaluable. For instance, a leader of a support group for adults with aging parents may want to study about nursing home care and housing for the elderly.

■ Would you be interested in serving as a leader of a counseling and support group? If so, what kind? For whom?

YES—NO For: _____

■ **If you listed a group, what kind of additional training do you think would be helpful for you to prepare for leadership of the group?**

_____

_____

_____

_____

_____

Enlist the Group Members

Use a variety of publicity methods to invite persons to participate—newsletter articles, worship service announcements, newspaper ads, letters, phone calls, personal visits, and so forth. Target your invitation to the common need the group will address. Explain that the group will try to identify common problems, needs, and concerns and discover ways to successfully deal with them in a Christian manner. Membership should be voluntary and for a specified length of time.

Size of the group is an important factor. Discussion groups should be limited to twelve persons at most. Eight to ten is an ideal size. If you have a large number of interested people, you may want to plan for a large group time for lectures, films, and so forth. Then divide into small groups of 4 to 8 for more intimate discussion. These smaller groups should include the same people from one meeting to the next.

■ **Check the maximum size for a discussion type support group.**
   □ a. Four
   □ b. Twelve
   □ c. Twenty
   □ d. As many as the room will hold.

   Explain in your own words how you could effectively provide a support group for a large number of people?

   _____

   _____

You can provide an effective group for a large number of people, but only if they divide into small groups for their discussion and sharing times. Trust and openness cannot develop effectively in a large group. Also, many people would not have opportunity to participate actively in a large group. The maximum number for a discussion group is twelve. Fewer would be even better.

Start with an Introductory Session

Get prospective members together for an introduction to the support group. Provide refreshments and conduct some ice breakers and get-acquainted activities. Ask for those present to discuss common concerns and suggest ways a support group might best help them.

Develop a Group Covenant

Work together with those who want to join the group and develop a group covenant. The covenant should include information about what is expected of members regarding attendance, participation, confidentiality, and so forth. It could outline the purpose of the group and how the group intends to support each other in achieving the purpose. You may want to use the covenant on page 11 as a model to follow.

Set an Ending Date

Decide to meet once a month for nine months or bi-weekly for a quarter. Set your own limit based on the needs and desires of group members. Once the ending date comes, the group can evaluate their relationships. Some may decide to continue to meet together. Others may choose not to participate any longer. This ending and new beginning allows the group to enlist new members and make changes that will better meet their needs.

■ **Select a type of support group that would be beneficial to some of the people in your church. On a separate sheet of paper outline and describe the steps you would go through to start that kind of group in your church. Bring your plan for a support group to your group session this week.**

Day 3: Managing the Dynamics of a Group

> **Today's Objective:** You will be able to describe seven ways to manage the basic dynamics in a group.

The skillful support-group leader is able to direct the forces (dynamics) of a group for the healing of human hurt. In the process of helping a group heal human hurt, a leader uses a number of activities in the management of the group dynamics. Let's consider some of these.

Establish a Covenant of Confidentiality

All types of counseling recognize the necessity of confidentiality for the counseling session. This is particularly true in group counseling. If all the participants do not understand that the session is completely private, the interchange will seldom go beyond a superficial level.

At the beginning of the session the leader says, "We are gathered here tonight under the covenant of confidentiality. This means that no one has the right to repeat anything that is said within the group." If a group's member fails to keep the covenant of confidentiality, he may be asked to leave the group. Trust and confidentiality are the basis for a successful group.

■ 1. What is one way to manage the dynamics of a group?

_____

   2. In the section on the previous page, underline what you would say to help promote confidentiality in a group.

Require Participation

Another fundamental dynamic of the group is that all the members must participate. Establish the expectation for participation by stating, "We do not have any onlookers in our group. We operate by the principle: No spectators, only participators." Throughout the sessions, you will need to work at involving all the members. This may require that you slow some down and prod others to get involved.

■ 1. What is a second way to manage the dynamics of a group?

_____

   2. In the section above, underline what you would say to encourage participation.

Provide Opportunities for Confession of Weaknesses

All types of counseling emphasize some time of confession. A group needs to get to the point where members can drop their guard and confess their weaknesses, failures, and problems in an atmosphere of acceptance and understanding. The model of openness by the leader is one of the strongest encouragements to openness for the group. Confession must be governed to protect group members. Here is a set of statements to guide confession.
1. Confession is not made indiscriminately but only to significant others.
2. Complaining and blaming others is not confessing.
3. We have no right to confess for others.
4. Boasting about our virtues is not confessing.

■ 1. What is a third way to manage the dynamics of a group.

_____

   2. Circle the statements in the section above that can help you guide confession in a group.

Promote Acceptance of Responsibility

Most people can readily find an excuse for their behavior. Some of these are just rationalizations rather than valid reasons. In a counseling group make an effort to push people toward accepting responsibility. One common expression is, "We cannot accept good reasons for bad behavior."

Jim Harris is refusing to undertake an action that all the group knows he should. His excuse is, "I can't." The group challenges him to change, "I can't" to "I won't." In this moment Jim realizes what he has been doing. This new posture means the individual accepts responsibility and has placed himself in control of his behavior.

■ 1. **What is a fourth way to manage the dynamics of a group?**

_____

   2. **In the section above, underline what you would say to manage acceptance of responsibility.**

Facilitate Identification

In a support group members are exposed to accounts of other people's struggles with life. Listening to these stories of difficulties faced, the bad decisions made, and the outcomes of self- defeating actions, listeners frequently come to see their own dilemmas in a clearer light. People are often encouraged in their struggles just by knowing that others are facing similar problems. They would be denied this opportunity of identification in one-to-one counseling. Encourage identification by asking, "Has anyone else had a similar experience he would like to share?"

■ 1. **What is a fifth way to manage the dynamics of a group?**

_____

   2. **In the section above, underline what you would say to encourage identification with the problems and circumstances of others.**

Encourage Dialogue

Members of a group react to each other. Before long, they are talking back and forth. Wise leaders encourage dialogue between group members. The leader might turn to another group member and say, "What could you say to Bill that might help?" or "What are some of the alternatives Bill might want to consider?" The process may be so effective that the leader frequently gets the impression that he might not really be very necessary. Group members can and will counsel each other if dialogue is encouraged.

■ 1. **What is a sixth way to manage the dynamics of a group?**

_____

   2. **In the section above, underline what you would say to encourage dialogue between group members.**

Foster Commitment

Any type of group activity calls for some type of commitment. Developing a group covenant (like you did at the beginning of WiseCounsel) is one way to foster commitment. Work together as a group to develop a covenant. Make sure each member has been able to give input for the agreement. Once the covenant has been approved by the group, you should keep the agreements before them and help members hold each other accountable for keeping the covenant.

■ 1. **What is a seventh way to manage the dynamics of a group?**

      _____

   2. **What is one of the best ways to do this in a group?**

      _____

   3. **Using the key words below as clues, describe seven ways to manage the basic dynamics of a group.**

      Confidentiality: _____

      _____

      _____

      Participation: _____

      _____

      _____

      Confession: _____

      _____

      _____

      Responsibility: _____

      _____

      _____

      Identification: _____

      _____

      _____

      Dialogue: _____

      _____

      _____

      Commitment: _____

      _____

      _____

One authority says that counseling groups are both the quickest and slowest way of helping people. Quickest because they frequently bring immediate relief, slowest because they call for a whole new life-style. Today, you have learned seven ways to manage some of the basic dynamics of a group. Many more dynamics are involved in the functioning of groups, but an awareness of these will help you function as a more effective worker with groups.

Day 4: Using Experiential Bible Studies in Support Groups

> **Today's Objective:** You will be able to identify five distinctives of experiential Bible study and describe nine steps to take in leading one.

One way to assure that valuable content will be considered in a counseling and support group is to study the Bible as a part of the process. Experiential Bible study helps people study and make application of biblical truths to their own lives. Though we are focusing on the use of experiential Bible study for support groups, you can also use this method at other times as well.

Distinctives of Experiential Bible Study

1. The Method is Personal. An individual thinks about his own personal experiences and relates them to the biblical passage, hence the title: experiential Bible study. It is an interactive approach.

2. The Leader Functions as a Facilitator. While the leader is available to assist in interpretation and provide background information, his or her main function is to guide the interaction of the group. The leader may discover as many new things about himself or herself as do the other participants.

3. It Enhances Interpersonal Relationships. The method tries to encourage group members to understand the interpersonal relationships of life. As they work together to apply biblical truths to life they grow in their relationships to each other.

4. It Is a Sharing Experience. Participants share their experiences with each other. This may become a practical demonstration of *koinonia,* the Greek word translated "fellowship" which literally means, "going shares". Many sharing groups in the church bring unusual blessing to the participants. Experiential Bible Study guides participants into a wide variety of subject areas about which experiences are shared.

5. It Calls for Action. The group members not only see the relationship of biblical principles to everyday life, but also commit themselves to do something, to go into action.

■ **In the following list, check the five distinctives of an experiential Bible study.**
- ☐ a. **The leader presents a well-informed lecture.**
- ☐ b. **The leader functions as a facilitator.**
- ☐ c. **It includes only private meditation on Scripture.**
- ☐ d. **It is a sharing experience.**
- ☐ e. **It calls for action.**
- ☐ f. **It focuses on mastery of Bible knowledge.**
- ☐ g. **It is personal.**
- ☐ h. **It enhances interpersonal relationships.**

This variety of Bible study will never replace the value of a diligent exegetical study of the Scriptures. It nevertheless brings a new element to the study of the Bible as it emphasizes the personal factor, group involvement, sharing, and action. The experience leaves the participant with a new appreciation of the Bible, its teachings, and its application to life. The distinctives you should have checked are b, d, e, g, and h.

Steps for Leading Experiential Bible Study

You may think that leading an experiential Bible study is easy. You will discover that it calls for you to carefully prepare and control the situation. The process will call for a number of steps:

Step 1. Arrange the Seating. Avoid any arrangement that makes the participants feel they are spectators at a performance. Place the chairs in a circle so that no space is between the chairs and each member can see all the others.

Step 2. Select a Scripture Passage. You could select any passage. Choose a passage that tells a story or teaches a principle. Focus on Scriptures that include applications especially appropriate for your group. You may want to study through a whole book like Ephesians, taking one portion at a time.

Step 3. As the Group Members Arrive, Greet Them Warmly and Confidently. Make sure they are introduced to each other. Create an atmosphere of warmth and acceptance.

■ **Describe in your own words the first three steps for leading an experiential Bible study.**

Step 1: _____

_____

Step 2: _____

_____

Step 3: _____

_____

Step 4. Read the Scripture Passage. You can do this in different ways:
• reading in unison
• alternating between leader and group
• one read from the King James Version and another from a modern version

Step 5. Identify the Key Truths. Provide members with brief explanations of words, the historical background, or other helpful information. Discuss the key truths members see in the passage.

Step 6. Reflect on Personal Experience and Application. Emphasize the importance of each individual's experiences or associations. You might say, "Think of some experience in your life that relates to the truths of this Scripture." Give them time to reflect on the application of the passage.

■ **Describe in your own words three more steps for leading an experiential Bible study.**

Step 4: _____

_____

Step 5: _____

_____

Step 6: _____

_____

Step 7. Model the Sharing. You must set the example for the group to follow. If I were leading the group, I would say, "We are now going to share our associations. Please remember we want every person to participate. "Let me lead off. When I think of (Bible situation or character), I remember a time when I . . .

Step 8. Share Experiences and Applications. As the leader turn to one of the group members and say, "Well, Jeff, why don't you share how this Scripture speaks to you?" At this step, the dynamics of the group become operational. Make these important emphases:

A Emphasize the importance of all the group members being "on task." Explain that they must pay close attention to whomever is speaking. Point out that the way members of the group listen may determine the contribution of the participant.

B Resist subgroups. Some insecure group members seek to subgroup. This generally takes the form of whispering to each other or making remarks that can only be heard by people who are close by. Stop this immediately. If it persists, it will destroy the interaction of the group.

C As you seat the members of the group, try to make sure that you position a good participant beside you. With this seating arrangement you can be sure of getting off to a good start. Try to position the shier members of the group in a place where they will have an opportunity to see a number of people in action before their turns come.

D Maintain a positive attitude. Don't let anyone say, "I'll pass." Make statements such as, "We want everybody to participate. We have a motto, No spectators, only participators."

Step 9. Focus on an Action Commitment. Try to help each member of the group decide what they will do in light of the experience of today. In some groups the action commitments are written down. At the next meeting of the group, the first order of business should be a report on these commitments.

■ **Describe in your own words the final three steps for leading an experiential Bible study.**

Step 7: _____

_____

Step 8: _____

_____

Step 9: _____

_____

This approach to Bible study calls for Christians to return to the practice of applying Bible truths to life in the context of a group. By studying the Bible experientially with a group, you increase the impact of the Bible on their lives.

Day 5: Conclusion

> **Today's Objective:** You will review and evaluate your work in WiseCounsel and determine a direction for your counseling ministry.

Review

As you have studied WiseCounsel, you probably focused your attention on the unit for the week and little else. You need to put all your study together into a big picture. Because you need this big picture to evaluate and set goals, I ask you not to skip the following exercises.

■ 1. **Write the stages, steps, questions, and decisions of the Ten-Step Counseling Model.**

TEN-STEP COUNSELING MODEL

STAGE ONE: _____

Step   1: _____

        Question: _____

        Question: _____

Step   2: _____

        Question: _____

Step   3: _____

        Question: _____

Step   4: _____

        Question: _____

       DECISION: _____

STAGE TWO: _____

Step   5: _____

        Question: _____

Step 6: _____

        Question: _____

Step 7: _____

        Question: _____

Step 8: _____

        Question: _____

Step 9: _____

        Question: _____

Step 10: _____

        Question: _____

        Question: _____

        DECISION: _____

2. For each subject below, turn to the page indicated and review the subject by reading the summary in the box or by reading the main headings. You do not need to review all the content. I only want to refresh your memory. Place an X in each box as you complete the review.

   ☐ 1. Reasons Christians Should Provide Lay Counseling, page 14.

   ☐ 2. The Demands of Counseling, pages 18-19.

   ☐ 3. Guidelines for Effective Questioning, page 27.

   ☐ 4. Ways Listening Helps People, page 67.

   ☐ 5. Guidelines for Listening, page 74.

   ☐ 6. Availability for Counseling, pages 80-83.

   ☐ 7. SOFTEN, page 87.

   ☐ 8. Expectations of the Counselee, pages 95-97.

   ☐ 9. Guidelines for Deciding on Issues of Confidentiality, page 100.

   ☐ 10. Guidelines for Handling Affection, page 106.

   ☐ 11. Guidelines for a Hospital Visit, page 117.

   ☐ 12. Stages of a Grief Experience, pages 120-122.

   ☐ 13. DO's and DON'Ts for Helping a Grieving Person, page 126.

   ☐ 14. Techniques for Behavior Change, page 144.

   ☐ 15. Guidelines for Marriage and Family Counseling, pages 128-131.

   ☐ 16. Guidelines for Negotiating, page 166.

   ☐ 17. Indicators of a Potential Suicide, pages 197-198.

   ☐ 18. Counseling a Suicidal Individual, pages 199-203.

Evaluation

A wise person knows both his or her strengths and weaknesses. The wise person tries to keep from overusing a strength, and he or she tries to grow stronger in areas of weakness. The wise person also realizes that he cannot be strong in everything.

■ Honestly evaluate yourself in the areas listed below by placing an X on the graphs. You will not be asked to share these responses with anyone. They are for your benefit.

STRENGTH   S ---- -x-- ---- ---- W   WEAKNESS

1. I believe I am adequately prepared to help counsel:

   S ---- ---- ---- ---- W   Persons in the hospital
   S ---- ---- ---- ---- W   Terminally ill patients
   S ---- ---- ---- ---- W   Grieving persons
   S ---- ---- ---- ---- W   Married couples with problems
   S ---- ---- ---- ---- W   Families
   S ---- ---- ---- ---- W   Persons who are lost
   S ---- ---- ---- ---- W   Youth considering career choices
   S ---- ---- ---- ---- W   Youth considering marriage
   S ---- ---- ---- ---- W   Youth with sex problems
   S ---- ---- ---- ---- W   Never-married singles
   S ---- ---- ---- ---- W   Divorced singles
   S ---- ---- ---- ---- W   Widowed singles
   S ---- ---- ---- ---- W   Senior adults
   S ---- ---- ---- ---- W   Persons with resentment
   S ---- ---- ---- ---- W   Persons with guilt
   S ---- ---- ---- ---- W   Persons considering suicide

2. Circle the group(s) of people that you anticipate having the most opportunity to counsel.

You can rejoice because you do not have to be strong in all of these areas to provide a valuable counseling ministry. In fact, some people may be strong in only one or two.

■ 3. Now evaluate yourself on the following skills. Use the same graph as you did in activity 1. If you have never used the skill and you are not sure how well you would do in real-life, write a question mark (?) beside the graph.

   S ---- ---- ---- ---- W   Asking open questions
   S ---- ---- ---- ---- W   Identifying a person's real problem
   S ---- ---- ---- ---- W   Making referrals to others
   S ---- ---- ---- ---- W   Modeling the role
   S ---- ---- ---- ---- W   Brainstorming alternatives
   S ---- ---- ---- ---- W   Exploring outcomes
   S ---- ---- ---- ---- W   Providing information
   S ---- ---- ---- ---- W   Communicating Christian values
   S ---- ---- ---- ---- W   Applying Scripture in decision making
   S ---- ---- ---- ---- W   Total body listening
   S ---- ---- ---- ---- W   Making known my availability to counsel
   S ---- ---- ---- ---- W   Building rapport in a relationship

4. Circle the skills listed above that you need to improve.

5. Read "The Church Study Course" on page 223 and fill in Form 725 if you have completed the requirements. Bring it to your group session.

Directions for Ministry

Now that you are better equipped to counsel people who have needs, you need to discover ways God would have you use these abilities. Think about, pray about, and respond to the following activities.

■ 1. I believe God wants me to use my counseling abilities in the following way(s). Check all that apply.
   a. Counseling individuals I encounter from day to day.
   b. Counseling people in classes or groups I work with in church.
   c. Counseling people I work with during the week.
   d. Leading a counseling and support group.

2. Look back through the "Review" and "Evaluation" sections. List below areas in which you want to do further study.

_____

_____

_____

_____

3. Do you sense God leading you to a specialized ministry to a particular group of people? If so, whom?

_____

4. Turn back to page 6 and read "LIFE's Core Curriculum." Do you need to study MasterLife to develop your walk as a disciple of Christ?
   ☐ a. Yes, I want to start as soon as possible.
   ☐ b. Yes, I will need to wait until (date)_____
   ☐ c. No, I've already completed a study of MasterLife.
   ☐ d. No.

5. Do I need to study another LIFE course?

   Which course?_____

   When?_____

A Parting Challenge

I have enjoyed being your tutor for the past thirteen weeks. Even though you have completed this course, you will still need to study and learn ways to more effectively minister to others. I encourage you to "Do your best to present yourself to God as one approved, a workman who does not need to be ashamed and who correctly handles the word of truth" (2 Tim. 2:15). Use your gifts, empowered by the Holy Spirit, to meet human need where ever you find it. Allow God's love to flow through your life day by day.

May God richly bless and use your counseling ministry for His glory!

For Further Study
☐ *Making Peace with Your Past* by Tim Sledge. Nashville: LifeWay Press, 1992.
☐ *Making Peace with Your Past Facilitator's Guide* by Tim Sledge. LifeWay Press, 1992.
☐ *Search for Significance LIFE Support Edition* by Robert S. McGee. LifeWay Press, 1992.
☐ *Search for Significance LIFE Support Edition Leader's Guide* by Johnny and Sallie Jones. Nashville: LifeWay Press, 1993.
☐ *LIFE Support Leader's Handbook* compiled by Johnny Jones. Nashville: LifeWay Press, 1993.
☐ *Untangling Relationships: A Christian Perspective on Codependency* by Pat Springle and Susan Lanford. Nashville: LifeWay Press, 1993.
☐ *Untangling Relationships: A Christian Perspective on Codependency Leader's Guide* by Susan Lanford. Nashville: LifeWay Press, 1993.

NOTES

Unit 1

[1]J. H. Powell, *Bring Out Your Dead,* (New York: Time, Inc., 1965), xiv.

[2]O. Hobart Mower, Anthony J. Vattano, *Integrity Groups, The Loss and Recovery of Community,* (Urbana, Ill.: Integrity Groups, 1975), 140.

[3]*Fort Worth Star Telegram,* June 15, 1976.

[4]Rudyard Kipling, "The Elephant's Child," *Rudyard Kipling's Verse,* (New York: Doubleday, Doran and Co., Inc., 1945), 607.

Unit 2

[1]Charles Kemp, *The Pastor and Community Resources,* (St. Louis: Bethany Press, 1960), 23. Used by permission.

Unit 3

[1]*Time,* February 10, 1986, 52.

Unit 4

[1]Helen Keller, *The Story of My Life,* (New York: Doubleday, Doran and Co. Inc., 1933), 23.

Unit 5

[1]Horace B. English and Ava C. English, *A Comprehensive Dictionary of Psychological and Psychoanalytic Terms,* (New York: Longmans, Green and Co. Inc., 1959), 437.

[2]Dale Carnegie, *How to Win Friends and Influence People,* (New York: Simon & Schuster Inc., 1937), 125.

Unit 6

[1]"Confidence and the Clergy," *Time,* October 1, 1984, 661.

[2]*Hospital and Community Psychiatry,* 1981, 106.

Unit 7

[1]Ten stages described in *Good Grief* by Granger E. Westberg, (Philadelphia: Fortress Press, 1962).

[2]Theresa A. Rando, *Grief, Dying and Death,* (Champaign: Research Press Company, 1984), 94.

Unit 9

[1]William James, *The Varieties of Religious Experience,* (New York: Longmans, Green & Co., 1928), 462.

Unit 10

[1]Smiley Blanton, *Love or Perish,* (New York: Simon & Schuster, 1956), 108.

Unit 11

[1]Sara Jenkins, *Past Present, Recording Life Stories of Older People,* (Washington, D.C.: St. Alban's Parish, 1978), 110-11. Used by permission.

Unit 12

[1]Bill Blackburn, *What You Should Know About Suicide,* (Waco: Word Books Incorporated, 1982, 88).

Unit 13

[1]John Telford, *The Life of John Wesley,* (London: Wesleyan Methodist Book Room, 1899), 147.

CHRISTIAN GROWTH STUDY PLAN

Preparing Christians to Serve

In the **Christian Growth Study Plan (formerly Church Study Course),** this book *WiseCounsel* is a resource for course credit in the subject area Personal Life of the Christian Growth category of diploma plans. To receive credit, read the book, complete the learning activities, show your work to your pastor, a staff member or church leader, then complete the following information. This page may be duplicated. Send the completed page to:

Christian Growth Study Plan
One LifeWay Plaza
Nashville, TN 37234-0117
FAX: (615)251-5067

For information about the Christian Growth Plan, refer to the current Christian Growth Study Plan Catalog. Your church office may have a copy. If not, request a free copy from the Christian Growth Study Plan office (615/251-2525).

WiseCounsel: Skills for Lay Counseling
COURSE NUMBER: CG-0184

PARTICIPANT INFORMATION

Social Security Number (USA ONLY-optional)	Personal CGSP Number*	Date of Birth (MONTH, DAY, YEAR)

Name (First, Middle, Last)	Home Phone

Address (Street, Route, or P.O. Box)	City, State, or Province	Zip/Postal Code

CHURCH INFORMATION

Church Name

Address (Street, Route, or P.O. Box)	City, State, or Province	Zip/Postal Code

CHANGE REQUEST ONLY

☐ Former Name

☐ Former Address	City, State, or Province	Zip/Postal Code

☐ Former Church	City, State, or Province	Zip/Postal Code

Signature of Pastor, Conference Leader, or Other Church Leader	Date

*New participants are requested but not required to give SS# and date of birth. Existing participants, please give CGSP# when using SS# for the first time. Thereafter, only one ID# is required. **Mail to:** Christian Growth Study Plan, One LifeWay Plaza, Nashville, TN 37234-0117. Fax: (615)251-5067.

Rev. 10-01

LIFE Support
Group Resources

LifeWay publishes an entire series of resources for specific life situations. These discipleship resources help persons understand difficult problems in the light of scriptural truth and find solutions for life change. The LIFE Support series includes resources for dealing with problems from alcoholism to caring for a chronically ill loved one. All of these resources combine individual study in a workbook format with group participation. Each study has group leadership helps either included in the member book or in a separate leader guide. Several leader guides can be downloaded at no charge at *http://www.lifeway.com/download.asp*.

    The LIFE Support Leader Handbook provides guidance for beginning and guiding a group ministry. It can also be downloaded at no charge from the above address. The LIFE Support series includes the following resources. Learn about these and other support group resources on the web site or by calling (615) 251-2816.

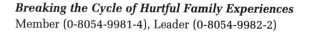

Breaking the Cycle of Hurtful Family Experiences
Member (0-8054-9981-4), Leader (0-8054-9982-2)

Conquering Chemical Dependency First Steps to a Christ-Centered 12-Step Process (0-8054-9972-5)

Conquering Chemical Dependency: A Christ-Centered 12-Step Process (0-8054-9983-0), **Facilitator** (Available at no cost on the Website. Use with both the First Steps book and the larger Member book.)

Conquering Codependency: A Christ-Centered 12-Step Process
Member (0-8054-9975-X)
Leader (Available at no cost on the Website.)

Conquering Eating Disorders
Member (0-8054-9977-6), Facilitator (0-8054-9978-4)

Enduring Triumphantly: Finding Victory over Chronic Illness (0-6330-1857-0)

Faithful and True: Sexual Integrity in a Fallen World (0-8054-9819-2)

Making Peace with Your Past
Member (0-8054-9986-5), Facilitator (0-8054-9987-3)

Moving Beyond Your Past
Member (0-8054-9927-X), Facilitator (Available at no cost on the Website.)

New Faces in the Frame: A Guide to Marriage and Parenting in the Blended Family (0-8054-9817-6)

Quitting for Good: A Christ-Centered Approach to Nicotine Dependency
Member (0-8054-9844-3), Leader (0-8054-9843-5)

Recovering from the Losses of Life
Member (0-8054-9874-5), Facilitator (0-8054-9873-7)

Search for Significance: LIFE® Support Group Series Edition
Member (0-8054-9990-3), Leader (0-8054-9989-x)

Strength for the Journey: A Biblical Perspective on Discouragement and Depression (0-7673-9105-5)

Shelter from the Storm: Hope for Survivors of Sexual Abuse
Member (0-8054-9979-2), Facilitator (0-8054-9980-6)

A Time for Healing: Coming to Terms with Your Divorce
Member (0-8054-9875-3), Facilitator (0-8054-9876-1)

Untangling Relationships: A Christian Perspective on Codependency
Member (0-8054-9973-3), Leader (0-8054-9974-1)

To order these resources: WRITE LifeWay Church Resources Customer Service; One LifeWay Plaza; Nashville, TN 372340113; FAX order to (615) 2515933; PHONE (800) 4582772; EMAIL to *customerservice@lifeway.com;* ORDER ONLINE at *www.lifeway.com;* or VISIT the LifeWay Christian Store serving you.